Martial Rose Library
Tel: 01962 827306

To be returned on or before the day marked above, subject to recall.

Performance Interventions

Series Editors: **Elaine Aston**, University of Lancaster, and **Bryan Reynolds**, University of California, Irvine

Performance Interventions is a series of monographs and essay collections on theatre, performance, and visual culture that share an underlying commitment to the radical and political potential of the arts in our contemporary moment, or give consideration to performance and to visual culture from the past deemed crucial to a social and political present. *Performance Interventions* moves transversally across artistic and ideological boundaries to publish work that promotes dialogue between practitioners and academics, and interactions between performance communities, educational institutions, and academic disciplines.

Titles include:

Alison Jeffers
REFUGEES, THEATRE AND CRISIS
Performing Global Identities

Marcela Kostihová
SHAKESPEARE IN TRANSITION
Political Appropriations in the Post-Communist Czech Republic

Jon McKenzie, Heike Roms and C.J. W.-L. Wee (*editors*)
CONTESTING PERFORMANCE
Emerging Sites of Research

Jennifer Parker-Starbuck
CYBORG THEATRE
Corporeal/Technological Intersections in Multimedia Performance

Ramón H. Rivera-Servera and Harvey Young
PERFORMANCE IN THE BORDERLANDS

Mike Sell (*editor*)
AVANT-GARDE PERFORMANCE AND MATERIAL EXCHANGE
Vectors of the Radical

Melissa Sihra (*editor*)
WOMEN IN IRISH DRAMA
A Century of Authorship and Representation

Brian Singleton
MASCULINITIES AND THE CONTEMPORARY IRISH THEATRE

Performance Interventions
Series Standing Order ISBN 978–1–4039–4443–6 Hardback
Series Standing Order ISBN 978–1–4039–4444–3 Paperback
(*outside North America only*)

You can receive future titles in this series as they are published by placing a standing order. Please contact your bookseller or, in case of difficulty, write to us at the address below with your name and address, the title of the series and one of the ISBNs quoted above.

Customer Services Department, Macmillan Distribution Ltd, Houndmills, Basingstoke, Hampshire RG21 6XS, England

Refugees, Theatre and Crisis

Performing Global Identities

Alison Jeffers
Lecturer in Drama, University of Manchester, UK

First published 2012 by
PALGRAVE MACMILLAN

Palgrave Macmillan in the UK is an imprint of Macmillan Publishers Limited,
registered in England, company number 785998, of Houndmills, Basingstoke,
Hampshire RG21 6XS.

Palgrave Macmillan in the US is a division of St Martin's Press LLC,
175 Fifth Avenue, New York, NY 10010.

Palgrave Macmillan is the global academic imprint of the above companies
and has companies and representatives throughout the world.

Palgrave® and Macmillan® are registered trademarks in the United States,
the United Kingdom, Europe and other countries.

ISBN: 978–0–230–24747–5

This book is printed on paper suitable for recycling and made from fully
managed and sustained forest sources. Logging, pulping and manufacturing
processes are expected to conform to the environmental regulations of the
country of origin.

A catalogue record for this book is available from the British Library.

A catalog record for this book is available from the Library of Congress.

10 9 8 7 6 5 4 3 2 1
21 20 19 18 17 16 15 14 13 12

Printed and bound in Great Britain by
CPI Antony Rowe, Chippenham and Eastbourne

This book is dedicated to all those who have shared their time and experiences with such generosity. Thank you Abas, Adman, Alan, Basil, Benjamin, Borhan, Cristo, Christophe, Louis-Denis, Eric, Eucharia, George, Girel, Hava, Herve, Jacqueline, Jean, Jonathan, Lito, Lancine, Maryam, Redley, Senodio, Rita, Robert, Pat, Timeyi, Tope, Ulrich and the many other people who have given their time and energies with such generosity.

Contents

Figures

Acknowledgements

This book owes its existence to all of those who showed me what it means to seek asylum and to live as a refugee.

Many colleagues have helped and advised me in the process of researching and writing this book. I am so grateful to my colleagues who made up In Place of War: Michael Balfour, Ananda Breed, Ruth Daniel, Rachel Finn and Charlotte Hennessy; Jenny Hughes and James Thompson were, and have continued to be, a special source of advice and support. My thanks too to other colleagues at the University of Manchester: Maggie Gale, Viv Gardner, Tony Jackson, Johannes Sjoberg in Drama, Peter Gatrell in History, Simon Parry and Helen Rees Leahy at the Institute of Cultural Practices and all my other colleagues who have all been helpful and supportive, often without even knowing it. Thank you to Amy Guest for her insightful work on editing and indexing the material. Helen Nicholson and Helen Gilbert from Royal Holloway University of London and Rea Dennis from the University of Glamorgan have all given me invaluable advice and support at different stages. Thank you too to colleagues in Sydney and Melbourne: James Arvanitakis, Paul Brown, Tom Burvill, Claudia Chidiac, Paul Dwyer, Emma Cox, Rand Hazou, Shahin Shafaei, Caroline Wake, David Williams for being so welcoming and accommodating and for introducing me to the possibilities inherent in thinking about refugees in relation to bureaucratic performance.

Many thanks to colleagues at Community Arts North West, Waters Edge Arts, Refugee Action in Manchester, the Medical Foundation for the Care of Victims of Torture in Manchester, Multiagency Services for Refugees and Asylum Seekers in Manchester, and Manchester Refugee Support Network. Special thanks too to Nigel Rose, James Lupton and Gerri Moriarty for their insightful comments and probing questions. Finally, thank you to Mum and Dad and to Alan, Tom and Caitlin for not commenting too much on the times when I have paid more attention to my computer than I have to them.

Preface

In the winter of 2004 a small group of asylum seekers from a number of African countries met in what would have been the drawing room of a large house in Manchester, built for a well-off family at the end of the nineteenth century, but now shabby and neglected. The city of Manchester, in the North West of England, grew and developed around heavy industry in the eighteenth and nineteenth centuries, the period in which this house had been built. Like many Northern English industrial cities it suffered a period of decline in the late twentieth century with the result that the area in which this house was situated has become run-down and is notorious for crime. In comparison with many Northern English cities, which have been unable to halt their decline, Manchester is having something of a renaissance as it remerges as a cultural and media hub in the region and nationally. This is not to say that pockets of extreme deprivation do not exist and the redevelopment of the city has proved rather uneven. Manchester is ranked second most deprived city in the UK in terms of income deprivation, third in terms of employment deprivation and fifth in terms of how widespread deprivation is within the city.[1]

Upstairs, in what would have been the master bedroom of this one-time grand Victorian house, a radio DJ was broadcasting music to the local community while the group of asylum seekers downstairs was enrolled in a training course organised by Radio for Refugees and funded by the British Home Office Refugee Integration Challenge Fund (Liddell & Manchester, 2005). The asylum seekers present were learning how to make and broadcast a radio programme that would go out live on air at the end of their ten-week course. As it was the first day of the course, participants were getting to know each other and one woman revealed that she had been a pharmacist back home in Uganda. Through tears she explained that she had got into trouble with some soldiers in her village because she refused to give them the drugs they demanded. Medical drugs were in short supply and if she gave in to the soldiers' demands she would have none left for the local people. She explained how one day a neighbour had come running to her pharmacy warning her not to go home as the soldiers were waiting for her there. Fleeing at once, because she believed she would not survive such an encounter, she had come to England not having seen or heard from her husband or children since, fearing that they might have been killed when the soldiers didn't get her. She then produced a large brown envelope overflowing with documents, letters and leaflets and explained that her application for asylum had been rejected because the authorities in the UK where she had fled did not believe her story.

Also present that day was Joy[2] from Nigeria who had boarded a plane for London having hidden at a friend's house in Lagos for some weeks. She had fled the Delta region of Nigeria with her young son fearing that her husband had been killed because he was a politician who had been vocal in the campaign for what he saw as a fair share of the oil from that region for his people. Word had come to Joy that it would be dangerous for her to return home as she and her son would probably be killed by the same people who had apparently murdered her husband and baby daughter that day. She had spent time in Lagos buying the papers, tickets and the passport she would need to flee the country with her son, her own having been left at home in the panic of her hasty departure. On arriving in London she claimed asylum and was held in Oakwood Immigration Detention Centre before being dispersed to Manchester[3] while the British authorities assessed her claim. She had recently been told that the authorities did not believe her story and that her appeal had also failed so she should await information about her removal back to Nigeria. Joy explained that she was starting an anti-deportation campaign.

Finally, by way of introduction, Derek from Eritrea, about 20 and hugely energetic, played the group a CD of his own music made in a friend's recording studio. The upbeat tempo of this love song, written and sung by Derek himself, represented what he wanted to do with his life. He was taking his big chance in the UK to become a musician. Infused with hope and optimism, full of enthusiasm for the opportunity to achieve recognition for talent and dedication, his introduction represented an alternative to the other two stories. Focusing on the future, Derek's story gave no detail about how he had arrived in the UK and the difficulties his family were having in being recognised as refugees or the challenging conditions in which they were living. These stories came out later but on that morning it was possible to see something of the spectrum of experiences, thoughts and emotions connected with violent expulsion from one place and uncertain arrival in another. These three sets of experiences provided an introduction to these individuals, some idea of why people became refugees and a valuable and salutary counternarrative to the seemingly inevitable sadness of so many refugees' stories.

And there was me. I was volunteering as a mentor in order to create an opportunity to meet people seeking asylum[4] as part of a case study on theatre and performance about and with refugees and people seeking asylum in the UK for a research project called In Place of War (IPOW). Set up by academics and applied theatre practitioners in the Centre for Applied Theatre Research at the University of Manchester, IPOW was funded by the Arts and Humanities Research Council and was charged with investigating the links between conflict and performance on a global sale.[5] On its simplest level, the intention of the refugee case study was to discover what kinds of theatre and performance forms were made by people who had escaped from war zones and travelled to the relative safety of the UK. Among many other activities during that period of research I became involved with a group of refugees in creating a verbatim play called *I've got something to show you* about an Iranian asylum seeker who had committed suicide in Manchester in 2003;[6] weekly drama workshops at the Medical Foundation for the Care of Victims of Torture in Manchester; researching and evaluating the Exodus Festival, a large outdoor music festival of refugee artists in Manchester in 2006 and field research in Britain and Australia among refugees, academics and practitioners with experience and expertise in the area of refugee theatre and performances of asylum.

As academics from a wealthy British institution, my colleagues and I at In Place of War were marked out as privileged in what Doreen Massey calls the 'power geometry' of movement through time and space (1994: 149). Our ability to access global travel for the purposes of research stood in stark, and sometimes uncomfortable, contrast to those refugees we encountered during our research in the UK. Who knows the number of miles we accumulated in our quest for knowledge? Many thousands I expect and our ability to travel at our ease, negotiating international boundaries safe in the knowledge that our British and American passports would grant us passage to, and protection in, any country set us apart from those whose travel had proved more constrained. Miwon Kwon has pointed out the paradox that academics and artists are often rewarded for being in the wrong place because under the 'seductive allure of nomadism' the more we travel for work the more valued we feel (2004: 160). At the same time, most of my research was only a twenty-minute bus ride away because Manchester, like most urban centres in Britain, is 'home' to many thousands of refugees and asylum seekers from China, Iraq, Iran, Afghanistan, Sri Lanka, Democratic Republic of Congo, Sierra Leone and many of the other states where poverty and persecution drive people beyond their borders in the hope of a better life elsewhere.[7] This bizarre telescoping of research locations which took me to the other side of the world and to the end of my street feels typical of this study where paradoxes, coincidences and outright contradictions came to dominate the work. This held true too when moments of clarity were closely followed by periods of overwhelming confusion. In such times it has been valuable to recall the words of anthropologist Michael Jackson that 'any essay that pretends to understand refugee experience is bound to reflect upon the fact that its own premises lie outside the experience' (2006: 76). However, this apparently reassuring idea is followed up with the provocative and challenging assertion that such essays 'may, as a consequence, be part of the very political problem that creates refugees in the first place' (Jackson, 2006: 76). Mindful of the challenges that this suggests it is my hope that this book will prove a fitting tribute to the many people who do understand what it is to be a refugee and who trusted me enough to share their stories, thoughts and experiences in such generous and surprising ways.

Introduction: Stories, Words and Points of View

> Illegals, refulciado, migrant workers, clandestines, imigrante, manonegra, asylum seekers, sans papiers.
>
> (Wild Geese, Banner Theatre)

> For whom is the border a friction-free zone of entitled access, a frontier of possibility? Who travels confidently across borders, who gets questioned, detained, interrogated, and strip-searched at the border?
>
> (Conquergood, 2002: 145)

An increasing number of stories told by refugees about their experiences are available in print (Arbabzadh, 2007; Eggers, 2006; Kenney and Schrag, 2008; Maric, 2009; Moorehead, 2005; Schmid et al., 2003). However, it is only in face to face meetings with people seeking asylum and with refugees1 that it is possible to comprehend the subtlety of these stories and the huge range of emotions behind them; anger, fear, anxiety, jubilation, hope, guilt and mistrust are just a few of the more obvious ones. In order to claim asylum refugees require a credible story of individual persecution to convince the authorities of their right to stay in the country to which they have fled. Without this they are vulnerable to refusal and their right to stay comes under threat, making it likely that they will be returned to the country they have fled from. Refugees' stories are troubling, troubled and troublesome. Troubling because they are hard to hear, especially if the listener enjoys the privileges of the West; troubled because persecution, trauma and suffering are essential elements of these stories, and troublesome because lives depend on their claims for truth. Studying the many theatrical ways in which refugee stories are presented compels the listener to understand how these stories function and operate. Some are valued for their 'truth', as a way to validate or authenticate the suffering of refugees, while others represent the depths to which people will 'stoop' in order to lie or perform their way into a better life. Interpreting refugees' stories for a western audience involves a process of translation; as a scholar of refugee theatre, the process of listening in performance requires a kind of double translation. I will show that it is important to listen to the listeners – the writers, actors and directors who create theatre and performance works concerning refugees, while maintaining the imperative to listen to refugees themselves.

Distance and proximity

Participant observation has proved an important way to meet and talk to refugees as well as to artists and others who are working with or on behalf of refugees. This method of research has been extended in two ways beyond the traditional definition of participant observation involving the researcher observing a community or cultural activity of which they are temporarily a part (Hume and Mulcock, 2004). First, in setting up an opportunity to work alongside refugees and asylum seekers, for example, in running the on-going participatory drama project mentioned in the Preface, I have deliberately *manufactured* rather than *encountered* research opportunities. The question of *role* is crucial in participant observation and, in taking on the role of leader/director, as well as being seen as a representative of a powerful cultural institution in the shape of a university, I will have affected the participant research in innumerable ways. The same is true of my role as a mentor to the participants in the radio project described in the Preface, for example, that put me in the position of trusted expert. My 'expertise', even if it was simply that of having lived in the UK all my life, inevitably put me in a certain position of power in relation to the refugees I was hoping to observe and interact with.

This leads to the second way in which the classic version of participant observation has not only been stretched but may even have been inverted. Traditionally, the participant observer is expected to place themselves in 'awkward social spaces' some of which would be 'difficult to inhabit' (Hume and Mulcock, 2004: xi) as the stranger. The 'field' of observation, in this case, was 'my field' and I was observing 'strangers' in my own environment, one which was hostile to their presence in many ways. Hume and Mulcock (2004: xii) argue that 'personal inadequacy and social failure' on the part of the researcher are perhaps an inevitable part of successful participant observation. In this case the refugee 'subjects' of research were just as often in this position as the researcher because of their fragile social and political position in a new home.

Ahmed (2000) questions the traditional position of the ethnographer as a 'professional stranger', dismissing it as inadequate for ethnographic enquiry and citing the controversy around Bell's writing on indigenous women in Australia. Power relationships within the ethnographic process inevitably affect that process but Ahmed suggests that the problem lies not so much in the process of translating the strange into the familiar as in the *concealment* of that translation. One way in which this process is concealed is by not drawing attention to the deixis in writing, the little words that locate the researcher and the subject of research within a matrix of power and influence (Billig, 1995). Ignoring this is impossible and unethical; it is a 'postmodern fantasy' that the I of the ethnographer 'can undo the power relations that allowed the "I" to appear' (Ahmed, 2000; 64). Ethnographic writers have used a number of strategies to approach this problematic area: inserting verbatim italicised speeches from the subjects of ethnographic research, for example (Nordstrom, 1997), or using elements of autobiography as cited in Bell's work (Ahmed, 2000). But these are not enough to destabilise, let alone invert, the power relations that are at play in an ethnographic situation. Ahmed rejects Bell's strategy of putting the autobiographical within the ethnographic in a bid to 'make friends' with the stranger/subject suggesting that the 'double vision' of Hortense Powdermaker provides a possible model of practice. From this position the knowledge of the subjects as *both* friends and strangers *admits the impossibility of being (with) them* (Ahmed, 2000: 72 emphasis in original) at the same time as allowing for a degree of humanity and compassion.

Ahmed's idea that 'the proximity of ethnography leads to a recognition of distance' (Ahmed, 2000: 72) echoes Jackson's words in the Preface to this book that speak of the impossibility of understanding the experience of being a refugee. This has many echoes for the research described here where setting out to 'get to know' refugees produced an ambiguous kind of knowledge. This ambiguity is reflected throughout the study seen in the images of host and guest in Chapter 2, in the indecipherability of some refugee speech in Chapter 3 and in the discourses of togetherness reflected in the title of Chapter Four, 'We with them and them with us'.

Hosts and guests

This book is not only about refugees but is also about those in the 'host' nations and their responses to the presence of refugees. Examining the cultural products made both *by* and *about* refugees reveals layers of thinking and practice that are dissected with discourses on performance, diaspora, migration and identity. Most importantly, these cultural expressions are strongly conditioned by the political and historical moment in which they are located because the growing numbers of refugees arriving in Western states since the late 1980s have frequently been viewed with alarm and the refugees treated with hostility, prejudice and even violence. Mistrust, and suspicion that has developed as a result, has generated a 'crisis' and it is against this background that all contemporary refugee theatre and performance takes place. The notion of the 'refugee crisis' is discussed in more detail in the next chapter but for now it is important to note that it is not simply a crisis of numbers but one that goes to the very heart of questions about the nation state, identity and belonging. This can be seen in the language used to describe refugees who come from a sedentary place, from 'us' who have no need to flee, to 'them', those who live an uncomfortable, insecure and less favourable existence. The etymology of the word refugee encourages this reading as the term *refuge* emerged in French indicating a 'shelter from danger or trouble' in the 14th century, based on the Latin *fugere* meaning to flee (Hoad, 1996: 395). The word was transmuted in subsequent centuries so that in the seventeenth century the word *refugie* came into being, based on the past participle of *se refugier*, to take refuge. Linguistically refugees are people who flee danger and seek safety elsewhere.

However, this over-simplified conception risks reinforcing binary notions of home and away where 'home' indicates safety, belonging, and rootedness while 'away' is designated as frightening, inhospitable, unknown. This emphasis on refugee *flight*, running away, implies weakness or passivity and exists in sharp contrast to the term 'asylum seeker', which implies activity and a vision of the asylum seeker as an active agent who wants something seems to create a sense of threat (Rotas, 2004). Sociolinguists have identified a process of negative semantic slide (Daly, 1986: xix) by which an apparently neutral word or phrase accrues negative meaning over time. The negative semantic slide of the term 'asylum seeker' illustrates how, 'common-sense racism', promulgated by the press among others, changed the meaning of the term asylum seeker 'from a legal term to a synonym for "illegal immigrant"' (Kundnani, 2001: 43). Although language and terminology inevitably differ across such a large number of countries and language communities most languages differentiate legally and linguistically between refugees and asylum seekers. In Germany refugees are called *fluchtling* while asylum seekers are *asyl-bewerber* (Peck, 1995: 109); the French for asylum seeker is *chercher d'asile* while refugees are *refugies*, and in Spain the term for an asylum seeker is *solicante de asilo* and refugee is *refugiado*. In most English speaking countries people waiting for their claim to be heard are called *asylum seekers* and can only be granted the title *refugee* if their claims for asylum are considered successful.

Other books have been written about the relationship between theatrical representation and immigration and they have been helpful in shaping this consideration of the relationship between refugees, asylum seekers, theatre and performance. The work of Karen Shimakawa (2002) on Asian-American theatre has proved illuminating in its use of theories of abjection; Lisa Lowe (1996) has offered a detailed and provocative insight into Asian immigration in the United States which provided ideas that are helpful when thinking about refugees in relation to cultural performance in Chapter 4. These works have opened up possibilities for reading refugeeness through discourses of immigration and, taken with Peter Nyers' (2003) concept of abject cosmopolitanism, show how refugees have challenged expectations by producing a counter discourse to that imposed by the dominant culture (Shimakawa, 2002: 20). Refugees are immigrants who have made a difficult political decision to expose themselves as immigrants who require political protection. They are framed in a particular historical and political moment, at a time when Western powers have become increasingly alarmed by the growth in the numbers of refugees claiming political asylum and by increasing movement in a globalised society.

It is in the interests of Western governments to blur the distinctions between refugees and economic migrants in order to obscure their increasingly draconian measures to deter them. For example, in France the so-called 'Pasqua Laws' passed in 1995 are cited by many (including French theatre director Mnouchkine whose work is discussed in Chapter 2) as responsible for the homogenisation of immigration (Fisek, 2008: 209). Refugees' claims for political asylum are based on rights enshrined in international law and yet it has become increasingly difficult to make the claim of being a refugee in all Western states where the suspicion is that immigrants are not 'real' refugees but economic migrants lying about persecution to gain access to a life outside their own probably war-torn and impoverished countries. The onus is on refugees to prove their persecution to the state before that state will offer the protection that is due to all refugees. Thus refugees become asylum seekers, immigrants in limbo, waiting to hear if their claims for protection have been accepted, enmeshed in the bureaucratic performance of refugeeness which is discussed in more detail in Chapter 1.

It is only in the twentieth and twenty-first centuries that the issue of refugees has become 'politicised and internationalised', and refugees have become 'increasingly constructed as a "problem"' (Kushner and Knox, 1999: 3). Writing during the 1980s about refugees tended to focus on the patterns of migration that followed the First and Second World Wars detailing population movements in and around Europe (Bramwell, 1988; Marrus, 1985). Marrus quotes two earlier researchers who said in 1944 '[t]he history of international migration in the past thirty years has been largely the history of refugees [...] ours might truly be called the era of refugees' (Marrus, 1985: 3). This notion of the emblematic nature of refugees for the times in which the writers were living is frequently repeated, and Rabbi Hugo Grynn's words that the twentieth century will be seen as the century of the refugee are often used (Kushner and Knox: 1999: 1). Arendt's work, particularly *The Origins of Totalitarianism* is influential in the development of thinking about refugees (Kushner and Knox, 1999; Malkki, 1996; Marfleet, 2006; Zolberg, 2002). She notes how, in the wake of the First World War, refugees were increasingly at the mercy of the state preventing great numbers from ever returning home.

Playing on the idea of the refugee as an object of knowledge in her critique of the growth of totalitarian states, Arendt calls refugees 'the most symptomatic group in contemporary politics' (Arendt, 1986[1951]: 277). In her view these states demonstrated a growing tendency among governments in Europe to place the 'shame' of being a refugee firmly on refugees' shoulders, at the same time removing from themselves any taint of guilt for producing the conditions that created refugees. Contemporary commentators have shown how the treatment of refugees can be taken as a kind of ethical measure with which to assess the degree of hospitality or largesse shown by a nation towards the stranger (MacCallum, 2002; Manne, 2004; Schuster, 2003). This sense of the figure of 'the refugee' as symptomatic of global inequalities and conflict remains prevalent, and refugees are often discussed in ways that would suggest they are sometimes significant as ciphers as much as for their materiality.

Refugee studies

Refugee studies, as a discrete academic discipline, emerged in the early 1980s and one of the most prominent sites for this is the Refugee Studies Centre (RSC) based at Oxford University. Established in 1982, and claiming an international reputation as the leading multidisciplinary centre for research and teaching on the causes and consequences of forced migration, the Centre has developed programmes of study into forced migration, an in-house journal *Forced Migration Review (FMR)*, as well as the *Journal of Refugee Studies*. The RSC library alone holds 39,000 bibliographic items, much of it so-called grey material that is not published or not available through the normal channels.[2] Consideration of culture or the arts generally is not a significant feature of Refugee Studies, as exemplified by the work of the RSC. Only one issue of *Forced Migration Review* has examined cultural practices among refugees, for example, with an edition in December, 1999 devoted to the examination of the art and culture for displaced communities (*FMR*, 1999: 6). Only one project in that edition examines the role that the arts might play in the reconstruction of refugees' lives in the West, with a project which took place in California looking at the ways in which involvement in playing traditional music was said to have been beneficial for Afghan refugees living there (Baily, 1999: 10). For the most part, like refugee studies generally, the rest focus on activities taking place in refugee camps close to the borders of the countries from which refugees have fled.

The fact that most of the world's refugees do not travel great distances and are often housed in camps along the borders of their own countries means that most research in refugee studies is concentrated there. The increasing use of incarceration for those who do arrive in Western states also prohibits research as these institutions are not easily accessible to outsiders. The idea, however, that it is not possible to access refugees outside these institutional spaces (Harrell-Bond and Voutira, 2007) is inaccurate and does not apply to all states. Refugees and asylum seekers live in community settings in many places but their dispersed locations, fears of authority, concerns about racism, prejudice and not least their volatile legal position often compel them to live in a covert way preferring to be seen as migrants rather than asylum seekers.

One further implication of the fact that the majority of refugees do not travel far beyond their own borders is the fact that it is generally the most mobile that can and do travel. In general the gender mix of refugees is fairly even across the world but in situations where it is necessary to travel extensively it is logical that those seen as stronger and more resilient will undertake the journey, which means that refugees in Western states are more likely to be young men. This is borne out in statistical terms; in North America, Latin America and the Caribbean young males constitute a higher proportion of those of concern to UNHCR (Merheb, 2006: 22). It also means that many refugees will have the means to pay for their travel to the place of refuge, even if that entails severe hardship on the families they are forced to leave behind.

Some scholars do take account of cultural thinking in relation to refugees; Lisa Malkki in cultural anthropology focuses on differences between Hutu refugees who settle in camps and those who are dispersed to urban settings in Tanzania. Malkki discovered that refugees who had been settled in designated refugee camps on the borders of Tanzania differed in their attitudes to their identity as exiles from those 'town refugees' who had dispersed into non-refugee neighbourhoods. Broadly speaking, those in the non-refugee setting began to conceive of themselves in a more cosmopolitan way than their counterparts in the refugee camps who classed themselves as refugees and who also maintained strict ethnic boundaries (Malkki,

1995). Malkki is critical of the conceptualisation of 'the refugee' as 'an epistemic object in construction' (Malkki: 1995a: 497) but her research methodology has been criticised by scholars in refugee studies for ignoring the grim material realities of displacement in the face of which questions of identity can seem superficial (Kibreab, 1999: 407). This impatience with cultural considerations in such extreme conditions is perhaps understandable but it is important to show how Malkki's work points to the importance of questions of identity in the move beyond the material considerations which tend to dominate a great deal of thinking in Refugee Studies.

Her work has made an important contribution to the conceptualisation of refugeeness showing how, for example, an over-emphasis on practical and material support for refugees can obscure important questions about cultural attitudes among the 'settled' communities to which refugees flee. Malkki suggests that we should pay as much, if not more, attention to what she calls the sedentarist position of a great deal of research on refugees. Ideas about home and belonging reveal how constructions of identity are based on assumptions about rootedness, taken for granted to the extent that refugees appear to threaten or disrupt the so-called natural order of things. Malkki's work provides a bridge between refugee studies and cultural theory (Verstraete, 2003: 227) and she uses Deleuze and Gautarri's images of roots and rhizomes (Deleuze and Gautarri, 1987) to suggest the importance of always becoming as opposed to reaching any totalising identity destination (Malkki, 1996). Nyers (2003, 2006) seems to agree concluding that cultural expectations, as much as legal definitions, are responsible for the contemporary image of refugees and he directs readers towards refugee activism which eschews traditional notions of invisibility and voicelessness as discussed in Chapter 3.

Thinking culturally about contemporary refugees leads to questions about borderlands, limits, margins and liminal spaces which have been much discussed in recent years across a range of disciplines concomitant with a growing interest in place (Cresswell, 2004: 103). In performance studies, noting that '[b]orderlands traditionally exist as sites of political contestation, risk, and risk-taking' leads Roach to suggest that 'the refugee is the cultural epitome of the postmodern condition' (Reinelt and Roach, 1992: 13). In Bhabha's conception any notion of 'building blocks' of identity gives way to interstices, borders and frontlines where 'the boundary becomes the place from which *something begins its presencing'* (Bhabha, 1994: 5 emphasis in original). For Hall 'identity emerges as a kind of unsettled space, or an unresolved question within that space, between a number of intersecting discourses' (Hall, 1996: 339). He notes that, traditionally, metaphors of identity have been located in images of depth, giving the example 'in here, deep inside me, is my Self which I can reflect on' and asks, 'what is replacing that depth?' (Hall, 1996: 340). Rejecting the obvious binary of 'shallow', he opts instead for destabilization, noting the 'decenterings in intellectual life and in Western thought that have helped to destabilise the question of identity' (Ibid.). So, if certainties about stability in questions of identity are severely shaken by this theoretical and conceptual de-centering how can we think about cultural identity in relation to refugees and questions of migration generally?

One way is to capitulate to the 'endless nomadic existence' which lies behind the argument that 'the self is simply a kind of perpetual signifier ever wandering the earth in search of a transcendental signified that it can never find' (Hall, 2000: 343). This is an unsatisfactory position, valourising refugees, as it does, as cosmopolitan citizens or ideal postmodern subjects, a stance which Gilbert and Lo have described as 'not only utopian but curiously indifferent' (Gilbert and Lo, 2007: 187). The alternative shows how it is important to reconceptualise the very idea of identity which has to be forged in a newly diverse or pluralised society. Identities, and concepts of identity, change throughout the individual's life and this does not happen in a vacuum but always in relationship to the Other: 'only when there is an Other can you know who you are' (Hall, 2000: 345). Hall's argument serves as a possible method by which to conceptualise a way out of the maze of deferral that Bhabha's more fluid concepts of identity conjure.

Hall's more concrete ideas about identity stop 'the spin of post-structuralist or post-modern instabilities long enough to advance a politically effective action' (Dolan, 1993: 417). The presence of migrants, forced or otherwise, offers an opportunity to re-define *all* identities as ethnically produced but the question remains: in whose hands does this re-definition take place and according to whose vision? This creates a paradox whereby subjects may be given an opportunity to define themselves in relation to the Other but in this very act of definition, made necessary by the presence of the Other, resentments and hostilities are built up by the imposition of the *need* to define. This often leads to the urge to ignore or dismiss the task and 'expel the Other symbolically – blot it out, put it over there in the Third World, at the margin' (Hall, 2000: 345).

In an effort to stop the need for re-definition from retreating 'over there' Brah has created the concept of 'diaspora space' defined as the space where 'multiple subject positions are juxtaposed, contested; proclaimed or disavowed' (Brah, 1996: 208). This uses ethnicity as a way to define *all* groups so that diaspora space becomes 'the point at which boundaries of inclusion and exclusion, of belonging and otherness, of "us" and "them", are contested' (Brah, 1996: 209). The point of using diaspora space is to undermine the grounds on which the native and the diasporic subject are founded, throwing the emphasis onto an account of the ways in which *both* identities are constructed within the nation space. In this way, for example, England becomes a diaspora space in which 'African, Caribbean, Irish, Asian, Jewish and other diasporas intersect among themselves as well as with the entity constructed as "Englishness", thoroughly re-inscribing it in the process' (Brah, 1996: 209). In performance studies there is an opportunity to re-envisage these general terms about meetings and encounters giving them a temporal and spatial quality in the theatrical space. This allows us to address specifics where diaspora space is small enough to examine moments of encounter; the space between two individuals on a stage, for example, or the space in which an audience and performers meet.

Practice and dynamic ways of knowing

This book is informed by practice, some my own but mostly that of other people;[3] by conversations, interviews and encounters with refugees and asylum seekers, with refugee artists, with artists who are deeply concerned about refugees, with advice workers, social workers, activists and refugee advocates. It presents an analysis of what happens when people flee fearing for their lives and the ways in which they create drama, theatre, music, poetry and performance to make sense of that journey and of their new surroundings. It considers refugee theatre and performance in the UK and the rest of Europe, in Australia, and in the United States. Different locations are more prominent at different times in the book depending on the kind of theatre under examination. Productions by companies like Théâtre du Soleil, for example, originate in France but tour internationally while smaller companies like version 1.0 in Australia are not set up to tour outside Australia. The participatory theatre which is examined in Chapter 4 is mostly located in Manchester in the UK because of access to this necessarily localised work. What has been labelled activist perform-ance in Chapter 3 is located in Australia and in the UK.

Conquergood's writing on radical research has provided a useful model for practical research, especially his notions about the radical potential of performance studies research. Quoting de Certeau's idea that 'what the map cuts up, the story cuts across' (Certeau quoted in Conquergood, 2002: 145) Conquergood shows how the map, 'offi-cial, objective and abstract' is one way of knowing; the story, 'prac-tical, embodied and popular' another. It is Conquergood's belief that performance studies offers a 'promiscuous traffic between [these] two ways of knowing' (Ibid.). Performance studies can open up the space between analysis and action or, more dramatically, 'pull the pin on the binary opposition between theory and practice' (Ibid.). This dynamic approach to knowledge synthesises bodily knowledges which are subjective, proximate and situated, with more empirical knowledges produced and encoded in text. This conceptualisation builds a complex picture that can encompass the individual and the general, the personal and the political. However, examining practice in theatre and performance also sets up the possibility for moments of incongruity and counter-intuition, for surprise and bafflement, as much as for neat theories, models and paradigms.

Conquergood's notions of dialogical performance which emerged from his model of 'mapping performative stances towards the other' (Conquergood, 1985) has also proved useful. Developed to conceptu-alise work among Hmong refugees in Chicago, he describes four 'moral pitfalls' into which the performance ethnographer might fall: the Custodian's Rip-off, the Skeptic's Cop-out, the Enthusiast's Infatu-ation, the Curator's Exhibitionism (Ibid.). His description of Dialogical Performance, where genuine conversation is enabled between researcher and subject, is an ideal towards which he strives. Despite the fact that he does not dwell on the political status of the refugees with whom he works, this model will be used as a performance ideal against which it is useful to discuss both professional theatrical and participatory performance about and with refugees respectively.

Refugee theatre has been created by citizens of the states in which refugees have sought asylum, and increasingly by refugees and asylum seekers themselves, but all these endeavours take place against a background of fear, suspicion and mistrust on all sides. Contemporary attitudes to refuge and asylum are conditioned by a sense of crisis and Chapter 1 shows the various ways in which this crisis has been manipulated and perpetuated and the effect that this has on refugees and on cultural expressions surrounding refugees. Suspicions about refugees' motives for seeking asylum and increased numbers of refugees generated by conflict and instability in many regions of the world have been heightened by fears that refugees are connected in some way to those instabilities.

Stories are multiply complex in a world where lives and futures depend on believable stories and this is explored in Chapter 1 when I introduce the concept of bureaucratic performance which is generated because refugees have to prove their individual persecution under the terms of the 1951 Refugee Convention. To convince the authorities of their right to stay asylum seekers are compelled to produce a convincing story of individual persecution in their previous home and to show that this persecution would continue were they to be returned. I analyse this moment of telling as a speech act with the capacity for success or failure but show how the outcome is more likely to be the latter on a political level despite its linguistic success. Using Kafka's parable *Before the Law* I show how 'the man from the country' is like a refugee who waits at the 'door of the law' imagining it to be open and accessible for all only to discover that this is not the case. Given the high stakes involved in bureaucratic performance I go on to suggest that theatre provides an arena in which a level of experimentation with names and identities can take place and in which artists have seized an opportunity to use the exploratory nature of theatre to educate and inform audiences.

Chapter 2 examines the range of theatre activity that has been produced by artists in the states to which refugees have fled. Continuing with Austin's ideas on speech acts I consider the nature of the etiolated speech of an actor on the stage and connections between this and accusations of parasitism against refugees. This suggests reasons for the popularity of verbatim theatre techniques in much refugee theatre and leads to questions about hospitality which underpin most theatre made about refugees by non-refugee artists.

All theatre about refugees attempts to create a better sense of under-standing of refugees among non-refugee audiences, sometimes by confronting misunderstandings based on myths particularly those about asylum seekers. I look at two contrasting approaches to staging asylum myths through Banner Theatre's *They get Free Mobiles...don't they?*[4] and the play *The Kindness of Strangers* by Tony Green (2004). Identifying theatrical tropes of home and nation accounts for the ways in which a large number of plays examine notions of hospital-ity and the ethical responsibilities of the host. Plays in this category include *I have before me a Remarkable Document Given to me by a Young Lady from Rwanda* (2003) and *Crocodile Seeking Refuge* (2005) both by Sonja Linden, *Two Brothers* by Hannie Rayson (2005) and *Asylum! Asylum!* (1996) by Donal O'Kelly.

This chapter goes on to discuss a number of plays that depend on the audience 'standing in the shoes of the refugee', a strategy intended to create empathy and enhanced understanding. I suggest that the strategy used by Australian company version 1.0 in their verbatim piece *CMI: A Certain Maritime Incident* shows how eschewing notions of empathy with refugees and using the words of citizens can raise the level of debate beyond pity and into a more ethical arena. Large scale productions *Le Dernier Caravansérail* by Théâtre du Soleil and *The Children of Herakles* by American Repertory Theatre are examined in relation to *Pericles* by Cardboard Citizens/RSC in terms of their canonicity but also their differing abilities to access the international touring circuit.

In Chapter 3 I ask what happens when refugees step outside the expectations of silence and invisibility that are so often imposed upon them. This chapter examines a range of refugee activist activities and frames them as 'impossible activism', so called because they are car-ried out by refugees themselves and thus go beyond expectations of silence and passivity. These include marches and anti-deportation demonstrations as well as various manifestations of self-harm includ-ing lip-sewing and hunger strikes. I argue that it is important to under-stand the temporal nature of performativity in order to appreciate these acts as pieces of 'wishful performance' where the possibility of re-ordering things in a more just and humane way can be glimpsed even if they cannot be carried out on a pragmatic or political level.

Finally, Chapter 4 describes and accounts for the growing body of theatrical and cultural events produced by refugees themselves.

Using ideas from cultural performance it is possible to identify the significance of the many refugee arts and cultural festivals that have grown and developed since the early 1990s. Using the Exodus Refugee Festival in Manchester as an example of this phenomenon I show how narratives of authenticity and togetherness vie for attention at this event and what these show about the festival in the wider cultural calendar of the city and the nation. The work of four actors who are refugees, all of whom have created multivocal solo performance pieces that relate directly to their experiences as refugees, is considered here. Finally, from participatory theatre practices I examine a growing range of work that takes place when refugees get involved with creative projects that are explicitly designed for their participation. Looking at these indicates how it is important to question assumptions about trauma and to understand how bureaucratic performance can act to encourage narratives of victimhood in theatre and performance.

In concluding I turn to an explicitly ethical consideration of the work beginning with a discussion of the work of Levinas, some of whose ideas have haunted this entire enterprise. I will argue that the political understanding of refugees brought about by conceptualising bureaucratic performance is a necessary prelude to a more ethical understanding. Thinking ethically about refugees begins with hospitality and responsibility for the Other, with small local acts of (necessarily) compromised hospitality that stand in for hospitality on a larger scale. Given the impossibility of aligning political and ethical needs and desires on a geopolitical level these are, perhaps for now, the best that can be hoped for. Theatre and performance have an important role to play in creating a more understanding climate and in showing the way in which these small acts can be achieved and perpetuated. Importantly, the act of creating theatre itself can be seen as a manifestation of the possibilities of generous action, of acting ethically with refugees and people seeking asylum.

1
Refugees, Crisis and Bureaucratic Performance

Sticks and stones may break my bones, but words will never hurt me.

— Playground chant

These people are not professional refugees; they don't know the magic code.

— Shahin Shafaei, Iranian refugee and theatre artist

In order to appreciate the cultural forms that are attached to refugees it is necessary to understand the legal context within which the definition of 'who can be a refugee' operates in the West in this particular historical moment. The first part of this chapter briefly deals with this question and I then go on to ask why refugees have been seen as especially significant since the early 1990s when the discourses surrounding them started to be couched in the language of crisis. Finally, taking up and exploring the concept of bureaucratic performance shows how, although tremendously significant, the language of international law is not adequate to the task of discussing the complexities of the ways in which refugees are represented in a wide range of cultural forms. Using ideas from Austin's speech act theory I will indicate some of the contradictions inherent in ideas about identity in relation to refugeeness in order to pave the way for discussions about the ways refugees have been represented and how they have chosen to represent themselves through theatre and performance practices.

Convention refugees or conventional refugees?

It is common in Refugee Studies to speak of 'Convention refugees' as a way to describe those refugees who conform to the 1951 Refugee Convention. The term 'Convention refugee' is often used to distinguish refugees from Internally Displaced People (IDPs)[1] who are defined by the UN as

> persons or groups of persons who have been forced or obliged to flee or to leave their homes or places of habitual residence, in particular as a result of or in order to avoid the effects of armed conflict, situations of generalized violence, violations of human rights or natural or human-made disasters, and who *have not crossed an internationally recognized State border.*[2] (my italics).

I emphasise the last part of this definition to show the important distinction between refugees and IDPs which lies in the fact that 'Convention refugees' *have* crossed a border having fled their own land and crossed into another's. One of the central arguments of this book is the suggestion that refugees who have crossed several borders and travelled to western states to claim asylum are forced to *play the role* of 'Convention refugees'.

To be considered 'legitimate' refugees must prove that they have fled individual persecution and that they fear persecution should they return to their own countries. In the course of arguing their case as 'Convention refugees' they become enmeshed in bureaucratic performance whereby they become *conventional refugees*, those who conform to cultural expectations of refugees, particularly in relation to suffering. They must become conventional refugees because, under international law, anyone has the right to claim asylum but only governments have the power to grant it. The onus is on the individual asylum seeker to prove that they have what the Refugee Convention defines as 'a well-founded fear of persecution'. This is something that the majority of asylum seekers fail to do. In Britain in 2005, for example, 6 per cent of asylum seekers were granted refugee status at the initial decision stage while an additional 11 per cent were granted exceptional leave or humanitarian or discretionary protection (Kyambi, 2005). In countries like Greece this figure is much lower while in Canada it is often higher (Merheb, 2006).

Asylum seekers are increasingly assumed to be 'acting the part' of a persecuted refugee but it is a 'performance' that will not succeed for most, and commentators believe that a culture of disbelief operates: crudely speaking, that all asylum seekers are assumed to be lying until they can prove otherwise. Legal definitions and the language of international law fall far short of encompassing the complexities involved in the many layered journeys that are undertaken by refugees to western countries. They also ignore the desire for refugees to represent themselves in certain ways that do not conform to the legal or cultural expectations placed upon them. However, despite the inadequacy of legal definitions to adequately reflect complex human experience, they strongly condition that experience and the many ways in which that experience is reflected on and expressed. My argument is that most, if not all, contemporary refugee theatre and performance is conditioned by this situation.

Who *is* 'a refugee'?

Travel, the movement of people from one location to another, is part of what it means to be human. Quotidian movements necessary to sustain life, from field or supermarket to home, are not usually classed as 'travel', that term being reserved for more significant journeys. Travellers create their own movement for pleasure; to encounter those who are strange to them or to re-encounter friends or family members in places which they could not experience if they remained at home. But people can become *compelled* to travel from their places of origin and three factors, choice, planning and return, differentiate the one who travels for pleasure or gain from those whose choices are more constrained. The *choice* of whether and when to travel is one which is available to those who travel for pleasure, and they can decide under what circumstances to travel in order to facilitate the ease of their journey and their reception on arrival. Linked with choice is *planning* because to take the decision to travel implies a level of planning which is not usually available to the traveller who is *compelled* to move. Doreen Massey suggests this when she talks about the unevenness of 'differentiated mobility' where 'some people are more in charge of it than others; some initiate flows of movement, others don't; some are more on the receiving end of it than others; some are effectively imprisoned by it' (Massey, 1994: 149). Finally, the question of *return* and the levels of complexity involved in that possible return are entirely different for those who travel through choice than for those who do not. The traveller who moves for reasons of pleasure is usually destined to return, but those who are forced to travel have a much more ambivalent relationship with 'home', perhaps unwilling or unable to consider a return.

Refugees and asylum seekers fall into the broad category of forced travellers (more commonly called forced migrants) but they are differentiated within this category by international law whereby they are given a special status, based on persecution in their place of birth. However, it must *not* be assumed that the terms 'refugee' or 'asylum seeker' are neat categorisations, universally accepted for all time (McMaster, 2001; Shacknove, 1985). As international refugee lawyer Guy Goodwin-Gill puts it 'When someone asks me *Who is a refugee? my reply is always Who is asking and why?'*.[3] Goodwin-Gill implies that, despite the apparent certainties of international law, definitions of refugeeness may be a little 'slippery' seeming to suggest that a certain degree of self-interest may be detected in both the question and in the answer to that question. Most western countries base their definition of what constitutes a refugee on the passage alluding to 'well-founded fear' from the 1951 United Nations Convention Relating to the Status of Refugees in which the term refugee was legally codified for the first time. This states that a refugee is someone who

> as a result of events occurring before January 1951 and owing to a well-founded fear of being persecuted for reasons of race, religion, nationality, membership of a particular social group or political opinion, is outside the country of his nationality and is unable or, owing to such fear, is unwilling to avail himself of the protection of that country; or who, not having a nationality and being outside the country of his former habitual residence as a result of such events, is unable or, owing to such fear, is unwilling to return to it. (Art 1 [AJ [2]/2)[4]

There are, however, other legal definitions of refugeeness and The Organisation of African Unity (OAU) 1969 definition recognised the UN Convention of 1951 but added a broader range of criteria on which refugeeness can be based, focusing on the breakdown of the bond between the individual and the state (Shacknove, 1985). In this definition persecution is not the primary driver of refugeeness and the OAU definition recognises that countries can let citizens down for a number of reasons not related to tyranny, such as extreme poverty, civil war or foreign intervention. The language and definitions of the OAU emanates in part from the challenges posed by decolonisation on that continent (Nyers, 2006: 104) and reflects the historical experience of Africa as much as the 1951 Convention does for Europe (Zolberg et al., 1989: 29). A further agreement, the 1984 Cartagena Declaration, builds on the OAU definition and has been adopted to protect refugees in Central America, Mexico and Panama.[5] The fact that several definitions of 'who can be a refugee' exist simultaneously in different geopolitical situations shows how refugeeness is constructed and how this apparently timeless concept has been taken up and adapted to suit a range of political agendas in specific historical moments.

For the purposes of this book it is the 1951 Convention which is of most relevance because the focus here is on refugees who manage to travel to western countries that have signed the 1951 Refugee Convention. The 'events occurring before January 1951' in the clause above refer specifically to the Second World War and its aftermath, during which an estimated 30 million people were displaced (Kushner and Knox, 1999: 10). Those who could not return were acknowledged as needing special care and protection under international law. Following Denmark, the first signatory to the Convention, most western countries have signed up to this international agreement to shelter refugees and not return them to their countries of origin. The notable exception is the United States which did not sign the 1951 Convention but did sign the subsequent 1967 Protocol which widened the scope of the Convention by moving it beyond the conditions specifically pertaining to the Second World War. By signing the 1951 Refugee Convention, and/or its 1967 Protocol, some 164 of the UN's 191 member states have undertaken to protect refugees and not return them to a country where they may be persecuted, a process which protects refugees from what is known as *refoulement* or compulsory return.[6] This means that under the terms of international refugee law the two main criteria for being a refugee in the West are 'persecution and alienage' (Turton,

2003: 13). To be recognised as a refugee under the terms of the 1951 Convention, or the 1967 Protocol, refugees have to have travelled outside their country of origin, to be able to demonstrate past persecution in that place and a reasonable fear that persecution would continue were they to return.

When the 1951 Refugee Convention came into being, western countries had a clear idea of what a refugee looked like; typically European, fleeing wars, religious persecution or oppressive regimes. Countries' obligations to refugees were similarly clear; to provide political refuge in the short term and the right to work and settle after that. Forty years later the picture had changed dramatically and by the early 1990s refugees were increasingly non-Europeans from poorer countries in the global south (Dummett, 2001; Marfleet, 2006; Pirouet, 2001; Schuster, 2003; Whittaker, 2006). Refugees were also present in much greater numbers and, while asylum claims to Western Europe averaged 13,000 in the 1970s, annual totals had risen to 690,000 by 1992 (Gibney, 2006: 145). Although it is notoriously difficult to represent displacement statistically, the United Nations High Commission for Refugees (UNHCR) estimated in 2005 that there were approximately 19 million people in the world who were displaced either within their own borders or outside them. Refugees accounted for just over half this figure at 9.2 million and asylum seekers were said to number 838,000. By the first half of 2008 the United States had the largest number of asylum claims with 25,400 new claims for asylum. Canada ranked second among the 44 industrialised countries with 16,400 new claims. France and the UK were third and fourth with 15,600 and 14,500 new asylum claims respectively.[7] Despite anxiety about asylum seekers in Australia, the highest number of unauthorised arrivals in any one year was 5870 in 1999/2000. In contrast, the number of people between 1997 and 2007 classed as 'overstayers' was between 40,000 and 60,000, the majority of whom were from the UK and the United States who had entered Australia on working holiday or tourist visas.[8] It is important to remember that, even though this study focuses on asylum seeking in western countries, the distribution of refugees across the world is very uneven. Pakistan, for example, is estimated to hold the largest number of refugees of any country accommodating 12 per cent of all refugees under the UNHCR mandate (Merheb, 2006).

Increasing global movement

At least three factors account for the growing numbers of asylum seekers in western countries since the early 1990s. Firstly, global migration in general has increased and the UNHCR estimated that migration had grown from 100 million in 1960 to 175 million by the year 2000. Inequalities arising through uneven economic development are a major cause of increased refugee numbers shaping international migration (Dummett, 2001; Marfleet, 2006; Pirouet, 2001; Schuster, 2003). This is partly the result of 'increased disparities in income and human security between North and South [because] 'impoverishment and outward migration are closely linked' (Merheb, 2006: 12). While states welcome increased flows of trade and they are much more ambivalent about flows of people and labour because trade is seen to generate financial gain while the people who make the trade possible represent a financial drain on a state's resources.

The second reason for an increase in the numbers of people seeking asylum in the West is globalisation which 'creates the cultural and technical conditions for mobility' (Merheb, 2006: 12). Growth in the numbers of international flights and price wars among airlines has enabled even economically disadvantaged people to fly. Between 1950 and 1990 international tourism increased by 17 times (Marfleet, 2006: 27) and international travel is quicker and easier than ever before. This, combined with 'manifold calamities – persecution, violence, war, hunger' (Dummett, 2001: 6), creates the conditions for people to leave their homes in large numbers in the hope of a better life. At the same time, communications technologies have boomed since the mid-1990s, with an estimated 1.4 billion emails sent every day (Marfleet, 2006: 218) and the global media network which beams 'idealised images of northern lifestyles into the poorest villages' (Merheb, 2006: 12) makes images of Western affluence more generally available.

The final cause of increased refugee numbers since the late 1980s is the changing nature of war (Dona and Berry, 1999; Kaldor, 2001; Summerfield, 1999). Wars that would once have taken place between professional armies have been surpassed by conflicts that impinge as much, if not more, on the civilian population. The ratio of military to civilian casualties at the beginning of the twentieth century was 8:1 and this has been exactly reversed to 1:8 military to civilians in the 'new wars' since the 1990s (Kaldor, 2001). The figure of 80 per cent or 90 per cent civilian casualties in contemporary conflicts appears to have been broadly adopted (Marfleet, 2006; Moorehead, 2005; Nordstrom, 1997) but the significance here lies in the human displacement that appears to be the deliberate result of these strategies and the ways in which this effects people in those countries effected and beyond (Thompson et al., 2009: 11). 'Refugee flows are not a by-product of fighting but the strategic goal of war itself' (Rieff, 2002: 130) and as war changes in its nature, increased numbers of refugees and displaced people are the direct result.

Whatever the reasons for the increase in the number of refugees the perception that refugee movement is 'global, diverse and increasing' (McMaster, 2001: 33) has created a sense of panic leading to the conception of a 'refugee crisis' and of refugees as a 'problem' needing to be managed. This is illustrated by a growth in refugee legislation across Europe and in Australia, Canada and the United States which has dramatically increased not only in volume but in the urgency of its rhetoric. In the early 1990s Australian immigration policy shifted its emphasis from humanitarianism to control (McMaster, 2001: 59) as 'a politics of transit was slowly replaced by a politics of control' (Puggioni, 2006: par. 7). Domestic conditions in America in the early years of Bill Clinton's presidency had a dramatic impact on attitudes to asylum seekers which led to the passing of tougher laws on political asylum (Schrag, 2000). In particular, because of the expedited removal provisions of the 1996 Illegal Immigration Reform and Immigrant Responsibility Act, anyone stopped in a US port can be refused entry if they do not hold a valid passport (Staeger, 2004: 76). In 2001 The Patriot Act, Enhanced Border Security and Visa Entry Reform Act in the United States tightened rules on visas even further and enhanced the authority to detain illegal immigrants.[9] Even Canada, with its reputation for a more liberal approach to immigration, has seen a tightening of regulations since the early 1990s (Staeger, 2004).

In Europe the dramatic changes to the political landscape with the fall of the Soviet Union, reunification of Germany and conflicts in Eastern Europe and the Balkan states created high levels of instability and a great deal of movement among people. In 1993 the Treaty of Maastricht took the European Union a step closer to political unity through the harmonisation of internal European borders with an eye to clamping down on illegal migration. A range of anti-immigration laws has created 'Fortress Europe' (McMaster, 2001; Pirouet, 2001) where restrictions on undocumented movement generally have impacted in a negative way on refugees. British legislation has taken advantage of the geographical isolation provided by its island geography and created a number of measures of exclusion that are intended to make it as difficult as possible for refugees to reach their shores. Asked in 2002 if there were any avenues by which asylum seekers might legally enter the UK, the Minister of State for Immigration, Lord Rooker replied 'No' (Gibney, 2006: 153). The increase in the volume of legislation has made it a necessity for refugees to use illegal means to enter most states, and this increases the level of suspicion and mistrust of refugees shown by the populations of many western nations.

Several studies have been carried out into attitudes of citizens towards refugees and asylum seekers (Campbell and Clark, 1997; D'Onofrio and Munk, 2004; Finney, 2005; Lewis, 2005).[10] These suggest a high degree of hostility towards asylum seekers in particular but many commentators have shown that these hostile attitudes are based on false beliefs (Pedersen et al., 2006). Myths or false beliefs about refugees and asylum seekers emanate in part from the press and are widely disseminated through print journalism in particular. While the attitude of the popular press towards race in general has softened in recent years (ICAR, 2004, 2006), the notable exception to this is seen in attitudes towards refugees and asylum seekers. This reflects the move from racism predicated on biological difference to that based on cultural difference (Gibson, 2003: 368). In this new or 'Xeno-racism' (Fekete, 2001) hatred circulating around black migrants has been 'generalised to contempt for strangers or foreigners in general' (Gibson, 2003: 368).

Although this will be discussed in more detail in the next chapter it is important to note here that the news media have increasingly determined the terms by which asylum is addressed creating 'an interface between state and popular racisms, providing a forum where the bureaucratic language of the first is translated into the populist language of the second' (Kundnani, 2001: 48). The British tabloid press in particular has been accused of inaccurate, negative and biased journalism around asylum seekers and coverage was extreme enough throughout the late 1990s to create a reaction in the UNHCR where United Nations officials 'criticised the British media for their hysterical coverage of asylum seekers and urged moderation from the government' (ICAR, 2004: 80). Asylum seekers have been set up as scapegoats in the British tabloids *The Sun*, the *Daily Mail*, the *Daily Express* and the *Daily Star* which are read daily by 22 million people, or about one third of the British population (Greenslade, 2005). This has resulted in a situation where the term 'asylum seeker' functions as a 'code word for a range of meanings, variously referring to people as illegal immigrants, scroungers or potential criminals' (Faulkner, 2003: 95). Because a great deal of theatre about refugees is concerned to challenge these ideas it is worth understanding a little of how this situation comes about.

Moral panic, false beliefs and sticky metaphors

One of the key concepts in the role of the media in shaping attitudes towards refugees, generating and perpetuating their association with crisis is 'moral panic'[11] which takes place when the media manipulates and defines false beliefs in order to create the framework through which to view the subsequent panic. This panic is characteristically disproportionate and volatile and it generates hostility by creating a consensus that a serious threat exists. Cohen, who first identified the phenomenon in relation to youth culture in 1987, has since extended and updated the categories of subjects that are prone to generating moral panic 25 years on from his original thesis. By 2002 asylum seekers had entered the lexicon of moral panic and Cohen concluded that the overall narrative about asylum seekers is 'a single, virtually uninterrupted message of hostility and rejection' (Cohen, 2002: xix).

Some false beliefs that have generated moral panic about refugees are specific to certain national jurisdictions and in the UK and Ireland a prevalent false belief is that these countries are host to many more asylum seekers than is actually the case. A survey in Northern Ireland in 2003 showed that many participants believed that the UK had more than 20 per cent of the world's refugees when the actual number is less that 2 per cent.[12] A MORI poll carried out in Britain in 2002 reported similar figures, with respondents estimating that the UK was host to 23 per cent of the world's refugees, with younger respondents (15–18 years) believing that Britain housed over 31 per cent of the world's refugees. Only 4 per cent of those asked knew the correct figure.[13]

In Australia there is a common perception that asylum seekers are 'queue jumpers' (Manne, 2004; Pedersen et al., 2006) because those who enter the country illegally are said to be jumping the queue by taking the place of those who have made an application from outside the country for asylum. This is only the case because the Australian government enacted legislation whereby the number of places available for official asylum cases is correspondingly reduced with each unofficial migration to Australia (Manne, 2004: 10). The Australian government refuses to acknowledge that the image of the queue suggests that refugees to Australia have some degree of choice, underplaying the fact that most people would not choose to migrate under such difficult and dangerous conditions. The idea of queue jumping is often accompanied by the false belief that those who pay smugglers to bring them into the country illegally must be 'cashed up' or rich enough to pay for their passage by boat to Australia (Pedersen, et al., 2006). Despite some of these local variations, myths or false beliefs about refugees and asylum seekers in all western states are remarkably similar; that 'parasitic' asylum seekers deprive native citizens of resources, receive favourable treatment from the government, and that they are 'illegal' (Ibid.).

Since the early 1990s the 'refugee crisis' in the West has been further exacerbated by the fact that national security and ethnic identity have become imbricated in both popular and political discourse. Specifically, associations of immigrants, refugees and terrorists have become linked in a 'metonymic chain', illustrated by the words of Conservative British politician Michael Howard when he said 'Firm border controls are essential if we are to limit migration, fight crime and protect Britain from terrorism' (Charteris-Black, 2006, 574). The impact of this drawing together of security and identity in a metonymic chain has been particularly marked for refugees and asylum seekers since 2001 when the terrorist attacks on major US institutions led to the widespread securitisation of asylum practices (Merheb, 2006: 5). The perception exists that asylum is somehow a terrorist's refuge in a post-9/11 world (Zard, 2002) and the bizarre circularity of this situation is highlighted by Gibney who points out that 'the attacks that fateful day led to war; war created refugees; refugees fled in search of asylum' (Gibney, 2002: 40). Following the events of 11th September 2001 the negative impact of the American reaction on countries like Afghanistan has been immense (Human Rights Watch, 2001) and subsequent wars there and in Iraq have had a nightmarish effect on those who would seek asylum from these countries but also on asylum seekers from Iran, Pakistan, Somalia and Eritrea; in fact any country seen as being predominantly Muslim. British politicians suggested that refugees coming from Afghanistan could prove to be a destabilising force if they were allowed to seek refuge in the West and David Blunkett, the British Home Secretary at the time, is quoted as saying 'the main aim is to stop people coming from that region and spreading across the world. That is also necessary for reasons of terrorism' (Ibid.: 9).

In Australia the impact of the securitisation of asylum on migration from Afghanistan, as well as from Iraq and Iran has been considerable. Many of those who fled to Australia had already been living as refugees in Iran having been internally displaced or having left Pakistan, Syria and Jordan (Human Rights Watch, 2001). In 1999 a route was opened up through movement by sea from Malaysia or Indonesia, often in small fishing boats, to one of Australia's Indian Ocean territories. Between 1999 and 2001 approximately 9500 asylum seekers arrived in this way and, although this is a very small figure in global terms, for Australia it was unprecedented (Manne, 2004: 6). Negative reactions to the presence of growing numbers of asylum seekers were exacerbated when 88 Australian citizens were among the 202 people killed in 2002 by a bomb attack on a nightclub in Bali. The bombers were said to be members of Jemaah Islamiyah, a militant Islamic group with alleged connections to al-Qaeda.[14] In 2005 Australia's emergent reputation as an increasingly relaxed, multicultural nation was rocked by a series of riots on the beaches of Sydney's suburbs. Despite reassurances by politicians that these were not race riots, it seemed clear that the roots of the unrest lay in tensions between Lebanese and Australian young people (O'Riordan, 2005). Respondents to surveys carried out in Australia in the early 2000s identified asylum seekers as a threat to 'the Australian way of life', refugee outsiders were criticised for not 'fitting in' (Pedersen, et al., 2006: 105) and it was suggested that they would cause 'cultural problems' (Dunn et al., 2007: 580). The presence of immigrants has become linked with questions of national identity at the same time as fears for security are rising. In Australia the perceived threat to security posed by the presence of asylum seekers, especially those identified as being from Muslim or Arabic backgrounds, is strongly linked to threats to national integrity.

In Europe the panic engendered by the September 11th attacks in Washington and New York in 2001 conveniently masked the fact that none of those involved were refugees. Indeed, in subsequent attacks in Madrid in 2004 and London in 2005, when bombs were planted on public transport networks, none of the perpetrators were refugees or from refugee backgrounds. The fact that many of those convicted for the Madrid bombings were seen as having integrated into Spanish life with a liking for football, fashion, drinking and Spanish girlfriends caused their neighbours to doubt that they had any Islamic fundamentalist agenda.[15] In London the perpetrators were British citizens, and products of the British education system. This was complicated by the fact that they were second generation immigrants whose parents had come from Pakistan and thereafter links with al-Qaeda, real or imagined, have muddled the situation to the point where *all* refugees appear to be a threat to public security and national integrity.

One way to raise the temperature of any debate and heighten the moral panic is through the linguistic strategy of the metonymic chain whereby metaphors are 'employed persuasively to provide cognitive frames for perspectives on social issues' (Charteris-Black, 2006: 565). Ahmed (2004: 91) argues that signs become 'sticky' through repetition, their history of articulation allowing them to accrue meaning over time. The sticky metaphors that have become 'attached' to refugees in both political and popular discourse are a strange mixture of the domestic (doors) and the apocalyptic (floods). Metaphors relating to natural disasters with an emphasis on floods and tidal waves can be found in early refugee scholarship with Marrus in 1985 describing how the 'flood' of European refugees had subsided and been overtaken by African states that were 'awash with refugees' (Marrus, 1985: 4) but these images of floods and tides have more recently been taken up in the popular press.

In the UK these are often linked to a number of military metaphors reflecting Britain's island geography and underlining connections between refugees and being under siege, defending frontiers and fending off attacks (Faulkner, 2003: 99). These military metaphors figure national borders as frontiers that are vulnerable to attack and suggest images of the nation as what has been called a 'spatial containment schema' (Charteris-Black, 2006: 575). This conceptualisation of a country as a closed container might be attractive because the quality of a container is such that, while it can be penetrated, it can also be sealed. The container of the United States is seen to be controlled by doors where 'genuine' refugees are welcome through the 'front door' while those who sneak in through the 'back door' are seen as deceitful and reprehensible (McMaster, 2001: 107).[16] Similarly, Canadian Immigration Minister refers to Canadian border policy as one of controlling doors (Nyers, 2003: 1087).

Metaphors for immigration to Australia are similarly powerfully figured in terms of front and back doors, the front door being onto the Pacific while the nation's 'back door' opens onto the Indian Ocean which borders with Asia (Balint, 2005). The cumulative effect of these metaphors is to suggest a feeling of being deceived and over-whelmed. While the front door presents the public face, the back door is more secretive and callers can be over the threshold before the house owner is aware of their presence. Similarly, sudden unpredictable flows of water have the power to drown or suffocate those overtaken by them. Both sets of metaphors, those connected to doors and those concerning water, have other possible readings that are less well known and have far less power to circulate than those promulgated by the national press. Instead of floods and tidal waves Winder suggests that 'we might do better to think of Britain as a lake refreshed by one stream that bubbles in and in and another that trickles out [...] without the oxygen generated by fresh water, it would stagnate' (Winder, 2004: 5). Equally, doors can be seen as thresholds or edges of possibility and potential. However these alternative readings are not widely circulated because they do not accommodate themselves readily within a narrative of crisis which demands less complex and more frightening conceptualisations.

Crisis and asylum

These conditions create and perpetuate a situation where seeking asylum becomes a threat that has to be kept in the forefront of public life. To do this all 'mainstream political effort is put into producing a crisis, an engineered crisis which is then met with the political discourses of "crisis management"' (Tyler, 2006: 195). A crisis is defined as a crucial moment or turning point, often as an emergency which, by definition, requires action to be taken. The discourse of crisis 'gives order to the world by marking off limits, assigning positions, and policing boundaries' (Nyers, 2006: 7). In order to produce a discourse of crisis it is necessary to suggest its oppositional relationship with what might be described as normality. However, the balance between the two states is not symmetrical but controlled by differential power relationships so that the crisis or emergency becomes pictured as 'that which is aberrant, unusual, not normal' (Nyers, 2006: 8). A crisis is therefore a construction, a way of conceptualising that which is 'not normal' and which can be seen as temporary or unstable. It is in the interests of the authorities to maintain the link between refugees and crisis because it instils and perpetuates a sense of fear and apprehension around refugees and those seeking asylum, allowing governments to maintain a veneer of humanitarianism towards those who are classed as 'genuine' refugees while dealing harshly with those who seemingly fail to meet the criteria.

The most overt way to maintain the discourse of crisis has been by legally differentiating 'genuine' refugees from so-called asylum seekers thus setting up and perpetuating the idea that 'true refugees' are those that can be recognised under the terms of the Refugee Convention while the rest (the majority) are merely economic migrants. Not under any political threat at home (extreme poverty and war not counting as a threat) they must be dishonest, greedy, a threat to national security and identity, terrorists, or all of the above and their presence, according to this logic, constitutes a crisis. Covertly generating a sense of crisis by creating the figure of 'the asylum seeker' allows states to be seen to *control* that crisis in a more overt way. Any asylum seeker who wishes to gain recognition as a refugee must, as we have seen, convince the authorities that they have a clear and credible story which demonstrates individual past persecution in their own country. They must also convince their audience that their persecution would continue were they to return. This must be couched in the language and terminology of international law so that it is recognised as operating within the boundaries of the 1951 UN Convention (Blommaert, 2001; Shuman and Bohmer, 2004). But the story alone is not enough and it must be rehearsed to create a credible *performance*, convincing in the telling as well as in the construction. A weak 'performance' can lead to failure no matter how strong the story/script and failure in these circumstances can be deadly. This is the essence of bureaucratic performance and it is vital to understand how bureaucratic performance operates because most, if not all, subsequent performances of refugeeness, including theatrical performance, are conditioned or marked by it in some way.

Asylum-seeking speech acts

The state has several options at its disposal when asylum seekers invoke the 1951 Refugee Convention but the option to accept the word of *all those* who make the statement has been ruled out so that the state demonstrates its belief in a small number of the claims while rejecting others as 'bogus'. In making the speech act *I claim asylum* the speaker seeks the title of 'refugee' that will allow him/her to stay under the protection of their new state but the fact that the vast majority do not succeed shows how the power to name is maintained by the state. With the name 'refugee' comes the right to personal safety and, eventually, legal entitlements while the withholding of that title leaves the speaker extremely vulnerable. This is not constative and refugees are not simply *describing* their state at that particular moment, but performative: in making this statement they aim to achieve something, to alter their legal status, to become a refugee.

Here I am clearly alluding to Austin's speech act theory which has provided a 'rigorous means of studying how performance embodies symbolic systems, and more radically, how such systems help to construct and constitute the body as such' (McKenzie, 2001: 41). I will show now how Austin's ideas relate directly to refugees and asylum seekers as a necessary prelude to understanding the full impact of bureaucratic performance on the lives of contemporary refugees and asylum seekers. By asking 'Can saying make it so?' (Austin, 1976: 7) Austin was concerned to differentiate between statements of fact or description and what he called performative utterances or performatives for short. With performatives 'the issuing of the utterance is the performing of the action' (Ibid.: 6). So, for example, someone naming a ship is carrying out the action of naming in saying 'I name this ship *The Queen Elizabeth*' (Ibid.: 5). While statements generally can be shown to have qualities of truth or falsehood according to Austin performatives are more likely to be felicitous/happy or infelicitous/unhappy; in short, they work or they do not, they succeed or fail.

Austin outlined six conditions that have to be in place for a performative to be felicitous or successful. First they have to be uttered according to convention or procedure which includes 'the uttering of certain words by certain persons in certain circumstances' (Austin, 1976: 14): Second, the people involved must be the appropriate people for the procedure: anyone can name a boat but for the procedure to 'work' as a performative speech act it must be carried out by the appropriate person, the monarch or another appointed person, who must say 'I name this ship *The Queen Elizabeth*' at the time and in the location where it has been agreed it will be launched. Third and fourth the procedure must be correct and complete. If any of these circumstances are not in place, suggests Austin, the performative will not work and there is said to have been a 'misfire'.

If we take these four conditions for a successful performative to the speech act 'I wish to claim asylum' it is possible to see how it should act or work in theory. The words are uttered by someone who wishes to take refuge in a country which is a signatory of the 1951 Refugee Convention. It is heard by the authorities in that country and, if it is correct and complete, it should automatically activate the terms of the 1951 Refugee Convention, providing protection to the person who has made the speech act. There is no reason for it to misfire and yet it does not work. Why not? The answer lies in the two final conditions for felicity or a happy speech act. These state that the procedure is designed for people who have

> certain thoughts or feelings, or for the inauguration of certain consequential conduct on the part of any participant, [so that] a person participating in and so invoking the procedure must in fact have those thoughts or feelings, and the participants must intend so to conduct themselves, and further, [...] must actually so conduct themselves subsequently. (Austin, 1976: 15).

If these two conditions on the part of the speaker are not in place, if the speaker is not genuine in their speech nor in their intention to live with the consequences of their speech, the performative will not work because the speech act is considered to be 'hollow' or 'empty'. In a culture where all refugees are classed as asylum seekers, on the basis that they are all lying until it can be proved otherwise, it is nearly impossible for asylum seekers to argue that they have the thoughts and feelings needed to be refugees.

The suspicion on the part of all states is that the speakers will not 'conduct themselves' as refugees but as people who live on government benefits at worst, or provide cheap labour in the underground economies that proliferate in Western states at best. In other words, happy or successful speech acts depend upon the perceived good will of the speakers and, as we have already seen, good will towards asylum seekers is in very short supply. So, even though technically a misfire has not taken place, the words of the refugee speaker are presumed to be hollow or untrue and the speech act fails as the result of what Austin calls an 'abuse'. Thus states can herald the fact that they are benign, that they provide protection for those who are persecuted, because they enact the 'correct procedures' whereby refugees can indeed invoke the rights enshrined in the 1951 Refugee Convention and claim asylum within their borders. However, they do this safe in the knowledge that, having developed and perpetuated a climate of crisis, they have clearly demonstrated all refugees' supposed duplicity, thus removing any immediate responsibility to make the refugee speech act 'work'. Thus the speech is act is not 'void' in Austin's terms. Procedures exist and the framework is there within which to make it, indeed these procedures are maintained at a considerable cost to the state. It is, however, 'unhappy' because it does not achieve what the speaker desires. A high proportion of refugee speech acts *must* be infelicitous or unhappy in order to maintain the political and economic status quo of the states in which they are uttered. In the words of an asylum seeker from Congo Brazzaville:

> I think the Home Office have just like a quota, you know. It's one hundred person this year [laughing] no more. They are just looking for how many person have we got here? It's ten...Let's stop there. Next month we take another ten.[17]

Austin differentiates between all locutionary acts (the speaking of an utterance), and illocutionary speech acts which produce effects without any lapse of time where the consequences are immediate. Locutionary acts in a third category, perlocutionary speech acts, also have consequences but those consequences are delayed, since the speaking of the act is not the doing of it. The refugee who wishes to claim asylum can make the locutionary act *I claim asylum* but is not permitted to make it as an illocutionary speech act, since the speaking of it is not the doing of it. They are permitted only to make a perlocutionary speech act, *I wish to seek asylum,* which will have a delayed set of consequences and that, more often than not, will fail to produce the outcome they desire. The state, on the other hand, maintains the power by making *only* illocutionary speech acts: 'The Secretary of State has considered your application but [...] has concluded that you do not qualify for asylum'.[18] The denial of refugee status is effective from the moment of utterance.

The difference between the asylum seeker's view of their speech act as a performative statement (by making it they are doing something to change their present situation) and the state's view of the speech act as constative (by making it they are creating a set of statements that can be judged for their truth or falsehood), shows how speech acts can become undermined, even deliberately institutionally sabotaged. Butler acknowledges that 'one can be interpellated, put in place, given a place, through silence, through not being addressed' (Butler, 1997: 27) but not being addressed is not the same as having an address *deliberately withheld.* Those 'lucky ones' (Zetter, 1999: 49) granted asylum and hence refugee status will have gained the title they sought, 'refugee', simultaneously becoming eligible for protection from the state, able to live with the rights and responsibilities of other subjects. Butler asks 'if performativity requires a power to effect or enact what one names, then who will be the "one" with such a power and how will such a power be thought?' (Butler, 1995: 203). The question of who holds the power to name is crucial in the case of refugees and is at the root of bureaucratic performance. Questions of what Pugliese calls the 'abyssal inequality of power' (Pugliese, 2002: par. 8) in the case of refugees and the state need to be considered in order to understand some of the reasons why the asylum seeking speech act may not work. The pain and frustration behind this inequality of power is shown in the writings of a refused and destitute asylum seeker:

> The UK, the country that I asked, has rejected my claim for asylum. Where am I going? Season of good will when are you coming my way so that the smile can come back to my face? Oh Christ is this your way of telling me that I have no rights? My life is a book of gold with the pile of dust on top of it. The more I am going forward the more enormous become my problems.[19]

Bureaucratic performance

One of the clearest ways to illustrate bureaucratic performance is through Kafka's parable *Before the Law*. Examining this rather strange and elliptical short story illuminates some of the complex ways in which refugees are affected by juridical practices in western countries, in particular the effect of naming. Kafka's parable *Before the Law* starts '[b]efore the Law stands a doorkeeper. To this doorkeeper comes a man from the country and prays for admittance to the Law' (Kafka, 2005: 3). The man from the country waits for admittance despite the fact that 'the gate stands open as usual' so there is no physical barrier to his admittance to the law which 'always remains open, marking a limit without itself posing an obstacle or barrier' (Derrida, 1992: 203). Thinking that the Law 'should surely be accessible to all and to everyone' he notes the fierce appearance of the doorkeeper and decides to wait until he gets permission. The country man curses his luck and grows old waiting to be admitted. Eventually, close to death, he addresses the doorkeeper 'Everyone strives to reach the law [...] so how does it happen that for all these many years no one but myself has ever begged for admittance?' (Kafka, 2005: 3). The doorkeeper roars in his ear 'No one else could ever be admitted here, since this gate was made only for you. I am now going to shut it' (Ibid.: 4) and there the parable ends.

This enigmatic story has produced a range of readings (Agamben, 1998; Butler, 1999; Derrida, 1992) some of which will be examined below. This story provides a key to understanding refugees' relationship to bureaucratic performance which goes beyond the Kafkaesque labyrinths of juridical practice in relation to refugees (although that is an important part of the picture) and shows the implications of the fact that the law is created at the moment when the country man asks for admission and is denied, despite the door to the law being open. Just as the reader of this story cannot know which law is at issue, moral, judicial, political, natural, in the story the man also does not know 'the law of cities and edifices protected by gates and boundaries, of spaces shut by doors' (Derrida, 1992: 192). The door proved not to be a passage to the law but the law itself however the ignorance of the system on the part of the man from the country renders him powerless. He cannot perceive his situation.

This is the situation that most asylum seekers find themselves in when they request asylum, far from home, often alone, ignorant of the language, systems, cultures and values of the place in which they find themselves. On the edges of possibility, at the door to the international laws of hospitality, the bureaucratic processing of asylum seekers' stories is characterised as a 'battle with unequal arms' (Charteris-Black, 2006: 436). Like the man from the country, asylum seekers in western states have 'no itinerary, no method, to path to accede the law, to what should happen there' (Derrida, 1992: 196). Asylum seekers find themselves at the mercy of a system that they do not understand; in the words of Shafaei at the start of this chapter, they do not know the 'magic code'.

For Agamben (1998: 47) *Before the Law* provides an 'exemplary abbreviation' of the structure of the 'sovereign ban', the ways in which the law creates its own power by setting up the norm and the exception. In this situation the 'essence of State sovereignty' does not lie in the monopoly to prohibit, sanction or rule but in the 'monopoly to decide, when the word "monopoly" is used' (Ibid.: 16). The sovereign ban places the subject in an impossible situation when 'the law affirms itself with the greatest force precisely at the point in which it no longer prescribes anything' (Ibid.: 49). The man from the country is held in the sovereign ban and the open door meant only for him 'includes him in excluding him and excludes him in including him' (Ibid.: 50). The fact that there is never any question of a trial or verdict, judgement or sentence makes the ordeal all the more terrifying and the man is 'prejudged' as a 'subject before a judgement which is always in preparation and always being deferred' (Derrida, 1992: 206). One thinks of the indefinite detention of asylum seekers in many states, discussed in Chapter 3, incarcerated for no reason that they can understand and with no knowledge of when or how or whether they might be released.

Beyond this story of 'law at a standstill' (Nield, 2008: 142) lies the 'state of exception' where large groups of people exist on the level of 'bare life' on 'an extratemporal and extraterritorial threshold in which the human body is separated from its normal political status and abandoned, in a state of exception, to the most extreme misfortunes' (Agamben, 1998: 159). In this reading the state of exception, created by asylum legislation under the influence of the United States' 'war on terror' and the walls going up around Fortress Europe, has created large numbers of asylum seekers who have been aban doned because they cannot be accommodated into the citizenry of any state. Recent moves to require biometric data at state borders provide further illustration of the 'state of exception', and the resulting 'disaggregation between the human and the citizen' (Nield, 2008: 142) that is produced. Asylum seekers already inside the state's border become a 'problem' that has to be 'managed'. The Australian government tried to deal with this problem through the policy of mandatory detention for all asylum seekers which proved so unpopular (and expensive) that moves were made to phase out. The alternative of allowing asylum seekers live in the community, as they do in the UK and elsewhere, created the need from the point of view of the authorities for them to be monitored in some way while their claims were being assessed. Governments resort to the technologies of the 'biopolitical tattoo' (Agamben quoted in Nield, 2008: 139) invented to detect crime, terrorism or, somewhat ironically identity theft, to mark and monitor asylum seekers. In the UK, for example, it was reported that the finger prints of infants from asylum seeking families were being taken,[20] while there have been moves to 'tag' asylum seekers[21] and to use voice recognition programmes to keep track of asylum seekers who are awaiting a decision on their legal status.[22] Citizens may experience unease or discomfort when crossing international borders but non-citizens, refugees, must bear the full force of the state of exception, of the suspension of their rights as citizens and as humans.

Bureaucratic performance then pictures the asylum seeker as the 'man from the country' who 'sits before the door of the law' awaiting judgment on their claims for asylum: it also demonstrates how refugees have no option but to 'sit and wait'. However, in this action, they are *ineluctably* placing authority with those on the other side of the closed door of the law and, by extension, of the entire judicial and political structure that would grant them their request for safety and asylum. Not only are they conjuring the law as they sit and wait, they are conjuring themselves, or *bringing themselves into being as refugees*. In approaching the door/border as those who would seek protection from the state within that space delineated by the border, they have no choice but to be produced at that border *as refugees* (Nield, 2006). This is the central paradox of refugee identity: refugees' bureaucratic performances for the state force them to work hard to create an identity for which they have no desire but which they passionately desire at the same time. This ambivalence is acutely captured in these words by Joy, the Nigerian refugee from the radio project in Manchester:

> Asylum seeker is not a person it's the situation which makes you become one. It's not the real you. You are different. You are person like them. You have intelligence. You have capability to work. I mean, I don't know how to put it but asylum seeker is not a person, is not a human being, is just a situation.[23]

The 'jarring, even terrible, power of naming' (Butler, 1997: 29) shows how the discourse which creates the subject 'need not take the form of the voice at all' so that interpellation may appear without a speaker on 'bureaucratic forms, the census, adoption papers, employment applications' (Ibid.: 31). In this way 'bureaucratic and disciplinary diffusion of sovereign power produces discursive power that operates without a subject, but that constitutes the subject in the course of its operation' (Ibid.: 34). This is what makes it possible to exercise power over the refugee without the need for the speaker's presence. The 'speech' of the state 'often takes its sovereign form, whereby speaking of declarations are, literally, "acts" of law' (Ibid.: 16). In France illegal immigrants are often referred, to as *sans papiers*, literally 'those without papers' and in the US illegal immigrants are designated as 'undocumented aliens'. This is a good example of the 'literacy of bureaucracy' (Conquergood, 2002: 147) and points to the irony that, although refugees are bombarded with *some* papers, those papers that matter, passports or letters offering refuge, are withheld.

When asylum seekers' claims for asylum are refused in the UK this is done through a letter which purports to come directly from the government, from The Secretary of State: 'The Secretary of State noted that you had provided no evidence of your claim, which he found to be vague and lacking in substance and credibility'.[24] Of course, the Secretary of State was not present at the interview in which the asylum seeker gave their evidence, nor did they have any direct hand in writing the subsequent letter. Nevertheless, the effect of the letter is such that, through bureaucratic performance, the state is enabled to exercise its sovereign power to produce a discursive power over the asylum seeker, denying him or her possibility of being interpellated as a refugee subject. The effect of interpellation is not 'descriptive but inaugurative. It seeks to introduce a reality rather than report an existing one' (Butler, 1997: 33). Thus asylum seekers are not simply *described* as 'failed asylum seekers' when their claims for asylum fail, they are interpellated as such, they *become* one from that point on (although they may have had to wait for years for this decision).

One way to counteract the wrongs done to the individual through labelling is to harness the power of 'creative resignification' through the strategy of 'catachrestic naming', defined as 'speech that either fail[s] to refer or refer[s] in the wrong way' (Butler, 1993: 217). Catachrestic naming opens up the possibility of 'occupy[ing] the interpellation by which one is already occupied to direct the possibilities of resignification against the norms of violation' (Ibid.: 123). By being creative with the injurious names granted to the subject, maybe through strategies of repeating those injurious names, it may be possible to experiment with ways in which they can be challenged. This could have the effect of challenging the original naming to see if the subject can *use*, or appropriate the name in some way to gain a sense of ownership over the injurious name rather than being dominated by it.

The 'playful' possibilities of catachrestic naming are *not* open to asylum seekers since they are not having speech inflicted on them, so much as having certain names *withheld*. Ultimately, the name that is being withheld is that of 'citizen' and, while the name of 'refugee' is not the desired name in the long term, it is a step on the way to the name of 'citizen'. The only name deemed possible by the authorities at the point of seeking refuge is that of 'asylum seeker'. The name that every asylum seeker dreads to hear is 'failed asylum seeker', making them vulnerable to imprisonment and deportation; the code words for a person with no rights

The problem with using bureaucratic performance as an organising concept is that it creates a tendency towards negativity placing an emphasis on failure. It focuses on those who do *not* gain refugee status at the expense of the stories of those who do, largely because of its emphasis on power. Although bureaucratic performance is far-reaching and is essential to understanding the situation that refugees find themselves in, it cannot move beyond that understanding to open out new possibilities for refugees themselves. This is the point at which theatre and performance practices generally show an alternative, suggesting what *might* happen if the door is not closed in the face of the refugee or if floods and waves of migrants are re-configured as an invigorating stream. Theatre is a place where issues are 'framed, problematised, opened up and made accessible to analysis and critique [...] an alternative form of border space' (Nield, 2008: 144). When bureaucratic performance reaches the limits of its usefulness, other narratives from theatrical and cultural performance take over, telling stories about some of the positive and complex experiences of refugeeness.

This is the moment at which catachrestic performances of naming *can* come into play since, within the theatrical frame, experimentation becomes possible. Catachrestic naming, rejections of naming, questions of identity that deny or confirm bureaucratic naming are all strategies that are seen frequently in refugee theatre and performance. One example which I will keep coming back to was seen in the words and actions of a young man in a production of *The Traffic of our Stage* in the Royal Exchange Theatre, Manchester (2005, see Figure 1). This participatory project with young refugees was a joint venture between the theatre and a local college and involved a re-working of Shakespeare's *Romeo and Juliet*. In one compelling scene a young man strode across the stage proclaiming 'I am Hervé. I am not a refugee' followed by many of the other actors who made the same claim in their own names. It seemed to me at the time, and I continue to believe, that these young participants in this drama project were excited about the possibilities of experimenting with naming and identity positions offered by the fictional space of the theatre. Their involvement in a theatre project in which they were encouraged to author their own work may have led to a situation where they could even begin to author their own identities beyond the theatrical space. These are some of the ideas that will be explored in subsequent chapters.

It is essential to understand the politics and political manoeuvering of state actors in relation to refugees in order to gain a full understanding of the theatre and performance practices that have arisen in relation to refugees since the early 1990s. Peter Nyers talks of the cultural expectations of certain 'qualities and behaviours that are demonstrative of "authentic" refugeeness' (Nyers, 2006: xv) and I will show how arts and cultural activities concerning refugees reflect,

Figure 1 Young people from the ESOL Department at City College, Manchester, participating in *The Traffic of Our Stage* at the Royal Exchange Theatre, Manchester 2005 (Photograph taken by Joel Fildes and reproduced with the permission of The Royal Exchange Theatre, Manchester)

but can also perpetuate, these cultural expectations of refugees: expectations of silence, passivity, trauma and victimhood. Understanding bureaucratic performance highlights the extreme ambivalence surrounding ideas about refugee identity and the ways in which that ambivalence taps into existing hesitations and uncertainties in ideas about national identity generally. Understanding bureaucratic performance helps those who have not had that experience to grasp something of the feelings of powerlessness and terrible frustration and impotence felt by so many asylum seekers in the West leading to a deeper understanding about the possible implications of the power of naming in the case of refugees and asylum seekers. Having set out the background against which refugee theatre and performance will be viewed and understood I will move on to consider theatrical explorations of hospitality through the figures of the host and the guest.

2
Hosts and Guests: National Performance and the Ethics of Hospitality

> Alexander: Think of yourself as a very important guest. You wouldn't insult a house that welcomed you.
> Henry: They don't welcome you here.
> Alexander: Maybe they express it differently.
> (Wertenbaker, Credible Witness, 2002: 203)

Theatre makers have taken responsibility for raising questions about the treatment of refugees and asylum seekers in the West, producing a 'growing corpus of theatre about asylum' in Australia (Gilbert and Lo, 2007: 191) and in the UK what was called a 'growing canon of asylum dramas' (Billington, 2001). Although the energy surrounding theatre about refugees may have slightly abated in recent years there is no doubting the impact of plays produced about the subject in the first decade of this century, not only in Britain and Australia, but also in other parts of Europe, the United States and Canada.[1] In addition, there have been numerous site-based performances and 'culture jamming' events where activists subvert everyday images and discourses to protest against the inhospitable treatment of asylum seekers (Gilbert and Lo, 2007: 189). Some of these para-theatrical events will be considered in the next chapter but the focus here is on the ways in which theatre seeks to generate a discourse about the ethical and political responsibilities of the citizenry in relation to refugees and people seeking asylum.

This chapter shows how theatre has been used as a tool for education and awareness-raising about refugees in ways that have opened up imaginative possibilities for empathy, solidarity and even political action creating, for example, a 'trenchant critique of Australia's asylum system' (Ibid.). Conceptualised as a locus for debate, theatre has become a place in which it is possible to create alternative narratives with one critic going so far as to suggest 'the asylum debate has moved into the theatre' (Billington, 2001). The communal nature of theatre going has shown possibilities for using the theatre event to gather and galvanise audiences for action, and for creating opportunities for ethical practice which could be characterised as a conversation, at its best a rich national debate about the possible limits of hospitality.

The 'right kind' of refugee story

The power of bureaucratic performance and the discourse of crisis affects all theatrical endeavours and the degree to which theatre makers understand and question this will influence the extent to which they enable audiences to perceive that, rather than living through a 'refugee problem', rich nations may have what has been called a 'hospitality problem' (Williams, 2008: 202). Opening up and exposing the discourse of crisis that has surrounded the asylum debate allows theatre makers to encourage audiences to look at the situation as chronic rather than acute, to see the presence of refugees as a long-term condition demonstrating the necessity for consideration and thoughtful negotiation around questions of the ethics of asylum and hospitality. However, the examples discussed here will also demonstrate some of the problems that have arisen through ignoring or downplaying the complexities involved. This has meant that refugees have gained a rather saintly glow in a number of productions and I will show how the representation of refugees generally oscillates between the extremes of gifted and traumatised (Pupavac, 2008). In their efforts to encourage empathy for refugees among audiences for this theatre there is a temptation to present only 'endearing refugees' and ignore the fact that 'a well-founded fear of persecution is not confined to nice people' (Ibid.: 285). As we will see, the 'association of refugees with parasitism is so strong that many theatre makers seem to think that they need to be represented as politically neutered to the point of victimhood in many fictional representations.

Implicit and explicit pressure to create certain narratives in relation to refugees comes not only from audiences because theatre needs financial support to take these stories into a public arena. The uneasy relationship between the sponsor of the work, and those who seek to undertake it can lead to theatre makers finding themselves 'operating in [...] structures whose sources of funding are [...] directly connected to the powers/institutions we want to question, that we need to question' (Schinina, 2004: 27). This creates a 'game-like opposition' between those doing the work that might be critical of those giving the funding for it: 'while the right hand holds populations down, the left hand doles out a modicum of funds and other resources allowing for a certain amount of artistic and academic expression, social theatre and other means of alleviating the sufferings of the oppressed' (Schechner, 2002a: 157).[2] The controversy surrounding the production of *Two Brothers* by Hannie Rayson staged in Sydney in 2005 shows this very clearly. By alluding to the sinking of the SIEV X[3] when the Australian Navy were accused of standing by and not rescuing drowning refugee survivors, and by directly referencing two real life brothers involved in Australian public life at the time, Rayson's play generated a political scandal. Marr reports how politicians made the displeasure of the government known to the Melbourne Theatre Company asking the chair of MTC 'Why do you insist on biting the hand that feeds you?' (Marr quoted in Brisbane, 2005: viii). This less than veiled attack on public funding for the arts demonstrates the vulnerability of theatre enterprises that criticise the authorities, showing how sensitive they are on the subject of asylum seekers.

Rayson and the theatre company who produced her work had apparently not abided by the 'rules of the game' but these games can be played out on more subtle levels where the requirements for certain kinds of refugee stories remain implicit. This is exemplified in Edmondson's critique of what she calls the 'marketing of trauma' in Northern Uganda where the narratives of young refugees that suited a particular agenda were manipulated and presented to audiences of potential funders. The young people involved, many of whom had been child soldiers, were required to present a narrative of 'unrelenting terror and suffering' which negated 'the skills and resources that these victims cultivated during the trauma itself' (Edmondson, 2005: 469). In this situation the more complex narrative was rejected because those involved were caught up in a situation in which (the right) narratives were seen as necessary for the organisation in order to provide them with the resources to help those victims of war to tell their story, to create further 'correct' narratives, in a bizarre circular 'game'.[4]

In the West, bureaucratic performance creates the need for the 'right' kind of refugee story in which complexities are smoothed out to create a simple linear narrative of individual crisis and flight. This need exists despite the fact that 'mass long-distance movement direct to countries of asylum' has become extremely rare and single journeys of flight have been replaced by 'several journeys, often separated by lengthy periods of residence in temporary homes in a succession of countries or even several continents' (Marfleet, 2006: 221). Stories about the poor treatment received by refugees when they arrive in a 'safe' country can be privileged over narratives depicting a largely unproblematic entry to that country. Questions about unfair treatment, lack of justice and experiences of racism are often preferred to narratives of resistance and resourcefulness on the part of refugees. Narratives in Western theatre therefore often require refugees to be portrayed as victims 'a deserving cause, worthy of sympathy, assistance, and a new life' (Jackson, 2006: 83). A liberal attitude among practitioners who seek to do cultural work with refugees may also lead them to ignore, or at least underplay, narratives which demonstrate any transgression on the part of refugees. Suggestions that refugees may have been in any way duplicitous about their entry to the country, despite the fact that legislation in most states makes this a necessity, usually remain unvoiced in performance.

Similarly, reasons for seeking asylum in the West which may not be due to persecution in the refugee's home country, are suppressed in many theatrical presentations in favour of simpler, but often traumatic, narratives of corrupt regimes, forced imprisonment and mistreatment in the refugee's place of origin. Rosello shows how '[t]he bad refugee stretches the definition; the real refugee must be innocent, powerless, a victim' (Rosello, 2001: 156). This deliberate down-playing of ambiguity and complexity on the part of some theatre practitioners may be seen as necessary in order to counter negative views of asylum seekers. It may also have the unintended, but unfortunate, effect of disempowering refugee subjects, creating an image of a victim in the minds of the audience or even a victim mentality in the minds of refugees themselves. Furthermore, for the non-refugee audience, such narratives may serve to reinforce negative and misguided attitudes

about the countries from which refugees have fled. It is
for an audience to accept simple narratives of corruptio
states, for example, than to take in the complexities of the ......
corruption, let alone the role of many Western countries in the creation and perpetuation of states where corruption takes place.

Etiolation, parasitism and authenticity

As we have seen Austin's conditions for a successful speech act can
only ever be partially in place in the case of the speech act *I claim
asylum* because the speakers of this performative fail to convince the
audience of their integrity in making it. Austin quotes Hippolytus
who gave his word on something with his tongue but not his heart
but to 'heart' Austin adds '(or mind or other backstage artiste)'
(Austin, 1976: 10). This is followed by a footnote in which he explains
that he does not wish to implicate 'all offstage performers' in an
implied lack of sincerity but 'objects to certain officious understud-
ies, who would duplicate the play' (Ibid.). An understudy, of course,
is a stand-in, someone who has learned all the lines and who may be
called upon to play the role when the actor cannot. Austin implies
that the understudy may not have learned the lines in good faith,
can only ever reproduce or duplicate them and cannot be trusted to
be sincere even in their acting.

For Austin even actors cannot be accepted as sincere when they
are acting and he dismisses their speech acts on stage as 'a parasitic
etiolation of language' (Austin, 1976: 22). Something etiolated is a
paler, weaker version of itself, like grass starved of sunlight for an
extended time. So theatrical speech cannot fulfil the conditions
needed for a successful speech act because the words are 'in a peculiar way hollow or void' (Ibid). To follow this line of thinking, speaking within the theatrical frame will always be considered an abuse
because the speakers are assumed not to actually have the feelings
they profess, marking theatrical speech out as existing in a special
set of circumstances and therefore not admissible for consideration
as a legitimate performance utterance. Etiolation carries inferences
of decadence and effeminacy (Parker and Kosovsky-Sedgwick, 1995:
4) but for our purposes it is Austin's notion that speech acts on stage
are 'parasitic upon [language's] normal use' (Austin, 1976: 22) that is
most striking.

Understanding parasitism in relation to refugee theatre goes some way towards accounting for the popularity of documentary theatre techniques and verbatim texts considered to be 'by far the most common type of "play" in this field' (Gilbert and Lo, 2007: 191). In Australia *Citizen X* by Sidetrack Performance Group in 2002 used extracts from letters to continue the 'quiet ethical form of activism' (Burvill, 2008: 238) of corresponding with detained asylum seekers, putting these before a public audience and 'bearing witness' to the thoughts and ideas of the writers of the letters. *Something to Declare* (2003) was compiled from the testimonies of asylum seekers by Michael Gurr and first staged by Actors for Refugees in Brisbane. It included fragments of testimony from asylum seekers interspersed with extracts from legal and medical documents and statistical reports in an effort to both inform and unsettle audiences (Gilbert and Lo, 2007: 193). *In Our Name*, which was performed at the Belvoir Street Theatre in Sydney in 2004, is based on interviews with members of the Al Abaddi family from Iraq carried out by writer and director Nigel Jamieson. *Through the Wire* (2004) by Ros Horan weaves the stories of four refugees in detention and was remarkable for the presence of Shahin Shafaei, the actor already mentioned, who was also a refugee and who performed 'himself' in the piece. In 2004 Australian theatre company version 1.0 produced *CMI (A Certain Maritime Incident)* a 're-contextualised verbatim play' based on an Australian Senate enquiry (Burvill, 2008: 23: 9). Elsewhere *Le Dernier Caravansérail* by Théâtre du Soleil was based on stories and testimonies gathered by the company in refugee detention centres.

In the UK *Asylum Monologues and Crocodile Seeking Refuge* by Sonja Linden (2005) are both based on verbatim theatre techniques and Banner Theatre in Birmingham used 'actuality' in the form of video footage to create *Wild Geese* and *They get free mobiles...don't they?* Although not strictly a verbatim play *The Bogus Woman* by Kay Adshead (2001) was based on refugee testimony provided for the writer by The Medical Foundation for the Care of Victims of Torture. In the US Ping Chong created *Children of War* in 2002 (considered in more detail in Chapter Four) as part of the series *Undesirable Elements* which is described as an oral history project based on the words and stories of the young refugees involved.

Questions of authority inform the decisions made to use these techniques, particularly when the theatre practitioners involved are not refugees, and it is impossible to approach the subject without some 'authoritative' refugee voices. Aston (2003) notes how Wertenbaker in writing *Credible Witness*, and Adshead the writer of *The Bogus Woman*, both stressed the role of research in writing their plays (performed within a day of each other in London in 2001). The importance of research carried out through speaking to refugees themselves lies in more than simply authenticating stories of seeking asylum, but in 'understanding how each play stages and persuades audiences of the truth value of the information that each presents' (Aston, 2003: 10). This can be seen as an attempt to sidestep any implication of etiolation, creating a sense of 'ontological authority' (Soto-Morettini, 2005: 314) by insisting that the voices on stage are those of 'real refugees', or that the words used in the play have been created as a result of 'extensive research' with refugee groups and communities.

There is, however, something more complex implied when parasitism is alluded to in the context of refugee theatre since it is a metaphor commonly used to describe asylum seekers themselves, sometimes classed as parasites living off the state. In extreme right wing British National Front literature asylum seekers have been explicitly referred to as parasites (Gibson, 2003: 380) and in 2003 a study of news stories about the Sangatte Immigration camp in Calais, Northern France revealed that the media used 51 different terms to describe asylum seekers, including 'parasites' and 'scroungers'.[5] The story of an asylum seeker from Nigeria confirms the result of the metonymic chain linking asylum seekers and parasitism:

> Like sometimes when you're friendly with people and they're friendly with you because they're not sure who you are [...] but the moment they know you're an asylum seeker, oh gosh, they think you live on benefits[6] and they have this attitude towards you. They will not like you any more. They will look down on you. They will see you as someone with no respect or regard any more.[7]

So, if the words of an actor in the theatrical frame are parasitical and refugees are often figured as parasites, when 'parasitical' words are placed in the mouths of 'parasitical' people what is the effect of theatre about refugees, on the audience and on the subject who is speaking? Considering parasitism in relation to refugees and theatre could fundamentally undermine any possible efficacy that could come about as a result of using theatre as a form to explore refugee issues. Most refugee theatre is produced to raise awareness among audiences in the host community, to educate people about the situations which have caused refugees to flee and the hostile conditions in which they find themselves in places of sanctuary in the West. The thinking is that refugees need to be understood and their situation brought to a wider public in order to create empathy but, if theatre is not trusted, is associated with fakery, falsehood, smoke and mirrors, can it really be the best way to represent refugees when they are themselves suspected of duplicity?

The aporia of hospitality

In order to avoid perpetuating narratives around parasitism, theatre concerning refugees needs to be reconceptualised as a debate about nationality, identity, citizenship and belonging. Understanding the parasitical undertones of the act of theatre and how they interact with the asylum debate is necessary in order to avoid xeno, or new, racism which focuses on questions of ownership and property rather than skin colour and also stresses the importance of transaction. Images of giving and taking are central to popular and political asylum discourses where the question of 'what [...] "they" give to the nation, or alternatively, what [...] "they" take from the nation' (Gibson, 2003: 379) is couched in many different ways. This parasitical conceptualisation has been effectively critiqued by comparing asylum seekers with tourists (Gibson, 2003; Tyler, 2006). Unlike tourists, who are seen to contribute financially to the nation, asylum seekers are, to paraphrase Derrida, the wrong kind of guests (Derrida, 2000: 61) figured as 'takers' but apparently giving nothing in return. Derrida asks what are the responsibilities of the 'host' nation to the 'guest', invited or not, arguing that the very word 'hospitality' has been parasitized by its opposite 'hostility' leading him to coin the word 'hostipitality'. Hostipitality can be thought of as an autoantonym, a word that means itself and its opposite, because of its parasitical origins. The autoantonym is sometimes called a Janus word after the Roman god of the New Year who is depicted as two-faced, looking both backwards and forwards.

This is particularly appropriate for asylum seekers who could be characterised looking both backwards to their old home at the same time as looking forward to new beginnings and possibilities in their new home. Unfortunately someone who is two-faced is also seen as duplicitous or untrustworthy so even relatively positive images of refugees are tainted. 'Like coins and leaves, stories are Janus-faced: the surface is a reverse image of the underside' (Jackson: 2006: 139). Even if troubling refugee narratives are accepted as legitimate vehicles for truth-telling in theatre, their shadow side as lifesaving commodity cannot be escaped but neither should it be ignored.

Hospitality works on many levels as 'an ancient classical tradition, a philosophical value, an ethical imperative, a political issue, and also a polymorphous individual practice' (Rosello, 2001: 6) and Derrida shows the impossibility of separating this range of readings, in particular the political and ethical readings of hospitality. At the same time, however, it is also impossible for the political and ethical to coexist and that tension 'is what hospitality is precisely all about' (Rosello, 2001: 6). Absolute hospitality is an aporia, or impossibility, always doomed to failure because, as soon as the host has generously offered the possibility of hospitality, he or she has simultaneously placed themselves in the position of being able to make the offer, creating a reaffirmation of mastery. 'Hospitality limits itself at its very beginning it remains forever on the threshold of itself' (Derrida, 2000: 14). Hospitality can only ever be a threshold because 'if there is a door there is no longer hospitality. There is no hospitable house. There is no house without doors or windows' (Ibid.). The aporetic nature of this 'double-bind' needs to be constantly approached because it is 'necessary to do the impossible' (Ibid.). Hospitality is always to come; 'we do not know what hospitality is' repeats Derrida (2000) in the sense that we do not *yet* know, or may *never* know.

Hospitality involves risk and for it to work both host and guest have to enter into a risky relationship in which each poses a potential threat to the other because both host and guest have to enter into the 'uncomfortable and sometimes painful possibility of being changed by the other' (Rosello, 2001: 176). The possibilities lie in the fluidity of the roles of host and guest to the extent that, if the guest is always the guest and the host is always the host, something has gone badly wrong and hospitality has been replaced by parasitism or charity. Fiction invites us to 'conceptualise oppositional practices of hospitality' (Ibid.: 174) and what is now discussed are the possible ways to think about the specific fiction of theatrical truth telling in relation to hospitality towards refugees and asylum seekers.

Victims, heroes and political actors

One of the most obvious and explicit ways to tackle the problem of misunderstanding around asylum is through 'mythbusting'. The most common mythbusting tactic is to re-state the 'myths', which usually include ideas of asylum seekers being 'bogus', 'parasitical', harbingers of terrorism and a threat to national security or identity, then to challenge them by posing a second 'truthful' discourse often through the use of statistical and other empirical information. This mythbusting information is produced by trade unions, local government bodies, refugee advocacy organisations and groups in the voluntary or third sector.

The mythbusting approach is pursued despite the fact that research has shown that 'the plethora of asylum fact sheets and myth-busting leaflets available do not appear to have much of an impact on public debate' (Lewis, 2005: 47). The reasons given for this are that they are partly 'not reaching the right people' and partly 'because they are not necessarily trusted' (Ibid.: 48). A survey of evidence from public information and communication campaigns about refugees concluded that '[s]uccessful campaigning in the area of asylum needs to do more than simply provide information or 'myth-bust' (Crawley, 2009: 7). Nevertheless mythbusting or dispelling asylum myths is still a common theatrical strategy, particularly in the UK and one popular way of debunking the myth of the parasitical asylum seeker is to point to the many refugees who are said to have made a positive contribution to the places to which they have fled. Historical contributions by exiles and immigrants as well as refugees are often conflated in refugee advocacy literature to support this argument (Teichmann, 2002) in an attempt to reassure those in the 'host' nation that refugees will not be parasitical in any way.

The discourse of mythbusting is used overtly by Banner Theatre who describe themselves as 'one of Britain's longest established community theatre companies, with 30 years' experience of working with marginalized and disadvantaged communities.'[8] Explicit about the socialist bias of their work, their productions have covered subjects like the British Health Service, unemployment, racism and all forms of discrimination. With their roots in the folk tradition under the influence of Charles Parker's BBC radio ballads of the 1960s and 1970s they have pioneered the use of what they call video ballads (Filewood and Watt, 2001). The video ballads use film footage of refugee, immigrant and activist subjects screened as part of the performance, interspersed with music and songs written for the piece. The form was initiated with *Migrant Voices* (Rogers, 2002) based on residencies with Iranian and Iraqi Kurdish asylum seekers in Salford and Birmingham and further developed in 2004 when they produced *Wild Geese*, based on stories of exile and migration from Irish, Chinese, South Asian, African and African-Caribbean migrants and refugees.[9]

They get free mobiles...don't they? is described as a 'live multimedia show, combining music, song, video, film and theatre' that 'speaks for Britain's newest arrivals as they dodge borders, bullets and bureaucracy in their quest for safety and security from war torn lands in Africa and the Middle East'.[10] In this play Banner sets out explicitly to tackle 'five myths about asylum seekers: it's got nothing to do with us; asylum seekers and refugees are robbing this country; asylum seekers are stealing our jobs; asylum seekers are stealing our houses; Britain is a soft touch for asylum seekers'.[11] Drawing threads through previous waves of immigration to the UK, Banner sets up a political analysis which lays the blame for the presence of large numbers of asylum seekers firmly with the British establishment, global capitalism and with past and present colonialism. Links are drawn between (white) working class subjects, refugees and migrants by setting them up in opposition to the capitalist system; as a line from one of the songs in the piece says, 'I'd rather shovel shit than be an entrepreneur'.

I would still argue that there is little room for audience manoeuvre in this didactic performance style and, arguably, anyone attending a performance with such a title is doing so because they understand the irony inherent in the title and have, therefore, already positioned themselves in sympathy with refugees. The possibility for dialogue is curtailed and Banner could be said to have fallen into the trap of over-identifying with refugees a position maybe best described as the Enthusiast's Infatuation, to use Conquergood's term. The enthusiast '[glosses] over important differences in the zeal to generalise' (Stern and Henderson, 1993: 29) in this case creating a tidy anti-capitalist model.

Banner's important work provides a politicised picture of refugee-ness which is embedded in the politics of race and class, and which provides a necessary corrective to the more politically neutral humanitarian message of some refugee theatre. Dave Rogers, the company's director and writer strongly challenges a liberal approach to refugee politics:

> There's all these things about social inclusion and blah, blah, blah [...] What does social inclusion mean? [...] included in what? Blair's Britain? And how can you talk about social inclusion when you have an outright racist policy towards refugees and asylum seekers? It's an absolute nonsense to talk about it.[12]

Banner's performances play in schools, community centres, trades union clubs and the like. By embedding their theatrical approach in the language of race politics they are bringing about shifts in understanding around refugees and asylum seekers to an audience who are not traditional theatre-goers. The structure of their work brings the experience of refugees directly to an audience through the video ballad technique, albeit still mediated through the apparatus of film making and editing. This style of performance is open ended and does not require the twists and turns of a linear plot, opening up the possibility to present a more complex and unfinished narrative.

The Kindness of Strangers by Tony Green (2004) takes a more traditionally theatrical approach to asylum myths. Performed in the Everyman Theatre, Liverpool in 2004 the play was based on a set of fictional characters. Green's refugee characters are complex and often compromised, sometimes by the tough environment of the Liverpool streets where they have been forced to make their homes but often by their own personal flaws and difficult histories. Green dares to show their daily realities as they navigate a world of prejudice, bullying and crime which creates the need for their duplicity. Like Banner he foregrounds the racial element of the asylum seekers' position in the UK by placing much of the action in front of a wall with graffitied slogans like 'Keep England white!' which forms the backdrop to many scenes.

The main action of the story lies with Mohammad who has paid Jimmy, a small-time crook and 'businessman', to find him a wife so that he can stay in the UK. Hooking him up with Macey, a mixed-race prostitute and mother of three, proved not to be the ideal that Mohammad had in mind and is an insult to his faith and traditions. There is a poignant humour in the discontinuity between his search for love and Macey's more business-like approach to the deal.[13] The humour in this play is something that could be said to be lacking from many of the pieces considered, for example, when Iraqi refugees Behrouz and Samir puzzle about the similarities of the Liverpool dialect with their pronunciation of Arabic.

> Behrouz: I know is English. But sound like Arabic. (Exaggerated Scouse:)[14] 'Chick-k-k-en.' 'Wick-k-k-ed.' 'Know what I mean lik-k-k-e.' Is all at back of throat. Is very strange. (Green, 2004: 30).

Elsewhere, Green plays with the representation of the asylum seeking characters by creating the convention whereby they assume RP[15] accents when they are speaking in their own language of Farsi. At one point Bherouz explains a local landmark to Samir:

> Behrouz: (RP)...Stella told me a wonderful piece of mythology about those birds...the Liver Birds?...Down by the waterfront?.... Local tradition has it that they are in fact different sexes: the female bird, she faces the river, awaiting the sailors coming off the ships...while the male bird, he faces inland to see if the pubs are open. (Green, 2004: 98)

The eloquence of Behrouz speaking in his own language sits in stark contrast to the awkward and broken English that the asylum seekers use in their interactions with English characters.

Traumatic narratives or narratives of hospitality?

The Kindness of Strangers addresses the duplicity needed to get around or to 'work' the asylum system. Berouz, for example, reveals that he will go underground if immigration officers come looking for him and when Samir complains that if one asylum seeker lies about personal history all asylum seekers are assumed to be lying Behrouz retorts:

> Behrouz: Oh you'd rather I'd been tortured? (Pause) [...] I'm sorry I've got no scars Samir. No wounds. No...badge of honour. I'm just a poor farm boy who wants a better life. That's my crime. String me up. (Green, 2004: 102)

It is rare to meet a refugee character in theatrical fiction who is given permission to be transgressive in the way that these characters are and this may be possible only in the more heavily fictionalised approaches rather than the verbatim or documentary plays discussed. However, the dramaturgy of the way in which the play is structured mitigates against this so that any disturbance of the image of the conventional refugee proves to be temporary.

Behrouz is a secondary character to the main protagonist Mohammad who is a much more conventional refugee in the shape of a heroic survivor. At the end of the play Behrouz has been attacked by 'some yobs [who] threw fireworks in his face' (Green, 2004: 147) in a suggested racial attack and the last the audience sees of him is a speechless figure completely shrouded in bandages. In order to fully demonstrate his pain to the British characters, and by implication, the audience, Mohammad performs the opposite manoeuvre, revealing his broken 'real' refugee's body when he is forced to take off his shirt to show 'his torso, completely disfigured with scars and wounds and burns' (Ibid.: 123). A similar scene in *Credible Witness* by Timberlake Wertenbaker shows another refugee character Amina, a Somali asylum seeker in detention, being forced to take off her shirt to reveal 'Thirty-four cigarette burns on her front. Twenty-five on her back...' (Wertenbaker, 2002: 232). The need for evidence of the corporeal wounds of 'conventional refugees' shows how important it can be for the figure of the refugee to be a heroic survivor in order to gain the sympathy of the audience. Wounded asylum seekers become a symbol for human suffering and, in the process, are made politically neutral. This suggests that it is difficult to represent asylum seekers as political actors and that their characters on stage must be neutered or incapacitated by their 'sadness' or 'trauma' in an effort to generate sympathy on the part of the audience.

This can be further explored through the work of Ice and Fire theatre company set up in London with the threefold aim of 'Honouring the real life stories of individuals who have been displaced as a result of conflict; channelling these stories into the production of high quality theatre; creating insight into the refugee experience through education and outreach.'[16] Founded by writer Sonja Linden, Ice and Fire have produced many plays about refugees. *I have before me a remarkable document given to me by a young lady from Rwanda* (Linden, 2003) was first performed in Britain in 2003. *Crocodile Seeking Refuge*

(2005) was Linden's second play which also focused on refugees before she set up Actors for Refugees in 2006 as a sister company to the Australian company of the same name, run by actor Christine Bacon. Their first piece, *Asylum Monologues*, was created in 2006 from a number of refugee testimonies and can be delivered as a piece of poor theatre by any actors in non-theatre locations. Linden began writing these plays during her time as a writer in residence at the Medical Foundation for the Care of Victims of Torture which describes itself as a human rights organisation that also provides assistance and therapy for individual torture survivors and this tricky balance between trauma and human rights is often reflected in her writing.

I have before me a remarkable document given to me a by a young lady from Rwanda by Linden is described as the most produced play about the Rwandan genocide in the United States with productions in eight cities in 2009 (Edmondson, 2009: 56). In it Linden focuses on the debate about the personal and professional difficulties of bearing witness to traumatic refugee narratives but I would like to explore what is being said about hospitality, which is much less frequently considered. Rwandan refugee Juliette's romantic hopes of finding a 'proper writer, a man of letters' who will coach her in her writing, are dashed when she decides that Simon, her English teacher, is 'a scribbler' (Linden: 2003: 12). Simon's insecurities about his pupil's expectations and his responsibility to her traumatic story, influenced by Linden's own experience of working with torture survivors through the Medical Foundation, dominate the narrative (Edmondson, 2009: 58). When Juliette wants to give up writing the book he is helping her with Simon describes how he feels let down:

> I've given up a lot of time on that book you know. Or perhaps you don't know. I've spent hours on it after our sessions, editing it, typing it up, and encouraging you, helping you, believing in you, believing this is important. Your 'mission'. The most important thing in your life. (Linden, 2003: 83)

Juliette has proved insufficiently grateful for his efforts on her behalf, failing to demonstrate '[s]ome of the relentlessly emphatic gratitude that refugees express when newly arrived' a performative gesture designed 'to keep the rest of the world at bay while the refugee re-groups and re-builds their inner lives' (Jackson, 2006: 71). Even while Juliette is sacrificing this possibility for herself she unlocks Simon's writer's block and enables him to start writing poetry again. In the final scene they have been invited to speak at a conference on 'Literature and Social Exclusion' and Simon has prepared a speech for Juliette to read. She begins reading her prepared speech but stumbles, symbolically crumpling it up as she 'finds her own voice' (Linden, 2003: 101) and addresses the conference without the aid of her British mediator.

This scene has been described as 'a classic reification of Eurocentric notions of resolving anguish through writing' (Edmondson, 2009: 60) but I want to focus on notions of hospitality that are brought up and the perceived risks of opening up the citizen's home to a guest, specifically that when hospitality is abused and the guest is conceived as a 'parasite'. Juliette comments 'English people are strange. I know Simon a year now but he has never invited me into his house. Africans would never be like this' (Linden, 2003: 96). Despite the fact that the material offer of hospitality was never made Simon's relationship with Juliette upsets his domestic life by throwing his marriage into jeopardy when his wife misunderstands his poems as love poems for Juliette and, even though Simon is not literally hospitable, the domestic repercussions of their relationship ripple through his home and family.

This is developed in Linden's second refugee play, *Crocodile Seeking Refuge* (2005) which examines the dilemmas and difficulties of the middle-class professionals who set out to 'help' refugees or to work on their behalf. Beginning its life as a verbatim theatre piece based on five refugee testimonies it transmuted into a much more conventional play which placed liberal lawyer Harriet at its centre, pushing the refugee characters to the periphery. The original refugees' verbatim narratives are placed in the mouths of fictional characters who are all connected in some way to Harriet. As they negotiate a place in their new culture and learn to live with their past experiences of trauma, Harriet's commitment to them and to other refugees forces her family apart. After she has invited a client, asylum seeker Zakariya, to live in her house she and Nick, her husband, become estranged from each other and it is clear by the end of the play that they have separated.

Asylum! Asylum! by Donal O'Kelly (1996) has strong structural similarities, focusing as it does on the Irish professional classes who struggle with the ethical dilemmas that the presence of asylum seek-ers poses. Here too the implications of inviting refugees into your home are explored and audiences are encouraged to read the individ-ual home as nation on some level. Bill, the father, is caught between his two estranged children, Mary a lawyer representing Joseph, an African refugee and Leo, his son, a tough immigration officer. Mary brings Joseph to live in her father Bill's house when his claim for asy-lum is rejected and Bill welcomes him like a son, symbolically remov-ing his own son Leo's belongings so that Joseph can move in. He reminds Mary and Leo about their responsibilities as hosts:

> Bill: We have a guest here folks, who we should be looking after... (O'Kelly, 1996: 139)

Joseph will only take up the invitation if it can be made on the basis of equality:

> Joseph: I don't accept charity. We'll make a deal. I'll be your... assistant, Bill. I'll be your house manager. In return you will pro-vide me with food and lodgings. (O'Kelly, 1996: 146)

When immigration official Pillar comes for Joseph to deport him back to Uganda and Mary does not cooperate he makes explicit the view that asylum seekers will invade the home usurping the hosts:

> Pillar: Right! Put your money where your mouth is! Throw your dad out on the side of the road! Give the whole fucking lot, lock, stock and barrel, to Joseph's folks! (O'Kelly, 1996: 168)

Pillar represents those who would take the gesture of hospitality to an absurd 'logical' conclusion by implying that to offer hospitality on an individual basis is to show weakness which will then be exploited on a larger scale; the fear that a charitable gesture may turn into a parasitical situation.

Any offer of hospitality is quickly dismissed at the start of *Two Brothers* by Hannie Rayson (2005) with the brutal murder of asylum seeker Hazem in a scuffle in the second home of politician James 'Eggs' Benedict a scene which, according to Burvill, 'resonates throughout our experience of the rest of the play' (Burvill, 2008: 240). Hazem, a

man without one home let alone two, was being supported by Egg's
brother, the more liberally minded human rights lawyer Tom, but he
was also a survivor of the sinking of a small boat containing asylum
seekers off the Australian coast. Evoking the sinking of the *SIEV X*,
when Australian naval boats apparently failed to intervene to save the
drowning refugees, Rayson peoples the event with fictional characters
and in her version among the officers on board was Lachlan, Egg's
son. Once again, when a professional family become involved in refugee issues, intense conflict about appropriate behaviour and attitudes
towards asylum seekers leads to the family being pulled apart, shatter-
ing domestic lives and culminating in disintegration.

Everyone in this dystopian play is compromised, leaving the audience to 'respond ethically to the other so violently negated in the
opening' (Burvill, 2008: 240). It falls to the audience then to repos-
ition the refugee characters as 'subjects who matter, "like us"' (Tyler,
2006: 194). The difficulty with this is that audiences will tend to
reconfigure the refugee subject as a humanitarian subject worthy
only of pity, a 'good' refugee who simply wants a better life for himself (and it usually is a male figure) and his family, a hard worker
with aspirations; someone, in fact, a little bit like themselves. To conceive of refugees who are making demands on home and nation as
anything other than deserving is just too difficult to contemplate.
The dramaturgy of humanitarian discourse requires innocent victims and narrates a simple tale of caring outsiders who are in a position to rescue the victim (Rieff, 2002: 54). The need to represent
refugees as abject figures similarly dominates the theatrical strategy
of creating empathy by allowing audiences to see the world through
the eyes of 'the refugee' and it is to this type of performance that we
now turn.

The (abject) shoes of the refugee

'Putting yourself in the shoes of the refugee' is a common way to
encourage those who are not refugees to consider the experience of
those who have been forced to leave their homes to seek asylum.
This approach asks for imagination and empathy and is very commonly used in refugee advocacy literature but it is in theatre that its
full potential can be explored with the possibility of a somatic re-
placement of the refugee body with that of the citizen. Theatre and

performance events which have made use of this technique include *Escape to Safety* in the UK (2003–2006), *An Unusual Encounter* (1998), The Container (Bayley, 2007) and *Pericles* (RSC and Cardboard Citizens, 2003). These pieces will be set in contrast with *CMI (A Certain Maritime Incident)* by Australian company version 1.0 which explicitly refuses this strategy.

Many companies have attempted to produce empathy on behalf of refugees by forcing audiences to experience some of the physical and emotional discomfort that refugees may experience on their route to safety. This is often done by alluding to a refugee's presence at the border: this moment of encounter at the political border is recreated at the border of the building or event as audiences seek to enter the theatre space in which the performance will take place. The meta-theatrical strategy of making the audience complete immigration entry forms in order to access a performance is frequently used to draw attention to the literal re-placing of the refugee within the theatrical frame.

In Cardboard Citizens' production of *Pericles* as the audience arrives they were treated with disdain by the actor/guards and ordered to fill in the SEF (Statement of Evidence) entry forms that all refugees must complete on arrival in the UK. Director Adrian Jackson said of this strategy 'so [the audience] came to a warehouse and they were treated very rudely. They could only cross the line one at a time. [The guards] are all Cardboard Citizens [...] they had great fun being rude to the audience'.[17] One critic reported the experience from the other side: 'I'm being told to stand behind the white line. They want to know where I was born. And why I have come here.' (Bassett, 2003). Similar performances of bureaucracy in the act of compelled form filling were used in *Asylum* (Urban Theatre Projects, 2001) which took place in a disused wallpaper factory in Sydney, Australia. Audience members arrived to be greeted by refugee actors playing stern officials speaking to them in the actors' own languages. They were gruffly commanded to undertake certain tasks as part of a 'selection process', the officials often having to resort to crude sign language to instruct them, before they could gain entry to a series of sound installations which preceded the play.[18]

Writer Clare Bayley staged *The Container*, her play about immigrants and asylum seekers, in an actual lorry container first for a young audience in Basildon, near London, and then at the Edinburgh

Festival in 2007. The audience were said to have emerged moved and shocked and one young woman reported 'I felt like I went on that journey with them. I'd never really thought about it. But I'll never feel the same way about immigrants again now I know what some of them go through to get here' (Bayley, 2007: 9). *Escape to Safety* in the UK also takes place in a converted lorry container has been touring the UK since 2003, experienced by an estimated 21,875 people (Nobili and Reynolds, 2005). More participatory than *The Container*, audience members are encouraged to place themselves in the position of 'an asylum seeker' and share their experience and perceptions as they are taken on a short journey through the container which has been designed to create eight small rooms in which an asylum seeker's journey is mapped out. Individuals move through the container listening on audio headsets to a number of refugee stories told in the first person. Beginning in a 'safe house' where the participants encounter 'Asif' who is waiting for papers to try to get into the UK, it moves to Rwanda where participants meet 'Maria' before moving through the third room which represents a border, and a fourth in which 'Ahmed' tells his story of being smuggled in the UK in a lorry. The seventh offers an experience of adjusting to life in the UK, while the final room offers an optimistic scenario of the friends of one of the 'characters' marching to demand her right to stay in the UK.

This replacing of the refugee body is taken to an extreme in *Un Voyage pas comme les autres sur les chemins de l' exil*, often translated as *An Unusual Journey*. Using theatrical conventions to create an interactive piece described as a giant role-play game (Mistiaen, 1999) it was first produced in Paris in 1998 by a conglomeration of human rights and refugee organisations, among them Amnesty International and the French organization Terre d'Asile. Supported by UNHCR, the impulse for the piece was said to be to 'take the asylum debate away from the specialists, and bring it to the people' (Mistiaen, 1999) and it marked the fiftieth anniversary of the signing of the Declaration of Human Rights. Abandoning any sense of a script, it was labelled a 'mise en situation', (literally put in the situation) and was hosted by several European cities as well as Russia and the United States (Mistiaen, 1999).

On entering the space, audience members were confronted by indifferent or suspicious guards who led them through the first part of the experience. Audience members were then asked to assume an identity chosen from twelve composite refugee identities. They followed 'their' character through the 90 minute representation of the journey to asylum in Europe. Many of the 'actors' in *An Unusual Journey*, who played the soldiers, aid workers, police and administration officials were refugees themselves taking audiences through experiences that mimicked some of the situations in which they had found themselves. Offering what Haedicke calls 'a dramaturgy that both transcended and transgressed representational performance' (Haedicke, 2002: 103), at the end of the piece it is revealed whether or not the refugee 'character' is allowed to remain in the country with the inevitable outcome that more 'failed' than were given leave to remain.

What makes these pieces remarkable is the way in which empathy works. Anger or resentment that *could* be generated when audience members are deliberately made physically and emotionally uncomfortable, is so often transformed into pity and sympathy. The potential to generate anger on behalf of asylum seekers often seems to be diminished by the need for representations of anguish, trauma and, particularly, abjection. Defined by Kristeva (1982) as both a state and a process, a way in which borders are established, abjection is never a fixed point but always unstable, a process of becoming rather than being: 'there is nothing either objective or objectal to the abject. It is simply a frontier [...]' (Kristeva, 1982: 9). For our purposes it involves differentiating between the bodies of the subjects that 'matter', citizens who can act and move in the world with ease, and refugees whose movement is more constrained. Placing the citizen in the shoes of the refugee would seem to be a good opportunity to transform understanding by experiencing the anger that people feel when they are being abused and mistreated but that is generally not what happens in these performances. Understanding how abjection relates to ideas about home and location and the ways that the dominant subject is 'established by the equation of his body with home' (Ahmed, (2000: 52) helps to explain why this may be the case.

By marking out the 'border which defines the subject' it is possible to mark out 'the centre from which other beings are expelled' (Ahmed, 2000: 52). In determining the centre from which the strangers can be expelled citizens create the familiarity of the home, 'the space one inhabits as liveable' and the strange space beyond the home, that which is classed as 'unliveable' (Ahmed, 2000: 52). Strange or abject bodies 'do not live *in* abjection: abject bodies are precisely the bodies that are not inhabited, are not liveable as such, or indeed, are *not at home'* (Ahmed, 2000: 52 emphasis added). The bodies that matter, in the sense that they have the power to delineate the zone of home, are those of citizens' and it is they who maintain the right to exclude or include those refugee bodies which do not 'belong' in that zone.

These borders are opened out in a theatrical exploration offering an opportunity to link 'the body, the image and the polis' (Shimakawa, 2002: 4). The 'unliveable' zone within which (abject) refugee bodies live becomes a kind of no-where, neither home nor not home, maybe beyond home. Citizens, however, use their mobility to mark out the place of home which can be called 'home' precisely because it is possible for them to leave it and enter it again with ease. Mobility is what marks the citizen's body as a body at home, drawing attention to the paradox that it is refugees who are classed as the 'mobile subjects' and yet their mobility is severely limited. Having left home under duress to arrive in the not-home, this move creates a not-not at home status by which asylum seekers are forced to remain in the place that they cannot leave but which is nonetheless 'unliveable'. The political designation they seek is 'Leave to Remain' but what this would actually give them is 'Leave to Leave', the ability to travel and to become mobile and to re-become 'liveable' subjects.

Refusal to stage the 'refugee body'

In their production *CMI (A Certain Maritime Incident)* Australian theatre company version 1.0 rejects notions of empathy and looks for an alternative way of engaging the natal Australian audience with questions about responsibility and hospitality. The ethical implications of this piece are discussed in the Conclusion but I want to look here at a reading of the piece that emphasises questions of belonging in relation to refugee theatre. It was based almost entirely on the words of Australian politicians, civil servants and military leaders in relation to the 'children over-board' scandal of 2001 and the parliamentary commission set up to investigate it. 'Children over-board' was the term commonly adopted to describe the claim of the Australian government in the run up to the 2001 federal election campaign that asylum seekers intercepted at sea had deliberately thrown their children overboard to force the authorities to rescue them. It was widely accepted to be untrue, even in the press, but once the story had emerged into the public arena the damage had been done and the political party that had made the claim won a convincing electoral majority largely on the issue of border control (Williams, 2008: 200).

The artists who created *CMI (A Certain Maritime Incident)* based the piece almost entirely on verbatim extracts from the enquiry set up after the elections to discover how the untruth had been placed and perpetuated within the public domain. In doing this they explicitly refused the more common strategy of staging the silenced voices of refugees so that 'the show was primarily about Australians' (Williams, 2008: 202). Refusing to stage the speech and bodies of refugees and show instead the obfuscations and evasions of the performative speech at the government enquiry represented a deliberately provocative challenge to the Australian audience asking 'who speaks for whom, under what privilege and with what force?' (Dwyer quoted in Williams, 2008: 202). There were no refugees to be pitied and no refugee stories to sadden or enrage an audience. Instead what audiences were confronted with was the illness and violation of the body politic and stories of the professionalism with which high ranking military men side-stepped and evaded the difficult question of how an untrue story had gained such a hold in the national rhetoric of asylum.

The beginning and end of *CMI (A Certain Maritime Incident)* produced a marked and sobering contrast to government rhetoric and served to remind audiences of the human consequences of harsh border policies. At the beginning of the piece audience members were forced to step over and negotiate a path through the naked bodies of the performers laid out like corpses (Burvill, 2008: 239). It was difficult for the audience to place any kind of context on this moment coming as it did at the beginning of the piece but audiences later drew associations between these bodies, drowning and the watery death of many asylum seekers who had died in trying to get to Australia by boat. The ending of the piece made this explicit by playing the accounts of the survivors of the SIEV X, the maritime disaster already discussed, which occurred only days after the 'children-overboard' scandal and in which 353 asylum seekers drowned. The audience listened to these voices at a remove deliberately distorted by a computer text-to-speech engine giving them a slightly robotic quality. On a screen at the back of the stage area their words were simultaneously projected onto 'continuous projections of featureless and endless ocean' (Burvill, 2008: 239) and the audience watched as an anonymous naked male body was laid out, washed and prepared for burial.

The effect was described as chilling (Burvill, 2008) and 'devastating in its simplicity' (Gilbert and Lo, 2007: 203). In rejecting the representation of 'the refugee body' and the trope of 'the face or voice of the refugee' version 1.0 emphasised questions of responsibility and hospitality. In choosing to focus on their own legislation and jurisdiction they rejected the emphasis on placing the citizen in a position of empathy and ask instead that audiences take on a level of responsibility *as citizens* for the situation in which they find themselves. By taking up the verbatim speech of politicians rather than the more common strategy of using the verbatim speech of refugees in works like *Asylum Monologues* (Actors for Refugees), *Le Dernier Caravansérail* (Théâtre du Soleil), *Citizen X* (Sidetrack Theatre) and *In Our Name* (Company B) they maintained the opportunity to create a more accurate and potentially radical critique of their own national legislation.

The role of audiences for all these pieces is complex, hailed in the moment of performance but understanding that the very act of being hailed in this setting demonstrates their desire to explore the possibilities for change. However, the hailing of the citizen/subject as a refugee subject does not have a lasting effect because hailing does not occur in a single incident but through a series of interpellative acts, direct and indirect, in the moment and historically situated. The audience asked to step into 'the shoes of the refugee' is *wrongly* hailed; they know that they are not a refugee outside the frame of the performance and social roles are reinforced rather than challenged because 'by hailing differently [...] the one who has the right to dwell and the stranger' (Ahmed, 2000: 23) fails to fundamentally question those boundaries. The strange subject is therefore identified as a body out of place and knowing what bodies are 'out of place' allows boundaries to be drawn around those other bodies that are in place, a process that excludes the strange(r) bodies. Communities are created by knowing who can belong and who is to be excluded so that 'knowledge is bound up with the formation of a community [...] with the formation of a "we"' (Ahmed, 2000: 55). Interpellation and, more specifically, deliberately inaccurate interpellation within a theatrical frame is thus used to displace the refugee body in performance by re-placing it with the citizen's body but all this does is to draw attention to the ways in which the citizen ultimately assumes the safety and security that comes with a sense of belonging.

Theatre crossing borders

The final section in this chapter examines what happens when plays about refuge and asylum negotiate international boundaries. By comparing three plays that have been created by companies with strong national and international profiles I hope to show how bureaucratic performance plays out on a global scale on the larger stages of prestigious international venues. *Le Dernier Caravansérail (Odyssées)* directed by Arianne Mnouchkine for Théâtre du Soleil and American Repertory Company's *The Children of Herakles* directed by Peter Sellars have, between them, had productions in France, Austria, Italy, Spain, Germany, the United States and Australia. Sellars' production of *The Children of Herakles*, by Greek playwright Euripides, began in the United States before travelling to the Ruhr Triennial Festival in Bottrop, Germany (2002). From there it moved to a number of international venues including the Romaeuropa Festival in Italy (2003), Forum Barcelona (2003) and MC93 Baubigny in Paris (2003), after which it returned to Cambridge, Massachusetts for the American leg of the tour. Mnouchkine's production of *Le Dernier Caravansérail (Odyssées)* was created in France in 2004 and continued on a world tour to Berlin, New York City and Melbourne (Figure 2). In comparison *Pericles*, the third play to be considered in this section, was produced by Cardboard Citizens and the Royal Shakespeare Company in 2005 never left London being performed twenty times in a disused warehouse in the run-down neighbourhood of Southwark (Figure 3).

All of these plays have a relationship with the canon through classical Greek theatre and literature. *The Children of Herakles*, by Greek playwright Euripides, is thought to have been performed between 430 and 425 BC, placing it within the lifetime of the real Pericles in the early years of the Peloponnesian War (Gener, 2002); *Pericles* by Shakespeare was a retelling of his story. *Le DernierCaravansérailis*

Figure 2 Scene from *Le Dernier Caravansérail* taken at the Lincoln Center, New York in July, 2005 (Photograph reproduced by permission of photographer Stephanie Berger)

Figure 3 Scene from Pericles by Cardboard Citizens/RSC, Southwark, London, 2003 (Photograph taken by Robert Day and reproduced with the permission of the Shakespeare Birthplace Trust)

subtitled *(Odyssées)* or *The Odyssey'* and has been described as Odysseus' journey in reverse (Choate, 2006). Homer's Odysseus famously made the long and arduous journey home, while these latter-day refugee subjects of Cixous' play leave home for foreign shores. The process of creating a canon is an exclusive one, the product of what is said not to belong, as much as that which is deemed suitable for inclusion. All three could be said to re-cite the canon, creating a canonical counter discourse in the terms proposed by Gilbert and Tompkins by whose definition the counter canonical piece 'actively works to destabilize power structures of the originary text rather than simply acknowledge its influence' (Gilbert and Tompkins, 1996: 15). Pollock has called the canon 'the retrospectively legitimating back-bone of a culture and political identity, a consolidated narrative of origin' (Pollock quoted in Smith and Watson, 2001: 120). The turn to the canon, the tool by which certain works are taken as the expression of culture or national identity, to explore what some see as an assault on national and cultural identity may appear paradoxical. Notwithstanding certain strong ideological challenges that have taken place since the 1970s, the works of Shakespeare and the classical Greek playwrights are traditionally seen as the pinnacle of Western theatrical canonicity. Re-citing the Greek and Shakespearean canon to address issues of foreignness, asylum and the rights and responsibilities of hospitality is both safe and challenging at the same time: safe, in that it serves to protect the work and the sensibilities of the audience, embedded as it is in Western cultural values and familiar to a Western audience, but daring for the same reason. Audiences may feel reassured by the presence of these familiar canonical texts, but these productions use canonical works to question or undermine a sense of ownership producing different relationships to cultural artifacts.

Representations of suffering

Mnouchkine's and Théâtre du Soleil's reputation is embedded in left-wing, French libertarian politics, having been set up as a workers' cooperative in 1964 in Paris by 'ten idealistic young students' (Williams, 1999: xi). Since this time their work has been written about and explored to the point where the company has become 'one of the most celebrated, indeed mythologised, companies in Europe' (Ibid.). Mnouchkine is recognised as a practitioner whose 'borrowings' from non-Western theatre styles and practices have placed her within the, sometimes, controversial bracket of intercultural theatre (Carlson, 1996). In recent years, Mnouchkine and Théâtre du Soleil have become increasingly involved with refugees and asylum seekers in Paris where the company is located, investigating practically and artistically the ethics of hospitality, questions of migration and the situation in which contemporary refugees find themselves. In 1996 the company sheltered 300 sans papiers in their building, many of whom were from the former French colony of Mali (Mc Evoy, 2006; Orenstein, 2002). This incident formed the basis of *Et soudain, des nuits d'eveil! (And suddenly the nights of awakening)* in which the recent history of Tibet became the main focus for their exploration of this experience which had marked them on both a personal and professional level (Shevtsova, 1999).

Their interest in, and commitment to, people seeking asylum was further pursued in *Le Dernier Caravansérail (Odyssées)*, a piece that was created over a two year period by interviewing asylum seekers at the Sangatte Centre in France, as well as in other countries, during their tour of *Tambours sur la digne (The Flood Drummers)* in 2001 and 2002. Indeed, five members of the company for *Le Dernier Caravansérail* were said to have been 'saved' from the refugee camps where Mnouchkine collected her interviews (Miller, 2007: 14). The production was performed in two parts, the first one called *Le Fleuve Cruel (The Cruel River)* which focused on the situations from which refugees flee (largely in Afghanistan), and the second one *Origines et Destines (Origins and Destinations)* described the problems that refugees encounter on their arrival in Western countries.

The play contained 36 actors who played one hundred and sixty-nine un-named characters in 62 scenes. Built on refugee testimony, the text is not credited to any single author, and the names of forty-nine people are listed as having collaborated on the script. The idea of creating a dramatic narrative from these accounts was apparently considered but then rejected by writer, and long-time collaborator, Hélène Cixous as 'too constructed and *aesthetic*' (Kustow, 2003, emphasis added). It was decided instead that the stories should be presented in their (apparently) verbatim state, giving the piece 'the intimacy and immediacy of a radio documentary' (Kustow, 2003). Fisek (2008) describes the process: the troupe recorded interviews with those refugees that were prepared to talk to them and these recordings were brought back to their French headquarters. Actor Shaghayeh Beheshti, who spoke Farsi, then translated these recordings into French. One copy went to the troupe of actors who began improvising scenes based on the story and a second copy went to Cixous who edited and ordered these into what Fisek calls a 'status-less' text (2008: 206). The status-less nature of the text suggests something that transcends both political and theatrical conventions and expectations. Miller suggests that having the play acted in Farsi, Dari and pidgin with French surtitles served to decentre the French language, something which she suggests is crucial to French identity (Miller, 2007: 14). The status-less nature of the piece of course also alludes to the fragile political status of the characters whose stories were being told. One remarkable piece of staging that is often referred to in this production was the use of small trucks to move the actors on and off stage, and at no point did any of the actors' feet touch the ground. Kustow suggests that this fluid staging becomes a metaphor for figures in endless transit, and McEvoy describes the effect of this theatrical device as 'cannily capturing external projections of strangeness and differences onto migrants' (McEvoy, 2006: 222).

Théâtre du Soleil's production has been called 'state endorsed migrancy' (Filewood, 2007) in which the play migrates across the world but always 'lands' in prestigious civic venues which embody the state, like the Lincoln Center in New York. Moreover, these venues have the theatre apparatus necessary to accommodate these large-scale productions; it was said to have cost AUD200,000, for example, for Théâtre du Soleil to add two extra days to their programme in Melbourne in 2005 (Filewood, 2007). Filewood's argument is that these prestigious touring productions are accepted in the civic arenas of the states that receive them because they do not pose any significant threat to the status quo. Their call for compassion is based on a liberal human rights agenda and, as such, creates only a mild frisson of excitement in the body politic of the host nations. In making this argument, Filewood is concerned to demonstrate the value of more politically oppositional work created by companies like the UK's Banner Theatre and he sets up a polemic in which Banner Theatre is presented as an example of good practice because of the strong anti-capitalist ideology which underpins their work, while the work of Mnouchkine is considered to be merely pandering to a liberal elite.

Although they are concerned to make a slightly different point something of the critique is also at the heart of Gilbert and Lo's discussion of the civic pride engendered by the company's visit to Melbourne in 2005 (Gilbert and Lo, 2007: 205). They go on to describe how it presented the 'aesthetic pleasures of orientalism' with 'elusive women in pale blue burqas; a starkly beautiful burnt-out hut [conjured] a generic Middle East' (Ibid.). The piece opened on 'a vast bare stage bathed in gray-blue and golden hews, with shimmering grayish blue curtains stage rear and on the sides' (Wehle, 2005: 80), and translations were provided 'in a *disturbingly beautiful* script that scrolls across various locations on the curtains and set pieces' (Choate, 2006: 95 emphasis added). This sits in clear contrast to the violence of the piece, especially in the first part in which women are hanged, men mutilated, children separated from their families, and girls are sold into the sex trade in a 'dog-eat-dog world' with a mafia mentality (Miller, 2006: 217). Miller suggests that it is possible to be 'swept away by the beauty, panorama, scale, virtuosity and melodrama of a Mnouchkine production' in such a way that 'any moral or political lesson is lost' (Miller, 2007: 59). Miller tries to exonerate Mnouchkine's work from such accusations by suggesting that her excessive formalism 'makes us aware in a process that both distances and pulls us in' to the action of the play. I am, however, more persuaded by Gilbert and Lo's argument that any 'conditions of ethical responsiveness are subordinated to the imperatives of voyeurism' (Gilbert and Lo, 2007: 205) which leads to the complex question of the aesthetic representation of suffering.

Das and Kleinman are clear that the links between 'aesthetic, legal and political forms of representation [are] at the heart of the problem of theorizing on the relationship between culture and power' (Das, Kleinman et al., 1999: 5). The theatrical representation of pain and suffering is a subject that has taxed a number of scholars; Diana Taylor, for example, talks about feeling trapped at the end of a particularly vivid depiction of a rape on stage in *Paso de Dos*, a play about the 'dirty war' in Argentina (Taylor, 1997: 2). The possibility that, in representing human pain, theatre makers may fall into traps of voyeurism, pity and the aestheticisation of suffering is a constant possibility. '[A]esthetic pleasure taken in the representation of suffering' (Mc Evoy, 2006: 214) has been called 'the elephant in the room' in relation to the theatrical representation of refugees (Filewood, 2007). Reflecting on this difficulty in her essay in the programme for *Le Dernier Caravansérail (Odyssées)* leads Cixous to suggest that spectacle 'first strikes, seduces and carries away, charms us, in such a way that we can forget that it's the golden and magnificent costume clothing terrible massacres' (Cixous quoted in Mc Evoy, 2006: 214). But it may be that Cixous' intentions not to aestheticise suffering were overtaken by the need for high production values in the global art market. Cixous acknowledges her struggle with the ethics of representing refugees in writing for the stage in a handwritten copy of her 'notes' reproduced in the programme for the event.[19] Her refusal to author a script from the stories given by refugees provided an opportunity to reflect on the nature of theatrical writing in relation to refugee testimony. Reproductions in the programme of Cixous' 'ethico-critical meditations' (Mc Evoy, 2006: 211) on the role of the writer and of 'the right to write' (215) in relation to the suffering of refugees are in themselves a rather aesthetically pleasing document, apparently handwritten in an artist's journal.

These are not new ideas for Cixous who has been collaborating with Théâtre du Soleil since the early 1980s. Although she writes across many mediums it is in theatre where she feels she can

> take on our cruel daily enigmas, the presence among us of the fight for life, the existence of death drives, the irresistible movement to action, the sudden assassination, or the external assassination which misogyny is, etc.
>
> – Why only in the theatre?
> – God knows: I do not. (Cixous quoted in Sellers, 1994: xxi)

It is in her theatre writing that Cixous feels she has come closest to giving a voice to the Other, partly it seems because she feels she can 'fade to the point of disappearing. I, the author, have to disappear so that you, so other may appear. My answer has come through writing for the theatre' (Cixous quoted in Sellers, 1994: 141). Some of Cixous' questions from the programme for Le DernierCaravansérail clearly articulate some of the dilemmas regarding the theatrical representation of the refugee 'Other' and are worth quoting at length:

> How do we avoid replacing the word from your lips with the sound of good intentions? How do we avoid replacing your foreign language with our French language? How do we keep your foreign language without being impolite or inhospitable to the public, our host in the theatre? How, without understanding each other's

words, can we all understand each other's heart? How do we avoid
appropriating other people's anguish when we use it make theatre? How do we avoid going wrong because we think we understand or because we are afraid we might not? How do we come as
close as possible to the other's place without taking it? How do we
avoid translating? That is, how do we avoid translating? We have
to translate. And if we don't succeed? That's what the refugee asks
on his/her journey. (Mc Evoy, 2006: 219)

Examining the deixis of Cixous' rhetorical questions reveals a ques-
tioner who represents 'us' the French-speaking citizen and 'you' the
non-French speaking outsider. On a second level of identity, the ques-
tioner is positioned as a theatre maker with responsibilities to an
audience in a 'deconstructive double-bind' (McEvoy, 2006: 219) that
illustrates both the necessity and the impossibility of translation in
its widest sense. This sets up a dynamic of visibility wherein the
speaker becomes visible through the visual representation of her writing, whereas the refugee respondents remain invisible represented, as
they are, by actors. For McEvoy this strategy is largely poetic and the
Other 'towards whom the text gestures, whose body and voice it
evokes, is finally absent and silent' (Ibid.). Maintaining the silent
absence of their refugee informants and presenting these dilemmas
instead to a Western audience suggests that Cixous' questions might
represent a performance of ethics as much as they do a practice.

To illustrate this it is helpful to once again consider Conquergood's
model of the four ethical pitfalls that are potentially involved in
'performative stances towards the other' (Conquergood, 1985) where
it is possible to see ways in which the strong commitment to telling
refugees' stories might combine with Cixous' 'difference' in relation
to those refugees to create what Conquergood calls the Curator's
Exhibitionism. In this stance the curator is so concerned to present
difference that their performances 'resemble picture postcards or
tourist souvenirs or mute, staring museum exhibitions that deny
humanity to the subjects' (Stern and Henderson, 1993: 29). This idea
appears to be borne out by Miller (2006: 217) who reported that the
effect of the hyper-realistic style of acting in presenting violence was
to 'mask' the characters in such a way as to set their experiences off
'in quotation marks, to be looked at, often deeply felt, but only partially understood'. The presentation of refugee stories envisaged in

Conquergood's Dialogical Performance ideal would be almost impossible to achieve within the framework of international touring theatre. Any piece of theatre which takes over two years to create and which travels to prestigious international festivals faces high levels of expectation, not least aesthetically in terms of visual and aural impact. The scale of the productions and the exigencies of international touring, the need for visual and aural pleasure, combined with the global reputations of those involved, all mitigate against the possibility of a theatrical presentation that is going to move beyond an over-simplified humanitarian message.

Audiences and citizens

The Children of Herakles by Euripides is very rarely staged, considered deeply flawed with its 'abrupt shifts of tone, a traffic of abstracted personae and a strange, schizoid structure' (Gener, 2002). American director Peter Sellars, however, saw potential in the story of the children of the dead Hercules seeking asylum in fifth century Athens for a re-staging of the work, feeling it would have clear contemporary resonance as it 'explores and questions the limits of democracy's role in the world-wide crisis of diaspora' (Ibid.). In answer to a question about the differences he found in touring a performance about refugees in Europe and the US Sellars acknowledges the political realities in the US which make refugees there 'truly exceptional. The United States has shut down all refugee programmes and immigration after September 11, so people are in limbo'.[20] This may give the figure of the asylum seeker slightly less potency in the US than it has in Europe and may account for the rather more considered tone of Sellars' production in comparison with work in Europe where narratives of crisis still form the dominant frame through which to read asylum.

In *The Children of Herakles* the classical device of bringing bad news, commonly used in Greek tragedy, is reversed by Euripides in an attempt to bolster the civic pride of the Athenians as they discuss what to do with the refugees in their midst. Euripides' strategy of making the original audience proud to be Athenian works for a contemporary audience, according to Sellars, because he 'filled the play with good news. His strategy was not to make the audience feel ashamed, but proud to be Athenian.'[21] In Sellars' own words 'if you're going to talk about refugees don't depress people. Don't make them feel guilty and hor-rible' (Sellars in conversation with Marranca, 2005: 38). In using the first hour of the evening before the performance for testimony, debate and presentation he required the audience to suspend their aesthetic judgement which, he hoped, would move them from the position of consumers to that of 'a citizen engaged in an actual debate' (Ibid.).

The overt address to the audience to place themselves in relation to Herakles' refugee children forms the undercurrent of the whole play, and Sellars made the controversial choice to place a group of young immigrant and refugee people on the stage throughout the perform-ance. In the German production the children of the eponymous Herakles were from the Kurdish community, from Rwanda, Colombia, Yugoslavia, Albania and Romania in Italy, and in Paris they included Moroccans, Algerians, Chinese and Vietnamese (Gener, 2002). The children, whose fates are being discussed in the course of the play, spend the entire evening looking at the audience. One critic finds himself fascinated 'by this silent gaggle of teenagers, who sit with chins in hands, trying not to fidget, staring out at us or just into space'.[22] Their apparent indifference to the piece being performed around them and their lack of engagement makes their presence their only contribution, nothing is demanded of them.

In presenting the young people in this way the production seems to reject the discourse of 'refugee contribution'. These young refu-gees are not being made 'special' in any way, quite the opposite, leav-ing the audience having to negotiate their role in this citizen/ supplicant relationship where the supplicants are making no effort to ingratiate themselves with their hosts. The young people are not heroic figures and presenting them in this way lifts their representa-tion beyond the false dichotomy of gifted and traumatised that has dominated refugee discourse. Instead the audience is presented with 'self-determining political subjects' (Pupavac, 2008: 274) who make no special claims to be gifted or unique, who demand neither sym-pathy nor pity but justice and a fair share.

The final play to be considered in this section is *Pericles* produced in 2003 by the Royal Shakespeare Company (RSC) and Cardboard Citizens, a partnership engineered by the Arts Council of England. Both organi-sations operate on very different scales, something that can be demon-strated by the fact that Cardboard Citizens had thirteen staff on its books, while the RSC had a staff of 500 at the time of the production (Jermyn, 2004: 2). As a large professional company the RSC was seen as having the technical expertise needed in terms of acting and design to stage Shakespeare's *Pericles*. The partnership with the more 'grass-roots' organization allowed the project to gain access to groups of refugees and homeless people who make up most of the constituency of Cardboard Citizens. Adrian Jackson, director of Cardboard Citizens and of the play, said 'for a tiddler like us to work with a behemoth like that [...] was a risk – the most obvious fear being that we would simply be steam-rollered' (Jermyn, 2004: 3). However, the opportunity to work with such a large company, and access to the resources that came with that, obviously outweighed those fears. Equally, the RSC was said to have 'gone out on a limb' with this 'edgy' project that was 'more like performance art installation' than a typical RSC production (Bassett, 2003). The deliberate choice of play identified contemporary preoccupations around refugees that resonated with Shakespeare's tale of exile:

> A high ranking politician is forced to leave his country because of the threat of war from a neighbouring nation, and thus starts an odyssey of exile and loss that develops its own terrible momentum; a young woman brought up by foster-parents is threatened with violence, then kidnapped by traffickers and sold into the sex industry in another country. These are stories straight out of today's papers – but they're not, they're the stories of *Pericles*.[23]

The set contained over 300 beds, ten washing machines, 300 desks and chairs, two forty-foot trailers, a fork-lift truck, a shipping container, two mobile auditoria and tons of old clothes (Jermyn, 2004: 4). Set in 'a vast warehouse, all corrugated steel and dirty concrete' (Bassett, 2003) that had been 'transformed into a Sangatte-like holding centre' (Jermyn, 2004: 7)[24], the audience was manoeuvred through six huge hangars in a promenade-style production. Each hangar was different: in one, audience members had to sit at desks to fill in a Home Office immigration form; in another 'child-size camp beds stretched out to the crack of doom in the half dark' (Bassett, 2003).

Metatheatrical strategies

Much of the power of these counter-canonical works in performance lies in their re-framing through the meta-theatrical activities which surround them, and which further dislodges them from their canonical roots. Sellars' production of *The Children of Herakles* used debate and discussion to create what has been termed a 'town meeting' that saw Sellars teaming up with the Carr Center for Human Rights, Physicians for Human Rights and the International Institute of Boston for the American premiere of *The Children of Herakles* in 2005. Refugee testimonies, presentations from political leaders and human rights specialists began the event, followed by the performance of the play which formed the centre point of the evening. At the end of the performance an informal gathering of audience, players and company members took place, accompanied by food prepared by immigrant communities from the area, the whole event running until the small hours of the morning. Similarly, Mnouchkine invited the audience to come early to La Cartoucherie, their theatre base in Paris, to eat and to study material that had been gathered up during the development of the play. There was a large map tracing various refugee journeys and source materials and relevant books were made available in the entrance hall of the theatre (Wehle, 2005).

For *Pericles*, Jackson set up similar conditions in which the audience encountered a range of refugee narratives in an installation before the beginning of the performance but he took this strategy one step further by interweaving the Shakespearean text in performance with a series of verbatim accounts from contemporary refugees as some of the stories from the research stage of the project found their way into the large-scale production of the full play. Productions of *Children of Herakles* and *Pericles* in particular called upon the authority of the extant text by significantly altering their reception to suit the subject of refugees and asylum. Both made significant changes to the staging of the text, Jackson by altering the ways in which the text was presented, and Sellars by adding layers of dialogue and debate outside the theatrical frame. Jackson, Sellars and Mnouchkine all made strong efforts to create the optimal conditions in which the performances would be received by challenging the audience to think through the issues that would be raised by the company in the hours that followed. This contrasts strongly with the often perfunctory 'after show discussions' which follow many performances of plays about refugees, and suggests the fruitful possibilities that exist for audience preparation before the event as opposed to debriefing after the event.

Thinking about these productions in relation to migration and travel locates them within a geopolitical frame that enables the travel of some people, while limiting the mobility of others. Examining the international reach of Théâtre du Soleil and the American Repertory Company alongside Cardboard Citizens/RSC highlights the different ways in which refugees and citizens are allowed to travel and negotiate state borders. Sellars' actors are always American and he rehearses every piece in the United States before taking them on the road (Marranca, 2005: 39). Mnouchkine's actors are international, originating from Iraq, Iran, Afghanistan, Kurdistan and Russia (Kustow, 2003). Both of these companies are able to tour internationally, crossing borders and entering the cities of Europe, the United States and Australia which offer them hospitality; global nomads with the freedom to travel as tourists in the major cosmopolitan cities of the world. The cast of *Pericles*, however, was made up of six actors from the RSC and six homeless or refugee actors from Cardboard Citizens, and the irregular status of these actors would presumably preclude this piece from being taken outside the UK (Jermyn, 2004: 1). The work of Cardboard Citizens began exclusively with homeless people and has broadened in recent years to include refugees. There are certain practical, material reasons for this in terms of the growing number of destitute 'failed asylum seekers' sleeping rough on British streets. It is also the case that, although the name Cardboard Citizens originally came from the cardboard boxes that many of London's homeless people lived in, there is an appropriateness about the title for refugees also, their status being demonstrated as unstable, flimsy and ultimately disposable. As Brah (1996: 182) suggests 'the question is not simply who travels but when, how and under what circumstances?' Sellars' and Monuchkine's prestigious place in what Gilbert and Lo call the 'global arts market' (Gilbert and Lo, 2007) and their freedom to travel with their companies stands in contrast to the limited mobility of the company that produced *Pericles*.

Theatre makers have been responsible for a surge in activity and a huge number of new plays that address issues concerning refugees and asylum seekers despite the inherent 'untrustworthiness' of the medium of theatre discussed at the beginning of this chapter. They have adapted traditional play forms to address the subject, seen in pieces like *The Kindness of Strangers, Asylum! Asylum!* and *Crocodile*

Seeking Refuge, for example. New forms of theatre have been created and developed particularly through experimentation with modes of presentation of verbatim speech seen in Banner's work, for example or in pieces like *Citizen X*. Verbatim plays have been identified as one of the most common forms of theatre in this field reflecting an urge to maximise the truth claims for the work and generate a sense of authority for the stories presented. Pieces like *An Unusual Journey* and *Escape to Safety* attempt to create a greater sense of empathy by allowing audiences to vicariously experience aspects of refugees' experience while pieces like *CMI* and *The Children of Herakles* ask that audiences direct their thoughts towards their responsibilities as citizens for those who would seek asylum.

The work discussed in this chapter has been instigated and carried out by citizens in the states to which refugees have fled with a view to educating audiences about asylum and improving understanding. Beyond this some have asked questions about the responsibility of citizens in a bid to understand how far personal and national responsibilities for hospitality can be stretched. They are all located in some relationship to refugee stories whether, as in *Asylum Monologues*, their strategy is to retell those stories in as 'faithful' a way as they can find or whether it is to reject that telling in the case of *CMI*. Many works aim to 'get closer' to refugees or at least to 'the refugee experience' with the goal of producing better levels of understanding which may lead to greater levels of empathy or to political action. The next two chapters examine the strategies that refugees themselves take up to articulate or refuse to articulate their own stories using theatre and performance.

3
Taking up Space and Making a Noise: Minority Performances of Activism

> We are "written" all over, or should I say, carved and tattooed with the sharp needles of experience
>
> (Gloria Anzaldua, 1990: xv).

In 2004 Merlin Luck, one of the contestants on Australian reality TV show *Big Brother*, emerged from the Big Brother House with tape over his mouth. He carried a placard which said 'Set them free' and his gestures were taken as a direct reference to the detained asylum seekers in Australia (Gilbert and Lo, 2007: 190). In October 2001 a 'sea of chairs' appeared overnight outside the immigration offices in Melbourne city centre. On each chair was the story of an asylum seeker placed there as 'a temporary reminder to the citizens of Melbourne of the existence of those made invisible' by the mandatory detention and off-shore imprisonment of asylum seekers in Australia.'[1] In the same year the words 'Boat People' were clandestinely projected (Figure 4) onto one of the 'sails' of the Sydney Opera House in an effort to remind non-indigenous Australian citizens that 'We are all boat people'.[2] The activists were suggesting that xenophobia towards asylum seekers is exacerbated by the fact that Australian citizens live in a land that has already been stolen from its indigenous peoples.[3] In this action Boat People campaigners placed the 'border panic' around asylum that had been induced by the government, the press and radio (Meikle, 2003) within the wider debate on citizenship and belonging. Luck's action of taping his mouth and the culture jamming of the No Borders and the Boat People activists are

Figure 4 Boat People image projected onto the side of the Sydney Opera House (Photograph taken by Tina Fiveash and reproduced with permission of Boat People)

examples of the range and variety of political interventions around asylum that are performative in intention and execution.

Refugee activism

As pieces of activist performance created by citizens they demonstrate solidarity with refugees and asylum seekers, taking place because refugees are *not* considered to be political actors. This chapter will discuss occasions when this view is challenged, when refugees have taken up political activities which focus attention on their precarious legal position. By contrasting their actions with those of the citizen activists concerned to act on their behalf I hope to show how difficult it is for refugees and people seeking asylum to act as political agents, the risks they take in doing this and the ways in which their actions challenge expectations that refugees should be quiet, both literally and politically. The 'refugee warrior' who has chosen the path of political action is a figure that emerged from conflicts following the decolonisation of African states in the 1960s

(Zolberg et al., 1989). Typically 'refugee warriors' are found in refugee camps along the border of the country from which they have fled. Those individuals who move further away, the South African activists from the ANC in Europe in the 1980s for example, are more often seen as political exiles (Zolberg et al., 1989: 124). However, refugee warriors represent what Zolberg and his colleagues call a 'contradiction in terms' (1989: 276), escaping violence themselves it is thought that they should reject it when they flee. Using the term refugee activist rather than refugee warrior in the context of the 'refugee crisis' of the last 20 years extends considerations of activism beyond the particular set of circumstances in which the notion of the refugee warrior was conceived.

Refugee activists are those refugees who challenge their treatment at the hands of the authorities simultaneously challenging cultural assumptions of refugeeness, namely silence and passivity. Just speaking up in a world where silence is expected can be read as a confrontational even potentially 'violent' act and, in the conditions in which contemporary refugees exist in the West, any association with violence or activism means that they risk, at the very least, losing sympathy and at worst undermining their grounds for asylum. Nevertheless some refugee activists do speak up, thereby rejecting the terms of bureaucratic performance, because they are not prepared to wait at Kafka's 'door of the law'. They speak out and demand action as this account of an occupation of immigration offices in Toronto by Algerian asylum seekers shows:

> From the outset the prior expectation of docility and patience on the part of the refugees (i.e. they should wait to be called upon) was shattered. The officials instead were faced with a loud, assertive group of non-status people, who were unwilling to be separated as (speaking) 'leaders' and (silent) 'followers' (Nyers, 2003: 1085).

Not only were these activists prepared to speak up they were also unwilling to be represented by someone else. It is a common trope in refugee advocacy to speak of 'giving voice' to refugees and, while this might sometimes be politically expedient, a more considered view of the ethical implications of giving and taking generally might provide a useful pause for advocates of this approach. Helen Nicholson

0) examines ideas of giving and taking arguing that 'the ce of the gift is fraught with paradoxes' (Ibid.: 161) when app... ied on an ethical level. Drawing from Mauss on 'the state of uncertainty associated with the gift' Nicholson emphasises the possibly coercive function of gift giving which leads to questions about the role being played by the giver and the receiver (Ibid.: 160). The assumption that the giver is in a position to offer something places the receiver in a position where a passive receiving is called for. The key is that the practice of giving 'always locates [the gift] in particular systems of value' (Ibid.: 162) and it is vital for subjects to be alert to the possible inequalities inherent in the action of gift giving as well as the instability of the gift itself.

To put this into a context in which the concept of 'giving voice' to refugees is so prevalent, being more alert to the ethical implications of gift giving should allow citizens to see that their role is not necessarily to give voice, but to 'create spaces and places which enable voices to be heard' (Ibid.: 163). However, the gift giver, like the host discussed in Chapter 1, cannot escape the implications of ownership in being in a position to make the offer. The host as the gift giver cannot avoid imbrication in systems of power because it is still within the 'gift' of the citizen to be able to *offer* the space in which refugee voices may be heard. In the act of critiquing and challenging the power relations which make refugeeness inevitable, it is impossible to extract ourselves as citizens from those very relations. When refugees are 'given a voice' they must usually accept that which non-refugees have deemed they *might* want or need and, more importantly, that which they are prepared to give them. This is, more often than not, a temporary voice in a temporary space. The impressive 'Assembly of the Refugees' in 2001, when the French National Assembly invited 577 refugees to meet and pass The Paris Appeal, called on governments to apply the Refugee Convention in a non-restrictive way (Nyers, 2006: 123). Despite the apparent success of gestures like this in accessing the civic arena for debate by offering refugees 'a voice', it is a temporary arrangement which may simply create the *appearance* of listening and which changes very little in reality.

This chapter shows that, despite a lack of political efficacy, the power of the Assembly of Refugees and other acts like it lies in symbolic and metaphorical qualities in the heterotopic space. For Foucault heterotopic sites are those sites in which all other sites within a culture 'are simultaneously represented, contested, and inv̶e̶r̶t̶e̶d̶ (Foucault and Miskowiec, 1986: 24). In the heterotopic site several incompatible sites can be brought together even when this would normally be impossible: Foucault cites the 'rectangle of the stage [where] one after the other, a whole series of places that are foreign to one another' can be simultaneously viewed (Ibid., 1986: 25). Heterotopic sites become sites of resistance, something which is achieved by 'disrupting the flow of meaning, unsettling because they have the effect of making things appear out of place' (Hetherington quoted in Tompkins, 2006: 95). Refugee activists can be seen to be 'out of place' in a number of ways. I have already shown that their activist status is seen as a contradiction which acts against expectations of silence and acquiescence. Refugees almost literally 'shouldn't be there' in the sense of being in civic space because they are required to be invisible. They should not be making a noise in public spaces because it disrupts the received notion of refugeeness with its emphasis on passivity or abjection. Refugee activists therefore appropriate certain spaces to create a heterotopia as a site for resistance. This has powerful potential because the space is not configured for this use, and refugee activists change its use (by walking in the road, for example) to suit their ends. It has even greater impact precisely because they are not the citizens for whom the space was intended, interlopers, the 'unsanctioned' taking control of spaces to which they are not entitled and altering their function. The power of this to disrupt, to anger and to militate is considerable albeit, once again, temporary.

Demanding to speak rather than waiting for permission creates a heterotopic space with the potential to lift refugee speech out of the normal economy of gift giving but this is not without risk. Refugees who make demands on the authorities may be more likely to be heard than those who passively await permission but when refugees shout the authorities usually hear only noise. Unwilling to understand the words beneath the noise, the authorities perceive only the 'violence' of refugees when they try to make their voices heard in public space and this will usually lead to them being dismissed. This seems to present a problematic no-win situation: either refugees must operate in a system of powerlessness (if they wait to be given to) or aggression (if they take without an offer). The title of this chapter suggests the significance of the nexus of voice and place where thinking about the power of the voice in the locations in which it is heard suggests a range of possible positions from which to view the apparently impossible activity of refugee activism.

Examining this interrelationship will show that, while citizens can act in public space, refugees are usually forced to operate in 'humanitarian space' which requires their bureaucratic performance of refugeeness. In humanitarian space refugees are compelled to perform their authenticity as refugees, eschewing any activity that is not about simply surviving (Rajaram, 2002). In emphasising their apparent helplessness and vulnerability to make their bureaucratic performance credible to a non-refugee audience, noisy refugees raise suspicions that they may be active agents with some sort of autonomy and that is seen as threatening and incompatible with their role as refugees. Considering refugee activism shows how taking speech is bound up with taking space and provokes fundamental questions which could be characterised as 'Who speaks? Who counts? Who belongs? Who can express themselves politically?' (Nyers, 2003: 1089). What happens when refugees have the audacity to be authoritative? And what happens when this is denied for so long that frustration and desperation become the only voice with which refugees can speak? Bearing this complex set of circumstances in mind I offer two examples of ways in which refugees have attempted to make their own voices heard, the first the noisy, public and disruptive action of a public demonstration and the other in which asylum seekers hope to make some noise through the silence generated by physically preventing speech in the act of sewing their lips together.

Taking up space

Campaigners and activists recognise the value of the 'modular tactic' of the demonstration which 'can be transferred across boundaries of context, complaint, location and identity' (Bogad, 2006: 50). The most common form of public demonstration uses the strategy of walking in the city, taking up public space, in the form of a march followed by a rally at an agreed destination. In common with many political campaigns, anti-deportation rallies make use of walking in the form of the march or procession in the city, and the larger the procession the greater the disruption that can be caused. If numbers are large enough the authorities are compelled to close major routes to traffic in and out of the city. Marches and demonstrations have been criticised for being over-formulaic, routinised into a mechanical response to an issue (Bogad, 2006: 50). Certainly there is not the same level of the wit or humour on show at an anti-deportation 'demo' as there has been in many protests described by Shepard and Hyduk in recent years (Shepard and Hayduk, 2002) where irony is such a strong feature of these actions: for example, the men and women of Church Ladies for Choice dress up as 'gals who lift spirits and provide comic relief at clinic defense and abortion-related demonstrations' (Church Ladies quoted in Cohen-Cruz, 2002: 235); or where anti-globalisation protestors made great use of irony by dressing up as Billionaires for Bush when a group of demonstrators created a stir at the Republican Convention in 2000 with 'nearly a hundred Billionaires in full dress [...] chanting, singing, burning money, smoking cigars' (Boyd, 2002: 252). A British anti-deportation rally is, by comparison, a rather earnest and humourless affair perhaps making up for what it lacks in wit, irony and satire with its noise and disruption.

The National Coalition of Anti-Deportation Campaigns (NCADC) has been behind over one hundred successful cases against deportation from the UK since 1995.[4] They support asylum seekers who have been refused refugee status and who are threatened with return to their country of origin, families under threat of being divided by the forced return of one parent, and lesbians and gay men who do not benefit from the marriage rules for deportation. Through large public demonstrations and marches NCADC, and other organizations like it, advocate on behalf of refugees and publicise their cause. The decision to start a campaign through organisations like NCADC is not an easy one, a fact articulated by Joy from the radio project who was introduced in the Preface. She felt that she had no option but to campaign against her removal back to Nigeria but was very aware that she had to make herself and her story 'sellable' to a British audience:

> If I really, really want to start a campaign I should now see myself as a commodity because a commodity is something that has come out to be sold. And it depends on how you are advertised [...] the example that without advertising a commodity you cannot get

people to buy them properly. So that is how I have to see myself. It takes a lot of guts.[5]

Once the campaign is under way it relies on the willingness and ability of the individual asylum seeker to speak about experiences in a public arena, often at demonstrations and rallies. An anti-deportation campaigner from Uganda reveals her anxieties about speaking in public before a large crowd at an anti-deportation rally:

> I guess this was the biggest crowd I had ever made a speech to. It's not easy to stand up and say I was abducted and raped when I was thirteen years old. But I have to because I'm fighting for my life all over again.[6]

In the refugee campaign the refugee's body becomes a guarantee, an indication of speaking and acting from the middle of a torment which has to be articulated for an audience.[7] Campaigners and advocates listen again to the refugee's story and yet they 'hear' a different story from that heard by the courts when the case was turned down. If both groups are hearing the same information, how can it be that they both arrive at such different conclusions? In his investigation of asylum appeals Ranger suggests that reading refugee stories 'with the grain' can reveal the mind of the Home Office or immigration authorities more generally, while reading them 'against the grain' enables the refugee's voice to be heard (Ranger, 2006: 219). Anti-deportation campaigns are a way in which reading against the grain is framed for a public audience but it is important to remember that this counter-narrative is also constructed and mediated.

Joy's campaign, for example, was initiated in 2005 in partnership with members of the Revolutionary Communist Group (RCG) who support a number of anti-deportation campaigns in the UK. The RCG advocates a policy of open immigration similar to that pursued by the No Borders movement and the No One Is Illegal network.[8] It is their belief that asylum seekers are victims of 'racist' governments and their campaign strategy is designed as much, if not more, to criticise the government as to support asylum seekers.[9] In 2006 Joy withdrew from the campaign and, although the RCG wanted to continue, without her personal endorsement this was impossible and

Figure 5 An anti-deportation rally outside Manchester Town Hall, Manchester, November, 2005 (Photograph taken by the author)

the campaign collapsed. In 2007 Joy was given Indefinite Leave to Remain on compassionate grounds with no official mention being made of her campaign.

Before it collapsed Joy's campaign formed part of an anti-deportation march organized by NCADC in November 2005 in Manchester city centre (Figure 5). Typical of many such demonstrations throughout the UK demonstrators assembled at an agreed location, in this case the University of Manchester Students' Union, where banner-making workshops were followed by a formal address by Manchester's Lord Mayor, Afzal Khan. This set the march off in the form of a mass procession, attended by a large number of police personnel, down a major arterial route to the Peace Gardens outside Manchester Town Hall. Several hundred people of all ages participated and elderly protest veterans marched alongside parents pushing babies and toddlers in highly decorated prams. Small children had their faces painted and most people carried placards. Some held rather badly painted banners which had been made for the occasion from old sheets, giving the march an informal, home-made aesthetic, a model of 'collective and individual Do-It-Yourself creativity' (Bogad, 2006: 52). A number of people who carried loud hailers instigated lively call and response chants with other demonstrators, including 'No borders, no nations, stop deportations'. Traffic was re-routed so that the march could take place causing widespread disruption of normal business and transport in the city centre on a busy Saturday afternoon. When the march arrived at its destination the rally began with speeches by asylum seekers from a platform outside which were followed by a 'Speak-out' in the main debating chambers of the Town Hall.

Using this example I want to examine the impact on refugee activism of walking which opens up the city space in a provocative way. Walking can be said to speak and has been called a space of enunciation (De Certeau, 1984: 99) and the act of walking in the urban system serves the enunciative function of appropriating the topographical system of the city which involves a spatial acting out of place. In De Certeau's definition, walking is to the city what the speech act is to utterances. It 'affirms, suspects, tries out, transgresses, respects etc., the trajectories it "speaks"' (Ibid.). Political marches and anti-deportation campaigns have a doubly enunciatory value in that the walkers gain the power to transgress their designated space on the city's pavements, at the same time as protesting volubly about the injustices done to asylum seekers.

Their right to do this inevitably arouses strong feelings on the part of those citizens who may be angry about these transgressions of the norm in public spaces. The public nature of this kind of refugee activism means that audiences are co-opted into witnessing, willingly or not, and this can lead to anger. When refugee activism is encountered in a public place the most common phrases used against it are couched in the language of physical violation. In particular, two heard most frequently are 'they don't need to wave it in our faces' and, even more emphatically, 'I don't want it shoved down my throat'. These images suggest that the body may function as a synecdoche for what the speakers think of as 'their' public space and usurpation of that space by those who seem not to belong there becomes a provocative, even potentially violent, act.

Making a noise

In refugee protest enunciation is also literal. The main debating chamber of Manchester City Council was turned over to refugee voices for the day during the 'speak out' when Darlain, an asylum seeker from Cameroon, 'conducted affairs from the head table of the debating chamber'.[10] The inverted political order took on a particular resonance when these troubling quasi-citizens took the space usually reserved for debating the business of the citizens of Manchester by their elected members, while the citizens themselves remained outside (on a cold November day). Giving up such a potent symbol of democratic activity as the debating chamber is significant because non-citizens have to interrupt the dominant political order not just to be heard but to be recognised as speaking subjects (Nyers, 2003: 1087). With the Lord Mayor addressing the start of the rally from the steps of the University of Manchester Students Union and a Cameroonian asylum seeker addressing assembled refugees and asylum seekers from the Mayor's position in the debating chamber, the event created a strange mirror image, like a refugee Feast of Fools, where the normal social order is inverted for a day. This pagan rite, adopted and adapted by the medieval Catholic Church, provided for a day to be set aside in which a brief carnivalesque break from the hierarchical order was permitted to those who were normally subordinate. Carnival, as a symbolic inversion of the contemporary social order, created a space of liberation so the carnivalesque refugee demonstration assumes the right to appropriate public space even if only temporarily; the right to be subversive.

Outside, the Town Hall, despite the disturbance of normal urban activity and the distortion of voices through loud hailers, it is possible that the demonstration was simply noisy, an annoying 'buzz' in the ears of shoppers. Although I cannot deny this possibility it seems that a more optimistic reading is possible: Rancière suggests that the first step in denying political agency to any subject is to 'begin by not seeing him as the bearer of signs of politicity, by not understanding what he says, by not hearing what issues from his mouth as discourse' (Rancière, 2010: 38). Political demonstrations place one world in the other, by bringing people to our attention that would otherwise remain unseen. Traditionally, says Rancière, all that was required to suppress subjects and to keep them out of the polity was to keep them in a domestic space which was separated from public life. Political demonstrations have the effect of 're-qualifying' these spaces making 'visible that which had no reason to be seen' so that 'what was audible as mere noise [is] heard as speech' (Ibid.: 38). It could be that taking the discussions inside the Town Hall was not simply symbolic but gave a platform on which 'distorted noise' had the potential to be understood as reasoned debate.

The state becomes extremely nervous when asylum-seeking 'quasi-citizens' start to 'make a noise' because this poses a critical question for the entire political system: 'who has the authority to protest, and under what terms and conditions?' (Nyers, 2003: 1071). In other words, who has the authority to be active? Only citizens are expected to be visible and articulate and noisy refugees unsettle conceptuali-sations of belonging by appearing to reject expectations of invisibil-ity and silence. This is what makes public speech and the action of the asylum seeker 'impossible', and yet it is an impossible acting and speaking that constitutes activist performance. The 'abject cosmo-politan' shows how to move beyond the literal sense of giving and taking that is reiterated in much refugee discourse. The expectations on the part of the citizen about the abjection of the refugee make it very clear that there is more at stake than the material concerns of taking jobs, houses, even livelihoods. The fear exists of something much more significant being usurped – the assumption of belonging that underlies citizenship.

In the previous chapter I suggested that refugee advocacy organisa-tions tend to stress what refugees have to offer, or what they can give as part of their 'myth-busting' discourse. An important feature of this discourse concerns the *contribution* made by refugees but the problem with stressing refugees' contribution lies in insistence that immigrants are givers to the nation and feeding the 'xenophobic anxiety that they might really be takers from it' (Honig, 2001: 199). An Australian anti-immigration activist seems to have understood this in his clear articulation of xenoracism: 'It is a form of theft for such people [asylum seekers] to break into richer countries, unin-vited, to share in the greater riches' (Wills, 2002: 86). Anxieties about 'taking' refugees are clearly demonstrated by activist performance not simply because of what they are saying but in the very act of say-ing *anything* in a public arena they are unsettling ideas about who has the authority and because 'the first target of taking-subjects is

[...] always speech' (Nyers, 2003: 1078). Demanding to be heard in the civic space is deliberately provocative and speaking beyond the sanctioned limits of refugee expression, for example in refugee arts festivals to be discussed in the next chapter, even more so.

Wishful performatives

In taking something that was not there, their right to speak in a public place, to be visible and political, Darlain and his colleagues were 'frame shifting [...] staging non-existent rights' (Honig, 2001: 101). The anti-deportation rally embodies what will be called a 'wishful performative' which originates from the idea of wishful thinking; by wishing something I can make it so. By turning wishful thinking into a wishful performative I hope to show the possibility of acting on the wish, of changing something, while still maintaining tenuous links with action and the inherently unobtainable possibility of success. Political realities undermine the possibility of true ethical engagement with refugees but wishful performatives allow us to take a step in that direction, to imagine ethical action even if it is doomed to political failure. In order to understand the anti-deportation march as a wishful performative it is important to understand the complex ways in which performativity relates to time because wishful performatives operate in the strange and complex world of the future anterior tense, *it will have been.*

In the first instance politicians make use of the language of the future anterior to justify the actions that created the need for people to flee from conflicts echoing the 'bizarre circular game' discussed in Chapter One where politicians make wars which create refugees who then flee in search of asylum only to be denounced by those same politicians. British Prime Minister Tony Blair used the future anterior in relation to the British invasion of Iraq when he said: 'if we are wrong we *will have destroyed a threat* that, at its least, is responsible for human carnage and suffering. That is something which I am confident history will forgive' (Blair quoted in Younge, 2006: 31 emphasis added). The action led to carnage and suffering in Iraq as well as untold suffering of refugees forced to flee as a consequence of the British and American invasion. In an illustration of McKenzie's central thesis (2001: ix) that performance 'can be read as both experimentation and normativity' George Bush's 'main weapon' around the invasion of

Iraq was conceived of as his language (Taylor: 2003: 5). This proved potent in the build-up towards the American invasion of Iraq when 'claims, boasts, declarations masqueraded as truths' (Ibid.). Performative language can be co-opted in wishful performativity, where all performative utterances are a kind of 'masquerade' in which 'a disguised form [...] apes a statement of fact while operating as a deed done' (Ibid.). Bush's language was allowed to act, his performatives were 'happy' because he was one of the most influential men in the world and performative language acts differently when it comes from an a *priori* position of power.

When refugees, arguably some of the *least* powerful people on earth, speak their desire for accomplishment their speech act is unhappy, considered to be simply masquerading. In this situation wishful performatives can 'conjur[e] a reality that does not yet exist' in such a way as to 'rethink the possible' (Butler, 1999: xvii and xx). Rather than simply naming something that already exists performativity 'works to generate that which it apparently names' making the 'temporal dimension of performativity [...] crucial' (Ahmed, 2004: 92). It generates effects which have not yet come into being by recalling what has already been said. Speaking of his work with Hmong refugees in the United States, Conquergood claims that 'performance as restored behaviour plays with time' (Conquergood 1992: 44). In examining the ways in which the traditional role of shaman is altered and mutated in its Western diasporic manifestation he alludes to Schechner's notions of restored behaviour, 'the habits rituals and routines of life...the key process in every kind of performing, in everyday life, in healing, in ritual, in play, and in the arts' (Schechner, 2002: 28). Restored behaviour offers groups and individuals 'the chance to become what they once were – or even, and most often, to re-become what they never were but *wish to have been or wish to become*' (Schechner quoted in Conquergood, 1992: 44 emphasis added).

One of the problems for refugees is that their future-creating performative statement *I claim asylum* is based on a constative account of events in the past. The process of claiming asylum involves uncovering past events in order to project those into the future: based on past persecutions in their country of origin, asylum seekers must demonstrate that they have, what the Refugee Convention calls, a 'well-founded fear' of future persecutions that might take place were they to be returned. Asylum seekers' ability to avoid projected future injustices depends on their ability to convince the authorities in the place to which they have fled about past injustices in the place which they have left. In other words, the felicity of their performance utterance depends on a believable set of past constative utterances but performativity struggles in the past tense; it is not at home.

Restoration of what once was and the hopes for what one *might* become can be clearly seen in the shouted rhetoric of the anti-deportation march. The performative chant 'Samuel will stay!', for example, performs a desire that naming it and reiterating it will make it so. The chanted speech act proposes three forms of restoration: one a simple replacing of what once was (Samuel's citizenship in his country of origin); the 're-becoming' of what he wishes to have been (a 'successful' citizen in his country of origin), and of what he wishes to become (through recognition as a refugee in the place to which he has fled). The refugee activist does not want Samuel to be forced to return and is thus chanting to restore something that was not there in the first place, Samuel's refugee status. It is possible to see two different tenses simultaneously in operation: the past: 'Samuel was persecuted in his country of origin' and the future: 'Samuel will stay' but the future anterior tense lurks behind this: 'if Samuel returns to his country of origin and he is persecuted, events *will have shown* that his claim to be a refugee was founded'. In the case of asylum seekers the 'overarching logic of the future anterior scripts [the] regime of torture' (Pugliese, 2002: par.16). This is the logic of medieval witch trials where, if the defendant drowned, it was seen as a sign that she was innocent.

Wishful performatives in the form of the reiterative chants are not 'contrasted with the real but [constitute] a reality that is in some sense new' (Butler quoted in Patraka, 1999: 5). The lack of any real political power on the part of refugee activists means that their reiterations will probably not be effective in real terms. Individual refugees are no less likely to be deported, and campaigners are equally unlikely to see a policy of open immigration across international borders. Jill Dolan has identified a similar phenomenon in theatre where 'utopian performances' in which 'small but profound moments' lift the audience 'slightly *above the present* into a hopeful feeling of what the world might be like' (Dolan, 2005: 4 emphasis added). Like utopian performances wishful performatives give a glimpse of 'how powerful might be a world in which our commonalities might hail us over our difference' (Dolan, 2005: 8). Like ' "wish"-oriented moments [of] theatre' wishful performatives demand that the impossible be achieved. Campaigners' actions are based on 'wishful thinking' in bald political terms, however, reframing wishful thinking as 'wishful performatives' opens up the possibility for evaluating success where it can be re-thought as ways to stage the impossible.

Taking space for impossible speaking

The state of being a refugee is thought to carry a certain stigma, a point made by two refugees from Nigeria and Zimbabwe during a joint interview:

> Speaker 1: It's nice when you still get some genuine people who take you as you are but generally when people know you are a refugee it's like a... Speaker 2: Stigma. People should take you as a human being for who you are and not where you come from.[11]

The ancient Greeks used the word stigma to refer to bodily signs which designated the bearer of these signs as remarkable in some way and beyond the boundaries of 'normal' society (Goffman, 1963). Slaves, criminals and traitors were marked on their bodies, forcing the bearers to carry scars as a visual representation of their social stigma. Some of the reasons for stigma becoming attached to contemporary refugees can be traced back to the negative refugee discourse which has been promulgated by the press, as discussed in Chapter 1. Feelings of stigma for refugees may also emerge from the dramatic change of social and professional status that many refugees find in their new home, something that will be discussed in the next chapter. However, a small number of refugees have taken the word stigma back to its original associations with bodily marks demonstrating their ambivalent social status to the observer and that is where I turn to now. Unlike the slaves and criminals of Greek society who would have been marked by their owners or by the law, these refugees physicalise their perceived stigma by their own hand, inflicting pain and injury on their bodies themselves.

Some asylum seekers have sewn up their lips, and sometimes eyes and ears, in a desperate attempt to draw attention to their situation and their 'monstrous silencing' (Pugliese, 2002: par.6). These extreme gestures seem to come about as a result of asylum seekers feeling excluded from the polis in such a way that 'the sole domain in which he or she now exercises any freedom is the domain of private emotions, the individual body, the domus' (Jackson, 2006: 70). This section examines the act of wounding the body, an action taken by a small but significant number of asylum seekers, and suggests that the individual and domestic combines with the public and political to reveal the complex way in which private and public domains interact in these extreme acts of protest. These difficult acts are an example of the 'delicate pivot' in performance studies (Anderson and Menon, 2009: 5). As scholars of performance part of our ethical obligation is to explore sites of violence remembering that 'enactments of violence are both spectacular in their cultural impact and embodied in their transaction and effect' (Anderson and Menon, 2009: 4 emphasis in original). To speak of them as performative is not to belittle the intense pain and suffering involved but acknowledges their impact beyond personal embodiment on a national and global stage.

In order to comprehend this phenomenon it is important to understand the way in which asylum seekers are so often placed in an unbearable position of uncertainty. Australia and the UK, two countries with a strong policy of detaining asylum seekers, are the sites of *most* self-harming refugee activity. A growing number of rejected asylum seekers in the UK are detained in holding centres often awaiting deportation (Bacon, 2005) with Britain allegedly having one of the worst records in Europe on the detention of asylum seekers.[12] In Australia under section 196 of the Migration Act refugees can be indefinitely detained regardless of whether they have committed an offence or not (Burnside, 2003: 183). Those held often cannot understand why they are in detention nor do they have any idea how long their imprisonment will continue. Their state of 'spatial confinement without temporal limits' places extreme stress on the mental and physical health of those who are held and subsequent breakdowns among inmates has led to increasing instances of self-mutilation as 'refugees fall back on the one resource left to them, on their one point of anchorage in the midst of the violence of indefinite incarceration: their bodies' (Pugliese, 2002: par.3).

In November 2006 riots broke out at Harmondsworth Detention Centre, one of the biggest immigration detention centres in the UK.

The 500 rejected asylum seekers who were being held in detention there reported that the conditions were appalling, that physical mistreatment was common and that solitary confinement was used for punishment as a matter of course. Prisoners spelt 'Help' and 'SOS Freedom' on the ground of the exercise yard with rubbish and paper so that the news crews filming from a helicopter above could see it. Like the survivors of Hurricane Katrina in 2005, who created messages on the roofs of their submerged houses in New Orleans, these messages, legible only from above, aimed to 'spell out' their anguish to an audience. However, unlike the residents of New Orleans who were able to use their hypervisibility to co-opt the 'techniques of representation and surveillance' (Anderson and Menon, 2009: 2) in their efforts to survive, images from immigration detention centres remain largely unnoticed, picked up only by refugee advocate groups and the left-wing press. Imprisoned and out of the public gaze asylum seekers are desperately worried that they have become invisible, nobody knows they are there and nobody cares; they feel as though they have been forgotten.

In Campsfield, a British Immigration Detention Centre near Oxford, 120 jailed asylum seekers went on hunger strike in 2006 and, in a letter which was smuggled out of the prison, described themselves as feeling like slaves and being treated as animals but their biggest fear was being forgotten.[13] In these conditions there is an urge to 'shout out' beyond the boundaries of their incarceration even if only to remind those outside that they exist. This urge becomes so powerful that extreme acts of defiance and disruption become necessary in order to be heard. As well as riots and occupations one of the most prevalent acts is that of self-harm.

The number of refugee detainees who are in danger of self-harming, or who have actually self-harmed in the ten holding centres in the UK, has almost doubled since 2004. Figures released by the Home Office under the Freedom of Information Act show that between April 2005 and February 2006, staff in detention centres initiated self-harm prevention procedures 376 times, compared to 192 times for the previous twelve months.[14] The most extreme form of self-harm is, of course, to take one's own life, and there is evidence of this happening both in detention centres and in the community beyond. In 2006 the Institute of Race Relations published *Driven to Desperate Measures* in which the deaths of 221 asylum seekers and migrants were catalogued (Athwal, 2006). Fifty-seven of these died at their own hand, and twenty-two suicides have been recorded in prisons, removal centres and in psychiatric custody. Some examples from detention include the death of Bereket Johannes, an Eritrean refugee who killed himself in Harmondsworth Immigration Removal Centre in 2006, and whose death was said to be the eighth in a detention centre.[15] One asylum seeker who was being held in Yarl's Wood Detention Centre was said to have hung himself so that his son could remain in the country.[16] Three gay asylum seekers who were not under detention are said to have killed themselves to avoid being sent back to Iran: Hussein Nasseri was found dead with a gunshot wound in July 2005 having failed to gain asylum and Esrafil Shirl, also from Iran, poured petrol over his upper body and set himself alight in Manchester in 2003.[17] A third Iranian, Babak Ahadi, doused himself with petrol and set fire to himself in his flat in Bristol in July 2005.[18]

Sewing and wounding

One method of self-harm among refugees which has gained a certain notoriety is lip sewing where refugees stitch their own lips together, sometimes as well as eyes and ears. This action produces a hunger strike (Richards, 2005) which mode of protest has been considered in detail elsewhere (Anderson and Menon, 2009) but hunger striking is not the focus here because it is a secondary effect of the primary action of lip sewing. In Australia, where mandatory detention for undocumented migrants was the norm through most of the 1990s, a number of commentators have considered this phenomenon (Gilbert and Lo, 2007; Pugliese, 2002; Wills, 2002). The mass lip sewing of detainees forced itself into a public arena when up to 60 refugees sewed their lips together in Woomera Detention Centre in 2002 (Goldsmith, 2002). An undisclosed number were reported to have done the same thing in Nauru, a detention centre on an island off the shores of Australia (Gilbert and Lo, 2007).

These examples became so notorious in that country that it was possible to stage a fashion shoot for the magazine *Australian Style* called 'Refugee Chic' where the models had fake stitches placed on their lips (Pugliese, 2002: par.37). A radio commercial for a well-known chicken dinner portrayed refugees unstitching their lips when they heard that 'with every quarter chicken combo, they're giving an extra quarter of a chicken away free'.[19] The Woomera lip-sewing incident gained national television coverage in Australia and has been argued as one of the reasons why Woomera was forced to close in 2003 (Cox and Minahan, 2004). Other detention centres still remain, however, and ten asylum seekers sewed their lips in a detention centre on Christmas island off the coast of Australia in 2010, the first reported lip sewing since 2004 (Hudson, 2010).

Elsewhere lip sewing has been identified in a small number of cases in the UK (Branigan, 2003, Oliver, 2003; Richards, 2005). Abas Amini, a Kurdish refugee from Iran and a political poet who had been in trouble with the authorities in Iran on many occasions, stitched his lips, eyes and ears in 2003 (Branigan, 2003). He faced a two year wait for a decision on his asylum claim, had his case adjourned five times and lost his final appeal because the British Home Office failed to send a representative to his hearing. This last event caused him to take his drastic action and after eleven days he agreed to have the stitches removed (Richards, 2005).

Another case was that of Shahin Portohfeh, an Iranian living in Coventry, who stitched up his eyes, lips and ears for six days in 2003 (Oliver, 2003; Richards, 2005). He reported that he had been sentenced to 74 lashes and faced death by stoning for having a gay relationship if he returned to Iran.[20] Similar protests have been recorded in Greece where six Afghan refugees sewed up their lips as part of a protest which took place outside Propylaea, one of the main universities in Athens. In an open letter to the authorities they stated 'Asylum is all we ask for; it is the only hope we and our families have of ever leading normal decent lives after all the hardships we have experienced in our own countries and on our journey to Greece'.[21] In a separate protest in Athens in the same year seven Iranian asylum seekers sewed their lips together as part of a public protest.[22]

The lip sewing of asylum seekers has been considered alongside staged incidences of physical wounding (including lip sewing) undertaken by artists like Ron Athey, Franko B, Marina Abramowich and Ulay (Richards, 2005). The power of the gesture of lip sewing in political protest and in art lies in the ironic way in which it gestures simultaneously to silence and speaking and Richards suggests that 'the sealed mouth becomes articulate' (Richards, 2005: 35). The lip sewing of Athey, Franko B and Ulay in the field of visual art all predate the 'refugee crisis' of the 1990s but Australian artist Mike Parr stages his extreme acts of bodily mutilation firmly within the asylum debate. It is to Parr's work that I now turn in order to understand the ironic way in which the gesture of lip sewing operates and what this might mean for the refugee protesters who have chosen this course of action.

Parr's durational art performances have challenged the artist's body in a number of ways. They include a ten day hunger strike called *Water by Mouth* (2001); *Malevich (A Political Arm) Performance for as Long as Possible* in 2002 where the artist nailed his arm to the wall of a gallery; *Close the Concentration Camps* (2002) in which he stitched up his lips and branded the word 'Alien' on his leg; Aussie *Aussie Aussie Oi! Oi! Oi! (Democratic Torture)* in 2003 and *Kingdom Come* in which he had electric shocks administered to his body that were triggered (often inadvertently) by visitors to the Art Space Gallery in Woolloomooloo, Sydney.

Parr's work has been described as 'ethical and unambiguously political' a response to the 'toxic language' of political debate in contemporary Australia which has manufactured a 'fear of the non-Anglo, non-Christian other' (Scheer, 2008: 44). Parr is specifically referencing the pain of those asylum seekers who have sewn up their own lips and eyes in an attempt to find a 'different order of communication' (Scheer, 2008: 45) from the arid bureaucratic and political channels which appear to be the only ones open in the asylum debate. In *Malevich* Parr links his rejection of formalist art (embodied in Malevich's *White on White* painting), with the White Australia policy[23] describing how his arm 'nailed to the white expanse of wall' seemed to provide 'a clear indication of the detention centers and the tabula rasa of the environment (geographical, psychological, and cultural) that located them' (Parr quoted in Scheer, 2008: 45). Parr's tortured body becomes a 'clean slate' on which he can make 'polysemic political statement[s]' (Austin, 2005) that amplify similar acts by asylum seekers who have been driven to their own desperate measures as a result of their treatment at the hand of the immigration system.

It would be easy to be critical of Parr on a number of levels. Some critics have suggested that he merely produces a kind of artistic parody of torture and mutilation where his body acts as a 'dramatised stand-in' for the body of the refugee (Austin, 2005). Equally, we could point to the ways in which his acts are so carefully managed in contrast to the conditions in which the refuges undertake theirs. For *Malevich (A Political Arm)*, for example, Parr's assistants following detailed instructions set out by the artist before the installation. These are worth quoting at length because they form only one of a series of instructions which make his act of self-mutilation possible:

> Every two hours exactly an attendant must offer me a glass of water with one teaspoon of glucose powder dissolved in the water. I am supplying the glucose powder and a drinking straw which will need to be held to my mouth. The glass with its straw will need to be held to my mouth. Every 6 hours the water will need to be offered with a multivitamin tablet [I will supply] and at that time 2 Panadol tablets will need to be offered. Two fingers can be pressed to my cheek to indicate Panadol. I will either nod 'yes' or shake my head. Every twelve hours I should be given one magnesium tablet in addition to the multi-vitamin.[24]

However, rather than criticise Parr for this level of preparation, the fact that he needs to set out such detailed instructions and to take such precautions adds strength to the conviction of refugees who have to carry out their acts without any of these strict protocols. This is an important consideration but one of the most powerful effects of Parr's lip sewing is the way in which it counteracts the claims of Australian politicians that lip sewing represents the barbarous customs of the refugee Other. Suggesting that the practice of lip sewing was previously unknown in Australia, the government is able to imply that it is a practice of savagery on the part of the foreign Other. The Minister for Immigration, Phil Ruddock, is on record as having said 'lip sewing is not known in our culture. It's something that offends the sensitivities of Australians. The protesters believe it might influence the way we respond. It can't and it won't' (Pugliese, 2002: par.9). Detained asylum seekers themselves have alluded to this debate:

> I was on hunger strike several times and last month I sew my lips. My protest was about freedom and basic human rights. This is not in my culture or your culture but sometimes silence is better than to shout. (Burnside, 2003: 98)

I am writing this letter with tears in my eyes and have sewn my lips. As you are aware we have been on hunger strike. We are requesting to leave this country. In reply to Mr. Ruddock's words that sewing lips is unknown in his culture, we have somehow to inform the Australian people it is unknown in our culture as well but Australian government has been causing us to do this action. We haven't been familiar with this action at all before we came here. (Ibid.: 136)

These arguments are made in letters that were exchanged between citizens and detained asylum seekers as part of a campaign for a more humane immigration system. As well as providing personal support for individual refugees the letters serve as a way for those directly involved to demonstrate their 'corporeal ventriloquism of anguish' (Pugliese, 2002: par.5) in writing when they cannot do it through the spoken word. Parr's work amplifies what they are saying: it is not the act of lip-sewing that is barbaric but the system which produced the desperation to act in this way.

Pain and the skin

The extraordinary action of refugees who silence themselves in order to create a voice can be further illuminated by thinking about the act of sewing itself. Richards suggests two places in which sewing is a more normative act: in the operating theatre and in the (usually) female act of domestic sewing (Richards, 2005: 36). Taking these in order I would first like to investigate the links between sewing and pain before looking at the feminine associations with sewing. In surgical sewing stitches are used to sew flesh together, to cover up a wound. Rather than containing a wound *unnecessary* surgical sewing actually creates one, extending and amplifying pain rather than ending it. Scarry suggests that in the moment of the infliction of pain, language disintegrates, and it is only after that moment that it can be recreated and shared stating that 'physical pain has no voice, but when it at last finds a voice, it begins to tell a story' (Scarry, 1987: 3). The essentially unshareable nature of the moment of pain due to its resistance to language shows how pain triumphs by separating the person expressing the pain from the one listening to that expression. The person feeling the pain has the certainty of the pain while the one listening feels distant to the expressions of the other's pain which are 'vaguely alarming yet unreal' (Scarry, 1987: 4). Scarry is interested in the deliberate infliction of pain on the subject at the hand of another. 'Dermographia', literally skin writing (Ahmed and Stacey; 2001: 15), focuses more specifically on self-harm and particularly on acts of self-harm by victims of abuse. A number of ideas particularly relating to the relationship between language, power and pain emerge from dermographia and are helpful in considering the act of lip sewing.

Skin has a phenomenological function to record a life lived and 'skinscapes' become an image of the skin as a vehicle for the storytelling of a life (Prosser, 2001: 52). Skin that is deliberately wounded by the 'owner' of that skin when more literal speech is impossible becomes 'a deeply eloquent form of testimony, where a plea is made for social recognition' (Kilby, 2001: 124). The wound can be conceptualized as a mouth which can 'speak what the actual physical mouth has been forbidden to utter' (McLane, 1996: 115). The infliction of pain on one's body serves three functions for the person who (self) inflicts it making it possible to 'restore their world': first localising pain rather than it being 'global, chaotic and incontrollable' (Ibid.: 112) creates a physical focus. Second, this reinstates the boundary between existence and non-existence of the self because it shows that the person inflicting the wound *can act* confirming 'agency through violence' (Ibid.). Third, doing this restores the boundary between self and other so that the self-harming subject can be defended from others' apparently arbitrary actions. Cutting at one's own hand shows how 'possession of [the cutter's body] is literally carved into her skin' (Ibid.: 116). The asylum seekers who sew their lips show how acts of self-harming take place within 'asymmetrical relations of power' (Pugliese, 2002: par.6) so that the act of lip sewing is one way to go about exercising a degree of power, autonomy and control. The deliberate infliction of pain on the body becomes a way to regain a degree of control in the situation where all power appears to reside outside the body of the one inflicting the pain.

One fundamental difference between those who cut themselves as the result of domestic abuse and the refugees who sew their lips concerns the negotiation between private and public spaces. The former rarely exhibit their wounds or behaviour in public while part of the aim for refugees is to draw attention to their situation because they feel ignored or forgotten. The self-harming refugees operate in a complex web of public and private space which goes beyond the individuals' state of mind. For those who inflict the pain and those who would interpret these acts it is vital that lip sewing 'reflects back to the nation the gestures of refusal and rejection that it violently deploys in the detention, imprisonment and expulsion of refugees and asylum seekers' (Pugliese, 2002: par.7). It is in the authority's interests to manage carefully any incidences of refugee self-mutilations because the lip-sewing refugee is not just a possible political flashpoint but, on a much more significant level, the refugee's mutilated body doubles as an emblem of the nation.

The guarantee of anamnesis which the 'mnemonically mark(ed) body produces in the national psyche' (Ibid.: par 7) means that the lip-sewing refugee stands as a symbol and visual reminder, in both the present (through the action of lip sewing) and the future (through the scars left by self-mutilation), of policies which cause such distress. There is, however, a fundamental problem in this act of remembering and this is the degree of control that the self-harming refugee has over what exactly is remembered. Speaking of the lip-sewing incident at Woomera, an Australian journalist implies a sense of infantilisation of the refugees involved and suggests two reasons why the lip sewers should not, in his opinion, be 'given in' to:

> the first, popular at fashionable dinner parties, is that the public is stupid, selfish, heartless, racist and scared of the other. The alternative, preferred by millions of parents who have raised toddlers to be civilised, is that we've learned that pandering to someone who is banging their head on a floor or holding their breath until they turn blue just reinforces bad behaviour. (Cox and Minahan, 2004: 3)

Pain causes the move from language to 'the sounds and cries a human makes before language is learned' (Scarry, 1987: 4), a movement to infancy. The journalist quoted above has connected the 'inability' of the lip-sewing refugees to speak, with the pre-linguistic phase of infancy, a connection which allows him to take a paternal role in relation to the nation's 'spoiled children'.

The self-harming refugees in the case of the two British examples make less use of the disruption inherent in heterotopic spaces because their acts are performed in private in their own homes. It is unclear at what point they 'emerge' from these private spaces into a public arena so that their acts do not command what Anderson and Menon (2009: 4) call the 'profound power to command attention' that usually accompanies the spectacle of violence in contemporary visual culture. Their dependency on media images to produce this emergence removes another layer of power because they are not in control of these images and the ways in which they are produced.

As I have shown, it can be in the interests of the state to maintain a silence on the issue of refugees who deliberately self-harm. However, broadcasting this act can prove another way to maintain control. Images of the wounded body of the refugee may just as well serve the interests of the state as the refugee's cause. In Butler's terms these subjects are speaking 'at the borders of discursive possibility' (Kilby, 2001: 126) and therefore risk becoming unspeakable. 'If the subject speaks impossibly, speaks in ways that cannot be regarded as speech or as the speech of a subject, then that speech is discounted and the viability of the subject called into question' (Butler, 1997: 136). The lip sewer's personal integrity can be called into question through images of their physical lack of wholeness which implies a psychological lack. It upsets the delicate pivot between spectacle and embodiment; non-refugee subjects may *see* the image but remain unsure how to *read* it. The lip sewers speak impossibly to the citizens who question their integrity (physical and otherwise), so that they may not be heard at all. Equally, they might also be 'speaking' to other would-be asylum seekers in such a way that their mutilated bodies become 'instrumentalised in terms of an exemplary model to ward off other prospective asylum seekers' (Pugliese, 2002: par.6).

Taking control

The feminine association with needles and thread has led to lip sewing being called a 'gendered, embodied and subversive craft' (Cox and Minahan, 2004: 5). This second association between lip sewing and sewing as a female craft links the paternalistic tendency to infantilise refugees with certain conceptions that also feminise. This is best considered through the historical example of Suffragette campaigner Lady Constance Lytton who understood the power of the humble woman's needle. She vowed to write the words 'Votes for

Women' on her body with a needle while in prison, intending to start with the V on her heart and ending with a full stop on her cheek. In the event, she was discovered after she had inscribed the first letter and forcibly prevented from completing the act. Notwithstanding the incompleteness of her act, she showed an acute awareness of the power of its reception by the public hoping that 'the last letter and full stop would come upon my cheek, and still be fresh and visible on the day of my release' (Howett, 1996: 35). Her act placed her in a position where her body became 'replete with shared political meanings' and a source of 'unity and pride' (Ibid.). As a Suffragette she was determined to optimize the potential of her imprisonment to further the cause of women's suffrage.

Resorting to an act of cutting the skin in an effort to respond to the violence of force feeding that was done on her body she also created an anamnesis of that damage to a wider audience. Using the literal marking of her body Lytton challenged any possible forgetting of the treatment of the Suffragettes in British prisons. Feldman (1994: 407) calls this lack of remembering 'cultural anaesthesia' which he defines as 'the banishment of disconcerting, discordant, and anarchic sensory presences and agents that undermine the normalising and often silent premises of everyday life'. Lady Lytton's inscription represents an attempt to overcome the cultural anaesthesia that is imposed on subjects through imprisonment. Her intentions were clear when she decided to commit the act in a place of enforced privacy in order to time the presentation of her inscription with her first appearance in public.

The sewing of the lips of asylum seekers takes place in a world where refugees are similarly silenced, often locked in detention centres in remote or inaccessible locations. The power of the act of sewing the lips lies in its counter-intuitive nature in a situation where refugees feel they 'have to do something big, noisy and violent like riots to send our voices out of detention' (Burnside, 2003: 92). However, Lady Lytton seems to have been able to manage her situation with much greater ease than the lip-sewing asylum seekers. She knew the date of her release and felt she could time her act to precision for maximum effect. This knowledge is not available to asylum seekers under indefinite detention, awaiting legal decisions which could lead to deportation. Lady Lytton did not have to contend with the multiplicity of media outlets that currently exist, nor with the corresponding levels of sophistication with which those media are managed. Contemporary coverage of news events and documentary, rather than providing anamnesis, actually perpetuates cultural anaesthesia. Feldman puts this succinctly:

> Generalities of bodies – dead, wounded, starving, diseased, and homeless – are pressed against television screens as mass articles. In their pervasive depersonalization, this anonymous corporeality functions as an allegory of elephantine, 'archaic' and violent histories of internal and external subalterns. (Feldman, 1994: 407)

There has been a similar tendency to visually represent refugees as a mass and this produces the 'anonymous corporeality and speechlessness' of 'generic refugees' (Malkki, 1996: 389). Comparing the depersonalised bodies of the wounded with our own 'progressively malleable bodies' (Feldman: 1994: 407), enables viewers to create a visual polarity between 'us' and the subjects we are viewing. The inability to control or manipulate the ways in which their acts are presented places the self-harming activist in a 'risky' position and, given the conservative tendencies of the media generally, it is unlikely that their representation will be allowed to produce sympathy or empathy. It is much more likely that, without adequate understanding of why they undertake their acts or any clear sense of what they wish to achieve, they risk reinforcing their abjection. The public audience is repelled rather than compelled by the extremity of the act, and an opportunity for understanding may be lost.

Considering space adds a civic dimension to the personal motivations of all of the activists considered because the act of taking speech necessitates taking space. The figure of the abject cosmopolitan illustrates how discourses about giving and taking lead to questions of rights, responsibilities and, ultimately, citizenship. In the demonstration refugee activists demand to be listened to in a public space and they appropriate that space with minimal negotiation or agreement. By sewing their lips, refugee activists commit an act which is intended to demonstrate how little power lies in their refugee's voice. The space within which the self-harming activist operates is less clear; locked away in indefinite detention or in an uncertain domestic space which the authorities have the right to enter at will.

Questions of choice and power are at the very heart of activist performance, and all activists display an urge to take control on both a personal and a political level, resisting the controls which place them in positions of powerlessness. Activists must regard themselves as commodities if their campaigns are to have *any* chance of success and their story must remain within the bounds of bureaucratic performance to create public credibility. In taking their campaign onto the streets they aim to get their message across to a wider audience but there is a danger that they remain behind the loud-hailer unable to speak a more complex story. The self-harming activists have to completely relinquish control in order to make their statement. In sewing up their lips (eyes and ears) they render themselves literally 'senseless' in an act of supreme will. However, they risk rendering the meaning of their acts 'senseless' in another way, leaving their audience unsure about their motivations and fragmented in their responses to these acts. Those who would speak on their behalf, as Joseph Pugliese (2002) and Mike Parr have done, have translated their acts to strong ethical effect. However, depending on this level of translation highlights the perilously thin line between rejection and efficacy which the self-harming activists must tread.

A number of refugees attempt to gain some sense of agency without recourse to desperate acts of self-harm in a way that increases their sense of control over their lives and their autonomy as individuals. Unlike the refugee protesters who are compelled to use megaphones to speak their stories in the public domain these refugees are using theatre, music and dance and it is to these performances that we turn in the final chapter.

4
'We with Them and Them with Us': Diverse Cultural Performances

> I'm live and let live, everyone's welcome, they should have a right to live their lives alongside us in Manchester, we with them and them with us'
> — English festival goer, Exodus Festival, Manchester, 2006

This final chapter will examine cultural expressions made by refugees themselves and is divided into three parts, in which I'll examine refugee arts festivals, refugee artists (particularly solo performers) and participatory theatre projects with refugees. Grouping diverse sets of practices in this way draws attention to questions of agency and control on the part of refugees. The examples show how the arts, especially performing arts, hold the potential to challenge preconceptions and validate refugee experience, some even pointing to a more hopeful and optimistic future for refugees and 'host' communities. Equally, they also demonstrate that the 'problem' of the refugee's voice is 'a deeply political problem, and one that cuts to the core of who counts as an authentic political subject' (Nyers, 2006: 124). However, bearing in mind the ethics around gift giving and hospitality discussed previously, these activities also show how 'giving voice' to refugees is *not just* a practical problem and *not only* a problem of rectifying unequal power relations. It is part of a deeply ethical practice and must be considered on this level as well.

I will show here some of the ways in which refugees and people seeking asylum use the arts and cultural expression to experiment with new identity positions and changed locations and how placing these expressions in a public arena has the potential to generate understanding and, more importantly, action. It is in this arena that refugees and citizens are most likely to meet and even interact. Some of these meetings are more thoroughly mediated than others but all of them raise questions of trust and, most importantly, the understanding that each group has of the other and the ways in which the ground of the meeting itself becomes questioned or at least productively unstable.

In contrast to the broad geographical sweep of the previous chapters the focus here is sometimes unashamedly local because this chapter discusses the small-scale and street-level, individual and community interactions. Concentrating on individual refugee artists and on community groups at grass roots level I will show where individual practice and participatory arts activities have played an important role in refugees' encounter with their new home. This chapter examines the phenomenon of refugee arts festivals, using the Exodus Refugee Festival in Manchester as an example (Figures 6 and 7), in order to analyse discourses of togetherness and their implications for questions of authenticity. The work of four refugee artists, solo performers in Britain and Australia, will be examined before looking at examples of participatory theatre projects in the UK.

Most groups that are set up to support and coordinate refugee arts activities reflect the twin ambitions of working with *both* refugee communities *and* individual refugee artists. Potential contradictions around this are compounded by a lack of clarity about the audience for refugee arts with one report identifying the 'need for arts projects to be clear about whether their work is addressing and serving refugees and asylum seekers or an external audience' (Gould, 2005: 11). This chapter inevitably plays out these oscillations between the individual refugee artist and refugees more generally, as well as examining who the audience for refugee arts is thought to be and who they actually are. I realise that including the refugee artists in this grouping may be seen to collude with their 'ghettoisation' in the marginal and excluded, but I take that risk in order to really examine the complex power dynamics that come into play when refugees try to speak for themselves in a creative way. On one level their inclusion here mirrors their struggle for recognition in the face of complex personal and professional negotiations around questions of identity but it also serves to show that the place from which refugees speak is often not their own place but one forced upon them.

Figure 6   Exodus Refugee Festival, July 2010. Manchester Town Hall Square
(Photograph taken by the author)

Figure 7 Testimony performing at Exodus Festival, Manchester, July 2010 (Photograph taken by the author)

Refugee festivals and cultural performance

One of the most notable innovations in arts and cultural work with refugees is the arts or music festival. These events have proved popular since UNHCR instituted Refugee Day in 2000 as an event to be held annually in June. Some countries have developed this into Refugee Week which is celebrated with a series of events designed to 'deliver positive educational messages that counter fear, ignorance and negative stereotypes of refugees, through arts, cultural and educational events that celebrate the contribution of refugees'.[1] Refugee Week has grown steadily from its inception, especially in the UK where 225 events were registered in 2002 (Blaker, 2003), and by 2006 the number had grown to over 450 events of varying scales, ranging from music festivals and art exhibitions to political debates, film screenings, conferences, school activities, sports and community events all attended by an estimated 250,000 people (Scott-Flynn, 2007: 6). One notable aspect of refugee week is the focus on refugee arts festivals like Celebrating Sanctuary in Birmingham and London and the Exodus Festival in Manchester which has been in existence since 2005.

Typically these refugee festivals involve groups of performers from countries that are represented by refugees in the host community performing mostly music and dance that is 'traditional' to their home location. Festivals are outdoor events which attract large audiences and often have stalls with food, clothing and other artefacts as well as information pertaining to refugees. Birmingham's event in 2007 was said to include 'performances from three Birmingham schools, musicians and dancers from Rwanda, Cameroon, Balkans, Iran, Congo, Angola, Iraq, the Middle East, Albania, Germany, Togo, the UK and more, with key speakers and [...] over 20 organisations displaying their work with asylum-seekers and refugees and involving themselves in discussion and activities with the public' (Scott-Flynn 2007: 9). It is possible to detect a certain degree of hyperbole in reports on refugee arts work which stress not only the numbers of refugees involved but also the ranges of locations from which refugees originate. The other frequent statistic is the number of 'local people' that these events are said to attract which allows organisers to make claims, both implicitly and explicitly, about integration and social cohesion, a concept that will be investigated below.

Festivals have been described as 'cultural performances *par excellence*' (Kirshenbaltt-Gimblett, 1998: 61) and refugee arts festivals fulfil many definitions of cultural performance. Cultural performance designates a huge range of activity which takes place outside the frame of the formal presentation of theatrical performance. Traced back to Milton Singer's work in the 1950s (Carlson, 1996; Guss, 2000; Kirshenblatt-Gimblett, 1998; MacAloon, 1984; Turner, 1988) cultural performance describes not only explicitly cultural events like plays and concerts but also the ways in which public and quotidian events can be read as performative in some way, 'occasions in which as a culture or society we reflect upon and define ourselves, dramatize our collective myths and history, present ourselves with alternatives, and eventually change in some ways while remaining the same in others' (MacAloon, 1984: 1). According to these accounts cultural performance can also be focused on a designated space where participants are conscious of communicating with those outside the 'group' and duration is a feature with events usually lasting much longer than traditional theatrical performances. Levels of training may differ for the participants in cultural performance, sometimes with no requirement for formal training, and the 'aesthetic elements of cultural performance are placed at the service of the cultural component of the activity which is designed to reinforce cultural values and to solidify social organisation or stimulate political action' (Ibid.: 26).

It is generally suggested that cultural performance is 'framed [and] set off from what might be considered normative' (Guss, 2000: 8). However, I am more interested in the ways that cultural perform-ance constitutes the normative rather than reading it as separated in this way. Turner (1988: 24) agrees that conclusions can be drawn about a society from observing the various ways in which culture is performed on the level of the everyday, but cautions against regard-ing cultural performances as 'simple reflectors or expressions of cul-ture'. The mode of 'reading' cultural performance should be reflexive rather than simply reflective, and the analogy should not be with the mirror but with the reflexive verb where subject and object are constructed within the same social, political or cultural context. Reflexivity has been defined as 'the capacity of human beings to distance themselves from their own subjective experiences' (MacAloon, 1984: 11) or 'the act of becoming an audience to oneself' (Kapferer quoted in Ibid.). Thinking reflexively about refu-gee festivals, for example, encourages an examination of audiences as much as the performers. It means that I will pay as much atten-tion to the promotion and official discourses of the event as obser-vations of the event itself. Cultural performances are noted for their reflexive qualities, enabling participants to 'understand, criticize and even change the worlds in which they live' (McAloon, 1984: 9) and refugee arts festivals are a good example of the ways in which reflexivity can work.

Derrida (2000: 3) notes that 'the foreigner is the one who puts me in question' which suggests that one way of looking at refugee festi-vals is to examine the role of the audience in the creation not only of 'refugee arts', but of refugeeness itself, by their very presence at a fes-tival of 'refugee arts'. A reflexive reading of cultural performance serves to challenge the audience's apparently stable identity encour-aging them to reflect, not only on their relationship with those on the platform, but with their own sense of identity in the position of the 'not-refugee' or citizen. Opening out the question of who the audience for refugee cultural performance is thought to be also points to assumptions about who is thought to be changed (or not) by the diasporic encounter involved in creating and viewing refugee arts.

Parkin et al.'s reading of cultural performance emphasises its inherently exilic qualities giving the example of Middle Eastern music which may be appreciated by an outsider, but which 'does not necessarily evoke in him [*sic*] the intensity of emotions experienced by, say, people from the region who are currently obliged to live as exiles outside it' (Parkin et al., 1996: xxii). The removal of cultural performance from its place of origin creates a multi-dimensional picture and shows how it is best to read refugee cultural performance through a diasporic lens, showing how not only the site of the performance and the performers themselves shift from home location to exilic location, but how the audience shifts and changes. It might be more productive to think in terms of multiple rather than single shifts. If it is accepted that in the home location there were always potentially two 'audiences', those directly participating and those participating through watching; cultural performance gains a third and fourth audience in its exilic location. The third is an audience of other exiles from different locations and the fourth an audience indigenous to the location. This natal audience is in turn doubled to produce the live and present audience and the unseen, not present or projected audience. It is in this 'doubling' of the audience that the operation of bureaucratic performance becomes pronounced because the second (implied) audience is that beyond the event who, arguably, remain to be convinced of that refugee performer's right to be there in the national space.

The Exodus Festival

The Exodus Festival[2] in Manchester, UK provides a case study for this discussion. Exodus as an organisation aims to 'impact on the cultural landscape of Greater Manchester through developing partnerships with Greater Manchester's creative and cultural sector, artists and groups amongst our refugee communities, and the wider Greater Manchester population'. Exodus sees itself as 'both producer and creator of cultural events and arts initiatives, including music, dance, theatre, spoken word, digital and visual arts, cross media collaborations [and] new writing'. It also claims to work 'in partnership to support community cohesion; to raise the voice of our refugee communities and to offer professional platforms for the breadth of their creative talents'. The choice of words in the phrase 'raise the voice in our refugee communities' is significant as it avoids the more common trope of 'giving voice' already discussed; raising a voice implies amplification of something already there and emphasises the potential of agency on the part of refugees.

By July 2006 Exodus claimed to have played to audiences in excess of 9000 and worked with 1378 participants. In its stated aims Exodus manages to sidestep the refugee artist/community divide that is the hallmark of many other companies, creating an emphasis on partnerships between artists and communities with the word 'refugee' mentioned only twice. Mindful of the power of branding, Exodus has created and promoted several events and initiatives which include Exodus Festival (2005–2010) for Refugee Week; Exodus Live, a series of band nights with refugee musicians; Exodus Shorts, a festival of short films by and about refugees 2005–2010; Exodus Stages in 2006 and 2010 with performances, writing workshops and staged pieces of new writing in several theatre venues throughout Greater Manchester. Cilla Baynes, Artistic Director of Community Arts North West who run the Exodus project discusses their approach to participatory work with refugee groups:

> This is a group of people [refugees and asylum seekers] that aren't getting access to cultural production, a voice and opportunities to express, enjoy, use the arts to create progression in their lives. And that might mean different things to different people in a community. For some people it might be about a sense of wellbeing, for some people it will be about professional development as an artist themselves, for many people it might be about communicating what is going on, for some people it's about making connections with other communities.[3]

Since its inception in 2003, Exodus Festival has provided a platform for the work of groups and artists from Afghanistan, Angola, Bosnia, Cameroon, China, Democratic Republic of Congo, India, Kurdistan, Liberia, Libya, Nigeria, Pakistan, Rwanda, Somalia, Sudan, Uganda and Zimbabwe. Since 2005 I have observed Exodus Festival in a variety of public spaces in Manchester including parks and other civic spaces as well as interviewing artists, audience members, stall holders and organisers for In Place of War in 2006 (Thompson et al., 2009: 95–99). The main elements include a large stage on which most of the acts perform, with a smaller secondary stage and/or workshop area. Food stalls run by refugee groups making and selling 'traditional' food play an important role in the event while several other stalls give out information considered relevant to refugees. A small number sell 'ethnic' clothing, jewellery and other artefacts and the whole event is emceed with a DJ playing music between the acts, creating a noisy, lively and upbeat atmosphere. The site is decorated with banners, flags and bunting, giving it a boundaried feel within the wider civic space and adding to the visual impact of the event.

Exodus Festival definitely lives up to the claim that in festivals all the senses 'olfactory, gustatory, auditory, tactile, kinaesthetic, visual' (Kirshenblatt-Gimblett, 1998: 58) are engaged. However, I want to look beyond the sights and smells of the Exodus Festival to examine the dramaturgy of the event because this shows the ways in which this event, and others like it, extend and deepen our understanding of the impact of refugees on the cultural and political map of the host nation. Refugee festivals are complex events made up of multiple elements with a potential myriad of readings of which I have selected only two: togetherness and authenticity. These vie for our attention at a refugee festival and identifying how they interact with each other will reveal a number of hidden assumptions behind refugee festivals generally.[4] Specifically, I will show how an emphasis on cohesion seen through the repeated discourses of togetherness can obscure the more complex ideas around authenticity and how authenticity in art forms, and in the shape of the festival itself, can operate as a code for the political authenticity of the participants.

Togetherness

There are many conflicting definitions of, and approaches to, community cohesion, a term that has been in common usage in the UK since the large-scale civil unrest in the Northern British towns of Oldham, Burnley and Bradford in 2001 and which took on a more urgent tone following the bombing of transport networks in London in July, 2005. Lack of community cohesion is thought to be generated by feelings of social and economic inequality and lack of social interaction between the different ethnic groups represented in many British towns and cities.[5] Existing tensions may be exacerbated by the presence of refugees and asylum seekers in areas of social and economic deprivation which are already racially diverse having been areas where Pakistani, Indian, Bangladeshi and African Caribbean families have settled during previous patterns of migration.

Diversity becomes a 'codeword' for racial difference and while some diversity is seen in a positive light 'the most "mixed" areas do not feature high on the scales of services or interest' (Kalra et al., 2005: 90). Looked at in this way a little diversity can go a long way and, while some is to be encouraged, too much diversity can be difficult to manage and may result in lack of social cohesion and, ultimately, decay or even social unrest. The increased 'diversity' that refugees bring with them, therefore, when they are forcibly dispersed to economically deprived towns and cities outside London, needs to be offset by activities that promote community cohesion, or so the official discourse goes.

The act of collective creativity is thought to be a way to promote personal development and wellbeing through increased communication, and to build confidence through developing and learning skills that participants are thought to lack. Specifically, in the case of refugees, increased social skills are said to generate the confidence necessary to promote integration with the 'host community' (Blaker, 2003: Gould, 2005; Harrow and Field, 2001; Hutton and Lukes, 2004). Collective creativity is also seen to provide a way of promoting positive images of asylum seekers whereby their right to 'be there' on a micro or local level stands in for the justification to 'be there' on the macro national level. Refugee festivals tend to promote discourses of togetherness, seen in official terms as community cohesion, and by framing refugee cultural performance within participatory arts, refugees are developing personal and social skills which will help them to feel more involved with the communities in which they are located. The increasing community cohesion implied in the festival or cultural event demonstrates how the use of public money for funding for the refugee arts events can be considered an investment in social cohesion, possibly even as insurance against social exclusion and the unrest that can follow. Participatory arts projects provide opportunities to develop skills, so this argument goes, increasing opportunities to build dialogue, create cohesion and, if not pave the way for social change, at least prevent social unrest. Artists and arts companies have been, sometimes reluctantly, drawn into this rather instrumental discourse (Belfiore, 2002) because of their reliance on funding from government sources, either directly or through some of the many 'quangos' (quasi-non-governmental organisations) set up by the British government to administer resources.

The need for a celebratory approach in order to promote cohesion has implications for the choice of the festival form itself. One alternative to the festival is the more challenging form of carnival which provides a place in which 'the nexus of debated (and debatable) space [in which] pluralism and difference emerge' (Gilbert and Tompkins, 1996: 85). There may have been very good reasons for rejecting carnival as a form with its roots in Christianity (or a reaction against it) and it is maybe not as culturally appropriate as the more inclusive festival form. However, the celebratory nature of the festival means that while pluralism and diversity are on view they remain highly managed by the spatial configurations and, in particular, the stage which creates a situation where refugee bodies are more presented than encountered. The staged presentation of refugee bodies at refugee festivals could be argued to diminish the potential for resistance especially when the refugee representations tend to the traditional 'authentic' performance forms. It may be that refugee bodies are not only made 'safe' for the audience but the discourse of safety, and the inclination to 'protect' refugees in these public settings, may prove counter-productive if refugees themselves remain distant and inaccessible to the audience.

This can be demonstrated most clearly by the group Afrocats, an accomplished dance group in Manchester made up of young British women of colour and young women from Rwanda and Burundi who are refugees. Afrocats are popular at the Exodus Festival for their lively and exuberant dances which are mostly derived from traditional African forms performed in 'authentic' costume. On stage at the festival the audience watches and enjoys their performance without any sense at all of who they are or why they come to be performing at a refugee arts festival. The fact that half the group is British further complicates this image. In 2005 when Afrocats decided to develop their performing skills beyond dance they created a theatre piece called *Nyubani Wapi?Where is Home?*[6]. The contrast between this play and their performances at the Exodus Festival could not have been clearer. In *Nyubani Wapi?Where is Home?* they discussed the complexities of their lives and the tensions that were created by the fact that the African girls potentially faced deportation back to their parent's countries on their eighteenth birthdays. As unaccompanied minors the British government had maintained a duty of care for the young women but, like all young asylum seekers on their eighteenth birthdays, they faced having to go into the immigration system where it was necessary to show that it would be dangerous for them to return to Rwanda or Burundi. The play ends with Kia's 18th birthday celebrations which slowly become more and more sombre as her friends begin to understand the implications of her coming of age in this situation:

> Kia: On the ninth of October, my birthday, I am expecting a letter from the Home Office which will tell me I have to go home.
> *Whole cast looks up to audience.*
> Kia: Where is my home?
> *Whole cast follows Imena off in a line to live music.* (Afrocats, 2005)

Neither the level of emotion captured in *Nyubani Wapi? Where is Home?* nor the political complexity of their situation can be evident in the Afrocat's performances at the Exodus Festival with their emphasis on celebration and togetherness. Looked at another way though, neither is there any opportunity to sympathise with the victimhood of these young women when they dance so exuberantly onstage at the festival.

An evaluation of the Exodus Festival undertaken in 2006 noted that the main impact of the event was thought to be that it brought people together (Thompson et al., 2009: 97). Bringing people together risks creating what Kirshenblatt-Gimblett calls a 'banality of difference' (Kirshenblatt-Gimblett, 1998: 77) where the emphasis on celebration de-politicises cultural events in such a way that refugee cultural expression becomes simply a 'rest-stop of smorgasbord culture' (Kalra et al., 2005: 93). Bringing people together implies an encounter between two groups who would not normally meet but who or what is being encountered at the Exodus Festival and by whom? Who does the audience think they are encountering when they attend a refugee cultural event and what do they think they are seeing? Diaspora space (Brah, 1996), as I have outlined in the Introduction, is the point at which boundaries between 'us' and 'them' are tested providing a reflexive physical space but, in order to create a meaningful encounter, it is necessary for both parties to have an accurate conception of each other. How much does the non-refugee's notion of a refugee actually change as a result of this encounter?

The celebratory nature of the festival and the distance between performers and audience obscures the fact that asylum seekers live in Manchester's 'diverse' areas because of their poor social and economic position and their forced reliance on benefits and lack of choice in housing. They are placed alongside those who are thought to suffer from social exclusion through poverty, lack of educational opportunities, inequalities in health and substandard housing. It may come as a surprise for some of the audience at the Exodus Festival that many refugees on the stage have had considerable wealth and status before they became refugees because people who manage to seek asylum in the West form a tiny number of people on a global level with most refugees staying close to their country of origin. It is often only those who can raise the considerable finances necessary who are enabled to travel further, meaning that refugees with the means to travel to the West are often professional people in their country of origin, journalists, politicians and business people with enough money and influence to leave.

This is frequently overlooked and there is often a tendency to perceive all refugees as exposed and helpless and therefore within the group of people vulnerable to social exclusion. Frustration with ideas like this is seen in the words of a speaker, who had been a high-level politician in the opposition party (MDC) in Zimbabwe (his reason for having to leave). His impatience with the British class system became apparent when he claimed 'the UK is not a just society – class divisions grow wider'. He continued:

> half of truth is a complete lie [...] the legal battle makes half of me permanently feel that here is not really where I should belong [...] I am not permitted to fully participate in the building of society [...] I am not using the skills I have [...] I am forced to go for jobs which are below my qualifications and experience [...]. Integration is not about getting British passport or having equal opportunities policies [...] there is a glass ceiling for jobs for black men from all different backgrounds (MARIM, 2007: 21).

Refugees, in general terms, are conceptualised as 'needy', 'poor' and 'disadvantaged' and, when they try to settle in Western countries, this conceptualisation transforms into ideas about 'social disadvantage' and 'social exclusion' in a system that is already complicated by questions of race and class.

Ideas about togetherness promulgated by festivals and similar events obscure difficult questions of trust, but without trust togetherness is impossible. Daniel and Knusden identify this fundamental challenge when they suggest that '[f]rom its inception the experience of being a refugee puts trust on trial. The refugee mistrusts and is mistrusted' (Daniel and Knusden, 1995: 1). The bonds of trust that maintain all social relationships have been broken in the case of refugees. Because of their experiences they find it hard to trust while non-refugees have been influenced by negative messages about refugees which teach them to be suspicious. Two local white security guards were on duty at the Exodus Festival 2006 lounging against a metal barrier and surveying the scene from the edge of the park. With their dark uniforms and shaved heads they looked a little threatening even though they seemed to be enjoying the sunshine and the fact that the event seemed not to need a strong security presence. When I asked them what the refugees' presence at the Festival might mean to them one said 'you can see they're not all parasites can't you? I mean, that's the term everybody uses'. I pushed a little further by asking what role music and dance might play in this, the following interaction took place:

> Security guard 1: I suppose it's more relaxed and you get all the different countries together.
> Security guard 2: They don't trust you and you don't trust them. You break that barrier and bring the trust back.
> Researcher: So, is an event like this useful in breaking that barrier?
> Security Guard 2: Hopefully yes. That's what it's based on isn't it? Lost trust on both sides.[7]

The security guards saw the festival as a way to rebuild trust, but trust is only possible when both parties have a clear view of each other and an honest perspective of their strengths and weaknesses. Festivals do have a role to play in this re-building of trust but they can become limited by the highly mediated representation of refugees and the need for celebration which obscures complex claims for authenticity. These claims are seen in the acts on stage and reflect out into wider claims for political authenticity but they start with the event itself.

Authenticity

Festivals are multifocus and multisensory events and studying them requires 'selective disattention or highly disciplined attention' (Kirshenblatt-Gimblett, 1998: 57). At the Exodus Festival, who or what remains 'disattended' and why? The large stage with its lighting rig and sound system, the food stalls and the temporary toilets create the look and feel of an outdoor rock festival while the publicity material and the performances themselves evoke a world music 'vibe'. At the same time, the neat rows of information stalls, many with craft activities, evoke a more traditional English cultural form from rural or village life; one audience member at the 2006 Festival said: 'in a way, the thing it reminds me most of, having grown up in the countryside, is a village fete. I think it's really English in some ways and I don't know if that's a bad thing either'.[8] The Exodus Festival appears to be a hybrid form with one foot in the world music festival and the other in a pastoral English idyll with other more contemporary elements like community multicultural festivals and political rallies further complicating the form of Exodus Festival.

At the same time, authenticity at the Exodus Festival is expressed in a wide range of terms including 'old/traditional, handmade, homemade, association with country of origin, local or grass roots, ethically sourced, live and multicultural' (Figure 8) (Thompson et al., 2009: 98). The focus here is on two related kinds of authenticity set within the multiply hybridised form of the festival itself: the authenticity of the art forms on display and their relationship to their diasporic location and, secondly, the question of the political authenticity of the participants. Exodus Festival is the ground on which, 'the diasporised meets [the] host in the scene of migration' (Kalra, et al., 2005). For some refugee artists and communities the festival represents an opportunity to 'maintain' the home culture for future generations, to assert an ethnic identity and to communicate that identity to a wider audience. The festival itself is a hybrid form but what other locations of hybridity exist at the refugee arts festival? A certain kind of hybridity is seen in those acts of the

Figure 8 A cake stall pictured with 'Eastern' carpets. Exodus Festival, Manchester, July, 2010 (Photograph taken by the author)

(mostly) younger refugee performers at the Exodus Festival, like the International Crew, who mix traditional dance forms with more 'Western' influenced music of rap and hip hop. But might this prove to be merely shorthand for, or caricature of, hybridity like the 'garden fete crossed with world music festival' image above? The idea of 'crossing' recalls the biological roots of hybridity which fail to take into account problematic notions of purity or authenticity on which an over-simplified picture of hybridity might rest. The true test of hybridity lies in the desire of 'culturally dominant groups' to assimilate. In being open to changing some of what Anthias calls their own 'cultural symbols and practices of he-gemony' they may make room for the new hybrid form (Kalra et al., 2005: 95). One-sided hybridity, which is ascribed to the marginal rather than the centre, can be tolerated only so long as it maintains that position on the margins making it important to look at where the site of hybridity is located and, if it is merely on the stage or on the festival site, there is a risk that only refugees are seen to be altered by the process of hybridity.

Questions of authenticity fail to acknowledge what Shohat and Stamm call 'power-laden and asymmetrical' relationships that under-lie hybrid forms (Shohat and Stamm quoted in Kalra et al., 2005: 83). The power of the economic giant that is the Western music industry dwarfs the small-scale and local traditional dance and music. Small-scale, community-oriented refugee music and performance are dou-bly disadvantaged by the fact that they are part of a culture which depends on transmission through the generations for survival. The dislocation posed by leaving the home in which this communication took place is magnified in the case of refugees by the often unplanned nature of their departure and the uncertainty of their destination. Not only that, but in the specific case of refugees, the forced nature of their relocation is often overlooked in discussions of hybridity where movement is implicitly conceptualised as being made through choice.

As I suggested in Chapter 1, it is vital to differentiate between planned travel and forced migration, not only because the circum-stances in which each takes place are so different, but because the ways in which each is managed differ at the point of destination. The refugee's outlook is very different to the traveller who travels for pleasure; going back to the tourist/refugee dichotomy discussed in

Chapter 2 a dramatic difference can be illustrated by the fact that, while the tourists' landscape is 'a beautiful spectacle to be consumed or admired', in the eyes of the refugee it may become 'a space that needs to be "penetrated", "traversed and "survived"' (Loshitzky, 2006: 752). This is an example of genre slippage, a situation 'when one man's [*sic*] life is another man's spectacle' (MacAloon quoted in Kirshenblatt-Gimblett: 1998: 47). Through genre slippage refugee festivals and events become a site where Western ways of knowing are reproduced and recycled (Rajaram, 2002: 251). At the refugee arts festival the audience/tourists watch/consume a 'beautiful spectacle' which, for refugees may represent nothing less than the survival of their arts and cultural forms and maybe even their social and personal survival.

This impulse is apparent in some of the artists at the Exodus Festival in 2006: the Chinese dancer who 'wants everybody outside China to understand what Chinese culture is all about'; the Kurdish dancer who said 'we are from Northern Iraq, so we don't have a country at the moment, so we are just like a community, and we came here to represent *how Kurdish we are*'.[9] Another member of the Kurdish group saw it as an opportunity as much for themselves as for the audience:

> there is only a few [Kurds] in Manchester. They come over here and they connect with each other, and they see each other and they singing and they hearing their music and we bring our food culture here as well and everything about showing people about our food, our culture, *our everything*.[10]

The festival provides a place to meet, to connect and to build solidarity at the same time as providing participants with the opportunity to display their cultures. This much seems obvious to an outside audience but perhaps the level of passion and commitment as well as the desire to represent themselves as embodiments or the very essence of that culture is less apparent to the observer.

Reading the festival on a political level shows how authenticity is challenged by bureaucratic performance which places the whole event in question. Through the logic of bureaucratic performance, all asylum seekers are under suspicion until they can prove their refugee status but, since asylum seekers cannot be distinguished from refugees through their appearance, all 'refugee' participants are placed under suspicion to some extent, bringing the discussion back to issues of visibility. Exodus Festival is literally visible to those who attend and to those who live nearby in the streets of Manchester but it is equally 'visible' as part of Manchester's cultural calendar. It has a relationship with the entire citizenry, paid for by public funds and embraced as an official cultural event which is publicised throughout the city. This takes it beyond any material consideration of its value to those who attend and participate, framing it as a performative event on a civic scale. The effect of this growing visibility on the event may lead to a loss of radical potential brought about by the organisers' need to maintain levels of safety for participants due to the increased attention paid to the event and increased participation by non-refugees. Attention from this non-refugee audience also excites anxieties about how the event might be 'read' by them compelling organisers to place themselves in the role of interpreters between refugees and non-refugees, curating a certain kind of refugee performance conditioned by the need for images of persecution and flight to protect the authenticity of the conventional refugee in the eyes of the British audience. The Festival can be a good way to guarantee that this image will be protected because, with its emphasis on music and dance, there is little opportunity for performers to go 'off message' in a public arena through direct communication with the audience. The implicit need for positive images of refugees merges with the need for stories about their 'contribution' means that refugee stories have to be managed so that refugees become 'framed' in the imaginations of the participants, running the risk that the more complex realities of refugee lives remain hidden.

This is exemplified by musician Jean Azip Blanchard, the main vocalist for Congolese band Britannia Rumba, who came to UK as a young refugee from Democratic Republic of Congo. At the Exodus Festival of 2005 he introduced Britannia Rumba from the stage, injecting the only overtly 'political' note of the whole day when he spoke about being proud of what refugees have to offer to British society. As one of the emcees in the 2006 Festival, Blanchard took the opportunity to talk about the need for refugees and asylum seekers to be confident by speaking up and showing their capabilities to 'British people'. By 2007 the message had changed and a slightly belligerent Blanchard, emceeing once again, said 'these are world class musicians, not just refugee musicians' and that 'we've got to get out of this ghetto that they've made for us'.[11] He urged the audience to 'get out there to our gigs, buy our CDs. Don't just come to free festivals like this. Get out to clubs in Manchester and show them what you've got'. Blanchard seemed to show his frustration with the limitations of the festival form and its lack of direct communication between performers and the audience. The need to manage the Exodus Festival so strongly comes partly from the urge to protect the participants but also from the need to protect or manage the various messages that emanate from such a public event especially when one of the stated aims is to create positive images of refugees. The next section describes the work of refugee solo performers who resist this framing by creating their own pieces of theatre thus managing their mode of representation and relationship to the audience to a much greater extent.

Refugee artists

There exist many romantic connections between refugeeness and exile, something that is often reflected in refugee advocacy literature: for example, '[a]rt is and always has been powerfully inspired by notions of flight and exile' (Refugee Action, 2007: 5). One of the difficulties with this position is that it can result in the work of refugee artists being predicated on pathos, where their work can only be authenticated through 'trauma, sadness, displacement and loss' (Rotas, 2004: 57). Artists like Rotas understandably become frustrated by the expectation that their work has to be, and will continue to be, refracted through the lens of expectations placed on refugee artists. At the same time, many refugee artists struggle with the implications of accepting or rejecting the label of 'refugee artist', worrying about the professional and personal impact of such a label on their sense of identity and professional standing. Rather than identifying themselves as 'refugee artists' many artists have tended to 'align themselves with the migrant "mainstream" for a variety of reasons' (Hutton and Lukes, 2004: 2). Rotas worked with another visual artist and refugee Margareta Kern, who fled the civil war in the former Yugoslavia, to curate *Leave to Remain* in London in 2003, an exhibition of eleven artists whose work was 'connected by a thread of enquiry into notions of belonging, home, identity and displacement' (Kern, 2007). Frustrated by negative representations of refugees and asylum seekers Kern hoped that the exhibition would provide visibility for her and fellow refugee artists. For Rotas, the exhibition offered an opportunity to 're-appropriate the term 'refugee' through an act of agency in which both refugee (artist) and non-refugee (viewer) enter into a dialogic relationship which effects a shift in the meaning of the word' (Rotas, 2004: 60). Kern later became disillusioned despite, or maybe because of, the success of *Leave to Remain* when she began to wonder what kind of visibility she was being called upon to produce as a 'refugee artist'. She began to ask questions about the conditions under which she was being asked to exhibit refugee art and who was benefiting (Kern, 2007) after noticing that she was being increasingly called upon to provide 'a voice' for refugee artists.

The refugee artists described below face many of the same dilemmas. They have felt compelled to create performances which reflect their own individual stories which are inevitably stories about their departure from their own countries and their seeking asylum in Western countries. When subjectivity is contested, which is arguably the case with refugee performers, 'autobiography, spoken or written, offers an affirmation of selfhood' (Caster, 2004: 111) but this is only part of the picture as these performers are doing more than reclaiming selfhood. In the act of taking speech they are taking space in the public arena, doing something that should be impossible and claiming a political voice. Their reclamation of selfhood needs to be witnessed by a public audience, ideally galvanizing that audience into action against the forces that caused the initial 'loss of selfhood', the fact of being a disbelieved asylum seeker. Questions of selfhood, witness and credibility inform the work of four refugee solo performers and I will consider their work with these questions in mind.

Refugee solo performers

Plays have been produced by at least four solo performers who are also refugees. *Come Good Rain* (2000) is described by its writer and performer George Seremba as an offering to the gods as 'a solemn promise, a collateral of sorts, in the form of this story, enacted and told' and as a 'thank you' to the people of Bweyogerere village for saving his life after he had been left for dead by government troops in the Namanve forest in Uganda in 1980 (Seremba, 2000: 9). It premiered at Toronto's Factory Theatre in 1992, then toured Ottawa, Montreal, and Los Angeles to critical acclaim. Seremba was nominated for Best Male Performer in the Dublin Fringe Festival 2004 and in the Best Actor category of The Irish Times Theatre Awards (2005). The play has subsequently been performed in British and Irish venues, including the Tricycle Theatre in London (1994), Galway Town Hall (2006) and Foyle Arts Centre, Derry (2007).

Sri Lankan refugee Redley Silva, wrote a one-man show called *Twisted Things* (Silva, 2003) which he performed in London in 2003 and 2004. During the play he describes how producing and acting a Sinhala version of Dario Fo's *Accidental Death of an Anarchist* (called *Saakki* in Sri Lanka) led to his arrest and accusations of criticising the police. Following a 'comradely warning' to desist, he was advised that he was on a 'hit-list' and left Sri Lanka in 1991.[12]

Nothing but Nothing: one refugee's story is a solo piece written and performed in Brisbane in 2005 by Towfiq Al-Qady, an artist and refugee from Iraq. Shahin Shafaei, an Iranian refugee and artist now living in Melbourne, wrote and performed *Refugitive* (2003) which he toured throughout Australia between 2003 and 2004 (Burvill, 2008; Hazou, 2008). In making *Refugitive* Shafaei refused to be cowed by bureaucratic performance and continued to tour the piece even though he was on a Temporary Protection Visa at the time and therefore at risk of being returned if he did not comply with its terms.

All performers use the same technique of the solo performance of multiple characters. Shafaei played several characters in his play including officials and other detainees as well as the main protagonist, The Man. This character is based on Shafaei himself as the publicity surrounding his piece stresses (Broun, 2003; Ho, 2003). Silva places himself in the narrative in the shape of The Narrator who uses direct audience address to tell the story of his persecution and flight from Sri Lanka, as well as playing policemen, solicitors and various army personnel. Seremba plays 30 characters, among them Idi Amin, as well as his own character named as George Banwika Seremba. *Nothing but Nothing* places the voice of the autobiographical refugee protagonist at the centre of the piece, and Al-Qady voices a variety of other characters including his mother, a soldier, his daughter and an immigration officer.

These polyvocal performances of multiple identities have clear links with the solo performance styles of Eric Bogosian, Danny Hoch and Anne Galjour, to name a few of the practitioners who have developed the form in recent years (Bonney, 2000). Using their own lives

as their material further links these refugee solo performers to practitioners like Tim Miller, Reno and John Leguizamo, for example,
who base their work on their own experiences, a form said to have its
roots in the early performance art scene in the United States, initially
collected under the title auto-performance.[13] Many, perhaps most,
experiments in solo auto-performance are grounded in the development of queer identities (Hughes and Roman, 1998). Following ideas
emanating from Hughes and Roman's collection of performance
pieces, it is possible to see many striking similarities between the
queer performer and the refugee solo performer which provides some
useful ideas about this small but significant body of work.

New identity formations

Queer identities have been described as 'dynamic and contingent'
and queer artists are involved in 'pioneering new identity forma-
tions' (Hughes and Roman, 1998: 5 and 6). Roman argues that all
queer people exist in a performative dimension, having to 'fashion
an identity around our gender and sexuality' (Ibid.: 6). Before 'coming out' they may have had to 'perform' as heterosexual and 'the
performative nature of queer lives involves a continuous negotiation
between our sense of private and public selves that does not always
amount to seeing these two areas as discrete' (Ibid.: 7). Asylum seekers face many similar challenges if they want to speak honestly about
themselves and their experiences because they cannot be distinguished by appearance or behaviour. The moment when they reveal
their political status becomes an experiment with a new identity formation, something that is clearly articulated in the words of Joy:

> And sometimes asylum seekers don't want people to know what
> they are or who they are. Like me for example, most of my neigh-
> bours are mostly white and they are very friendly, they don't
> really know who I am they just see me as somebody who lives in
> the street who laughs and plays with them sometimes. They don't
> really know who I am. And last week, sometimes I really do feel
> shy; I don't really want to talk about who I am or why I have come
> to this country, but last week I was kind of tempted to talk to one
> of the neighbours and I told him 'Oh the reason why I am here I
> actually am an asylum seeker?' I wanted to introduce him to my

campaign but I didn't know how to introduce it so I came off with [quiet voice] 'Oh I am an asylum seeker. I'm not sure if you know anything about asylum seekers and why they come here'?[14]

Joy's conscious decision to reveal her political status shows a complex layering of personal and political identities which is reflected in the solo performances of the refugee actors.

In one way these plays operate on a personal level for the individuals concerned but they cannot fail to resonate on a more public level too. Gannit Ankori suggests that for Palestinian refugee artists 'experiences of loss, displacement and exile are imagined [...] not only as traumatic separation [but as] the visceral and excruciatingly brutal rupture between the Self and one's very own body' (Ankori, 2003: 59). These auto-performances of refugeeness may grant the actors involved a level of agency and the benefits of acting as a therapeutic activity, perhaps serving to re-unite self and body to use Ankori's terms. In *Come Good Rain* Seremba describes how he went back to view the location of his shooting and to give thanks to his rescuers. Silva's play came directly out of work in London with a drama therapist with whom he had trained.[15] For Shafaei there seems to be two senses of exoneration: one is for himself, and he describes how the piece provided 'a lot of relief and release for me'.[16] The other is in relation to the refugees whom he left behind in detention. He claimed 'I could see my face in the mirror'[17] as a result of doing this performance, alleviating guilt perhaps, but also giving himself permission to live with a new identity and maybe even to heal a rupture which his forced migration may have produced.

This differentiates Shafaei's work from the work of theatre companies like Actors for Refugees which aim to give 'a face to the faceless and a voice to the voiceless'[18] because he operates more like the activists discussed in the previous chapter creating a sense of agency by taking his voice rather than waiting for it to be given to him. The way in which he did this provides a strong contrast with those refugees who are forced to sew their lips or go on hunger strike. The refugee solo performers have all used performance 'as a way to bring into being a self [...] a way to talk out, talk back, talk otherwise' (Heddon, 2008: 3) which stands in contrast with the individual refugee activists who render themselves unable to talk. Unlike them, the solo performers exercise a much stronger degree of control over their encounter with an audience placing less reliance on mediatised images to communicate their experience.

Shafaei, for example, did undertake a hunger strike at Curtin Detention Centre which was necessary to achieve a personal, short-term goal but his preferred mode of representation for this act is within a theatrical frame. His change of political status enabled him to shift his act from the private to the public sphere where he has not only the political status of refugee, but can meet an audience with the assurance of his professional status as an actor. His skills enable him to indefinitely re-present a hunger-striking refugee to a range of audiences, without compromising his physical capabilities. Shafaei's experiences allow him to carry a level of authority as a refugee and an actor but he was equally enthusiastic about meeting the audience informally after the performance. Particularly difficult and noisy exchanges with audiences in his after-show discussions were welcomed as a kind of victory because this demonstrated to him that he had had an impact.[19] In this way, the solo performer's speech is much less risky than the self-harming activists because it is much less prone to intervention and therefore to misunderstanding.

The work of these performers creates 'dynamic sites for the performance of identities constitutive of subjectivity' (Smith and Watson, 2001: 143) but their real significance lies beyond the private sphere extending into the public arena where their performances become 'sites for the staging of transgressive subjectivities' (Harte, 2006: 228). All these solo artists draw attention to the body and always, to differing degrees, to the traumatized body. Seremba describes his shooting in the play:

> George: The first bullet hit the right leg. I was down on my knees, actually squatted. Before I knew the left arm was grazed. (Another shot is heard.) The body was *now* contorted as another got a bit of skin just above the forehead. But this time, the body moved back and forth, never still and unwilling to give them a clean shot at the chest or stomach. (Seremba, 2000: 57)

At the moment of extreme pain he becomes detached from his body, describing it in the third person: 'the body moved back and forth'. From a similar position of detachment, Silva tells the audience about his beatings by the police in Sri Lanka, but it is not until the last scene in his refuge in London that there is any focus on the physical effect of this treatment and his escape. This scene is set in a toilet as he describes his first days in Britain and the desperate loneliness and isolation that he faced, despite being provided for by Amnesty International (who sponsored his flight from Sri Lanka). Taken to hospital by his solicitor because he was 'in a pretty bad state [...] in severe depression and chronic constipation' he concludes the play on an ambiguous note: 'they gave me anti-depressants and laxatives. After a few days I was able to go to the toilet!' (Silva, 2003). Shafaei's depiction of a hunger strike begins with the character of The Man doubled up in pain as he is thrown back into his cell. He has to negotiate with his stomach throughout the play, cajoling it into giving him a little more time:

> The Man: I know that I am at the end of the way...please cooperate with me for the last part dear stomach. I should speak my last words, maybe to the wind, to carry them to first brave pen to write, to write the truths... please, please...(Shafaei, 2003)

In Al-Qady's piece he is marooned in a small boat off the coast of Australia describing his suffering and that of the passengers:

> Please give water...water
> What happened?
> Nothing to drink.
> Water is finished.
> No water!
> Please sky, water! (Al-Qady, 2006)

The mutilation of Seremba's body, the constipation of Silva's, and the starvation of Shafaei's and Al-Qady's, suggests connections with Kristeva's ideas about the abject body: the body as the site of decay, 'the cadaver at the border of the condition of living' (Kristeva, 1982: 3). We are faced in these plays with strong images of blood, vomit and shit, fluids that leave the body, reminding us of 'the in-between, the ambiguous, the composite' (Ibid.: 4) something to which, according to Kristeva, we are attracted and repelled at the same time. Yet, despite the gloomy connections with abjection, Shafaei's work is called a 'Message of Hope'. Although these motifs might encourage a reading of these works as stagings of abjection, these particular 'abject bodies' are the bodies of refugees located within a specific time and at a particular historical and political moment making it vital to look beyond the psychoanalytic reading of Kristeva to one which seeks to locate these bodies in an historicised and politicised location. The abject body is a 'real' body which has to be encountered by the audience and the self-conscious display of these bodies within the frame of theatrical performance for an audience particularises ideas about abjection. The solo performers are not *refugees manqués*, but 'real' refugees who have chosen to display their damaged bodies in public to an audience, causing that audience to question what might be so important as to drive them to that action.

For the refugee performers in their personal journey of healing, placing a narrative structure on their experience may have created 'a stay against confusion' (Kearney, 2002: 4) but the performed autobiographical story in their hands moves beyond the level of personal therapy because it requires an audience for completion. These pieces operate on a public or political level to compel reflections on identity on the part of the spectator, to make a narrative event out of the narrated event. To 'speak one's past is always an invitation to others to think and possibly speak of their own' suggests Rosen (1998: 17). The autobiographical impulse can only be fully realised by the dialogic act of speaking and listening because the audience is as much part of the process as actors. Hughes (1998: 4) suggests that, for the audience, part of the attraction of attending solo performance lies in 'knowing that there is a good chance that the performer is also the writer and the stories we will hear really happened'. One journalist, reporting on Shafaei's performance, begins 'Have you ever met a refugee, and heard his or her story yourself?' (Broun, 2003). The importance of the encounter with 'the genuine article' is reflected in the reception to Shafaei's work in Australia in particular where it has been government policy to deliberately obscure the humanity of refugee subjects.

The value of the work of refugee autoperformers lies in creating a level of political exposure on the audience's part because they cannot hide behind the idea that they are seeing a fiction. In being compelled to come face to face with the teller of the tale, they simultaneously have to face their own sense of responsibility as a citizen. Yet the refugee actors, despite their terrible experiences, are privileged because they have the background and training necessary to present themselves within a theatrical frame. The final part of this chapter examines what happens when refugees with little or no training or experience of performance create and perform plays based on their stories.

Participatory theatre

Participatory theatre places the creative agency of the participant at its centre and a number of participatory drama and theatre projects have been carried out with refugee groups in a range of locations (Cohen-Cruz, 2006; Kurashi, 2004; Salverson, 2006 and 1999; Schinina, 2002; Thompson et al., 2009; Wehle, 2004). Within the academy these often fall inside the category of applied or social theatre although professionally they would more often be categorised as community or participatory theatre (the preferred term here). Typically projects involve a group of refugees, often with little or no experience of theatre or performing arts in general, working with artists to create and perform a piece based on their own stories and experiences. Participatory theatre is thought to fulfil many of the functions of confidence building, encouraging social skills and challenging negative images described in relation to refugee arts festivals. In addition it provides a safe space in which to explore and experiment with identity creation and a place in which participants can begin to understand and order their experiences.

The UK in particular has seen a huge growth in arts and cultural activities among community groups made up of refugees and asylum seekers since the early 1990s (Alibhai-Brown, 2002; Barnes, 2009; Blaker, 2003; Harrow and Field, 2001; Kidd et al., 2008). In 2005 Creative Exchange[20], identified 76 projects in Britain with a high concentration of projects in London (Gould, 2005). In Place of War (2004–2007) identified a similar picture with a growth of activity in other areas, particularly in Manchester with the establishment of the Exodus Refugee Arts project already discussed. By 2008 the authors of *Arts and Refugees in the UK: history, impact and future* were able to show that over 200 arts projects existed in the UK, most in Britain's urban centres, London, Manchester, Birmingham and Glasgow (Kidd et al., 2008). Arts Council England (the body charged with distributing public funding for the arts in England) has no specific policy towards funding refugee artists or refugee communities. Broadly speaking, many refugee artists should benefit from the positive polities towards international artists and or what ACE calls Black and Minority Ethnic (BME) artists. Refugee communities could potentially benefit from funds as they are seen, accurately or otherwise, as economically and socially disadvantaged thus qualifying for support for arts and cultural activities under the banner of 'social inclusion'.

The background of bureaucratic performance against which refugees are invited to retell their stories in a theatrical setting is often not explicitly addressed in these pieces but I would argue that the impact of bureaucratic performance can be seen in the ways 'authentic' refugee stories are sometimes crafted and manipulated in order to 'give voice' or allow refugees to tell 'their story'. As we have seen, refugees need a convincing narrative based on individual persecution to make their asylum seeking speech act successful and even those with the most believable stories, backed by sound evidence, struggle to translate their personal stories into terms of political persecution (Schuman and Bohmer, 2004). I want to focus on the extent to which the exigencies of refugee stories told in the juridical arena, particularly the need for trauma, affect those told in participatory theatre.

Trauma and participation

The ubiquity of the word 'trauma' to describe a range of generalised conditions has become problematic and leads to suggestions that it has gone beyond the medical condition and moved into the cultural arena (Bracken, 2001: 736). Of course some refugees will receive diagnoses of PTSD, a formal diagnosis of trauma, and many more will receive some form of medication for depression and other mental health problems. Some refugees who may have suffered trauma have benefited from sensitive approaches to sharing their stories with experienced facilitators outside the psychiatric realm (Cohen-Cruz, 2006: 106). However, assumptions of trauma in relation to refugees underplay differences in culture and world view, ignoring ethical issues by leaving questions about the responsibility for trauma with the individual rather than on the context that created the trauma, and potentially undermine refugees' own processes and techniques for coping with rapid change (Bracken, 2001; Bracken et al, 1997; Summerfield, 2002). At the same time storytelling, the technique by which traumatic narratives are usually uncovered, has been reified to the point where it is sometimes forgotten that it is not a neutral act but is 'inter-twined with multiple acts of narrative creation' (Thompson, 2005: 216). In his story one Bosnian refugee rejected assumptions of trauma. 'We are not mad [crazy], we are betrayed and have been through hor-rible experiences and we are coping with it' (McAfee, 1998: 38). Despite assumptions of trauma, and even when there is evidence of trauma, it is vital to remember that refugees' stories are of survival. It may be tempting to dwell on representations of trauma in some refugee per-formance because the alternative is to portray refugees as 'mad' in the sense of angry, as active agents of change, to an audience who are bet-ter prepared to accept an image of depressed passivity.

Children of War was directed by Ping Chong in 2002 as part of *Undesirable Elements*, a series of oral history performance events. Created and performed by young refugees from Somalia, Sierra Leone, El Salvador, Afghanistan and Kurdistan, all of the participants were said to have experienced the traumas associated with war and conflict before their arrival in the United States (Kurashi, 2004). *Children of War* was performed in prestigious locations in the United States starting in 2002 in George Mason's University Theater Space, touring to the Headquarters of the World Bank in Washington DC, the Ford Foundation and the Headquarters of the United Nation's High Commission for Refugees both in New York. The setting for the play is described as stark, with a semi-circle of chairs arranged in front of a backdrop showing a map of the world. Kurashi (2004) and Wehle (2004) describe how the performers read from their scripts, re-telling their stories in the setting of a rehearsed reading, some-times reading each other's stories, chanting certain phrases and clap-ping in unison to introduce new stories, giving the piece a ritualistic effect.

A therapist from the Center for Multicultural Human Services (CMHS), who was herself a refugee and survivor of torture, worked with the group and the piece was said to serve a double function of raising awareness among the audience while providing a therapeutic function for those involved. The final stories performed were 'ghost-written [by Chong] autobiographies, woven together, then read by their real-life subjects' (McGray, 2003) and it was performed by young people between 13 and 18 years old who had told their stories to Chong at the beginning of the project. CMHS interviewed 80 young people and selected those who were thought to be '*traumatized enough* to serve the project's educational mission and reap some therapeutic benefit, yet psychologically sturdy enough to confess to horrifying personal histories in front of hundreds of strangers' (McGray, 2003, emphasis added). Thus, participation in the project was not offered either to those who may *not* have been labelled as traumatised or who were considered to be *too* traumatised. Those who were 'rejected' at this stage were offered some therapeutic counselling, and Chong subsequently chose five young people from within this group after individual interviews which lasted for two hours each. This level of selection is troubling, especially when the emphasis on the final theatrical product may lead to the young people being selected on an artistic basis as much as one predicated on the welfare of the participants. More significantly, by searching for young refugee participants in a setting where 'trauma' is a necessary attribute, the enterprise risks pathologising all refugee experience in a potentially harmful way.

Cardboard Citizens' *Pericles* project, already discussed in Chapter Two, provides another model. While maintaining its status as a product within the apparatus of professional theatre, it was also underpinned by a participatory theatre model which stressed the active participation of a large number of refugee people. Initially a small company of five actors, three of whom were refugees, performed a scaled-down version of *Pericles*, (which became known as *mini-Pericles*), to an estimated 400 people at fourteen refugee centres in London. Participatory dance workshops with refugees ran alongside this with the aim of recruiting refugee participants to take part in the final production. Thirteen people were recruited during four dance outreach workshops which were attended by more than 60 people (Jermyn, 2003: 4). These dancers created The Wedding Dance with professional choreographer Liam Steel which was performed during the full production as part of the Pericles and Thalsa wedding scene from the play; in addition the dancers took on many minor roles throughout the production.

The participatory element of the production was key to the project's success with Jackson trying to engineer a genuine exchange 'of expertise, experience, and dare I say it, ethos' (Jermyn, 2003: 11). Although Jackson's project seems to be located in a more 'ethical space' than *Children of War* it may not have provided the same opportunities as Chong's project for the exploration of personal experience or a way to develop a stronger sense of self through negotiations around what to tell and what to keep silent. Both projects demonstrate an interesting interaction between the professional theatrical model and the more open and inclusive form of participatory theatre as well as approaching the subject of trauma in very different ways.

Saying and not saying

The final part of this chapter examines *A Letter from Home*, a project which discovered that creating and performing narratives in participatory refugee theatre projects is as much about what is not said, or what is kept, as it is about what is made public (Thompson et al., 2009: 113). *A Letter from Home* was directed by Janine Waters and incorporated narrative, testimony, dance and live music with a mixed group of about 20 adults and young people, refugees and asylum seekers from a range of African countries. Some members of the group were part of Britannia Rumba (including Jean Azip Blanchard mentioned above) and some had experience of dancing with Afrocats (also already mentioned). The rest of the group had no training or experience of public performance.

What follows is a critical account of three scenes from this piece which are included to show some of the possibilities and challenges of theatrical strategies for staging violence and in being aware of the ethical responsibilities in creating opportunities for refugees to represent themselves within a theatrical frame. Wade shows how a consideration of the staging of violence beyond the practical exigencies of 'blocking and stage images' leads to an exploration of the ethical relations materialised by theatre production and 'whether their stagings demonstrate impulses of ownership or domination' (Wade, 2009: 16). The scenes show how recognising sensitivities around showing and reporting extremely violent acts opens up discussions about responsibilities to participants of these projects at all levels.

In one scene a young refugee actor gave a convincing performance of anguish, watched by fifteen or so fellow actors and musicians and an audience of about one hundred people. Playing the character of Wana the actor fell to the floor, visibly distressed, crying and pulling at her clothes, telling the immigration court in the UK 'the one thing I don't want to say', the story of the brutal killing of her boyfriend and her rape by 'rebel soldiers' (Figure 9).

Figure 9   The character of Wana tells her story to the immigration judge in *A Letter from Home*, John Thaw Studio, University of Manchester, June 2006 (Photograph reproduced with permission of In Place of War)

In the audience we knew that, within the fictional frame, the original story of violence took place in an unnamed African state, just as we knew that this subsequent re-telling of the story of violation was taking place in a 'British asylum courtroom'. Outside the theatrical frame we also knew that similar stories were played out in non-fictional British courts less than a mile from the theatre in which we were sitting, as asylum seekers made their case to be allowed to remain in the UK. As has already been discussed asylum seekers whose stories have *not* persuaded the authorities of their authenticity have been unable to perform to the required standard and stand accused of being unconvincing in the bureaucratic performance of those stories. In re-staging stories of refuge within a fictional frame that is peopled by refugees who are directly affected, participatory theatre practitioners tread a precarious line between producing validation on the one hand, and victimhood on the other. Anecdotal evidence abounds about the ways in which asylum seekers are 'coached' by their legal advisors, in often contradictory ways, in the *performance* of their 'victim's narrative' for the courts: they should cry, they should not cry, they should remain calm, they should show how the situation is affecting their mental health. Participatory theatre practice is commonly accepted as a process based on encouraging agency in those who participate in it as well as in those who watch. Yet, as Wana literally throws herself at the feet of the judge asking repeatedly, 'Why do you not believe me?' she is positioned as a supplicant, simultaneously at the mercy of a silent audience and, beyond the theatre, of those who maintain the power to decide whether to grant asylum or not. How are theatre practitioners to honour the experiences of the participants in projects and to challenge prejudice against those participants without resorting to demonstrations of victimhood?

Paying attention to two other scenes from *A Letter from Home* it is possible to read the play as challenging the image of asylum seeker as victim, both theatrically and politically, and to re-read the scene above on a more political level. The first scene to be considered took place in the same courtroom where the judge, played by a statuesque African man, listened again to Wana's story then stood to deliver his judgement. 'Surely you can't mean to tell me', he began in a calmly reasonable way before advancing towards the audience and shouting angrily, 'that because there's trouble in Africa we should let them *all* come in!' 'Yes!' shouted another actor. Having created this moment of confrontation and surprise he commanded, 'Somebody hand me my guitar!' at which point the band sprang into action and African rumba music filled the theatre. The scene then moved away from dialogue and transformed into a rowdy adversarial dance between Wana, her solicitor and the two immigration officials. Wana leapt from her chair, gyrating towards the immigration officials and confronting them with a show of provocative, energetic and playful dance. One official then stood up throwing her file on the chair behind her and, making a hand gesture which appeared to set up a challenge to Wana's dance, enthusiastically 'danced' the challenge back to her. Following a second call-and-response dance sequence between Wana's solicitor and the second immigration official, the whole company took to the stage as the reverential tones of the courtroom were replaced by the chaos of the dance hall. Theatrically this had the obvious effect of moving the character of Wana from a position of supplication, recreating her character as a young woman with some sense of agency. It also emphasised the element of performance in the giving of testimony, as though the spoken testimony was reiterated in dance and music which might create an awareness of the extent to which the state of becoming a refugee is dependent upon performance and performance conventions.

The second factor that might mitigate accusations of the perpetuation of victimhood is seen in the self-reflexive framework within which *A Letter from Home* was produced. This was perhaps best exemplified by the Brechtian device whereby a message was flashed onto the back wall of the stage, 'Please take out your mobile phones and switch them on'. A number of slides followed, giving information about the Democratic Republic of Congo focusing on the recent war there and the four million dead as well as the on-going conflict. Then our attention was drawn to links between the enormous mineral wealth of DRC, especially the element coltan an essential component in mobile phones and computers, and the continued unrest. Thousands of people have been killed and displaced, we were told, so that international companies can gain mining rights in mineral-rich areas of Eastern Congo. Finally we were informed that The University of Manchester, in whose building we were sitting, had invested considerable sums of money in companies involved in human rights abuses and that British arms are known to have been used in the conflict in DRC. The slide show ended by suggesting that the university was currently considering withdrawing investment in arms manufacture as the result of a student-led campaign and asking us to switch our mobile phones off again. This was probably the least theatrical scene in the whole play, but the most dramatic. Interviews with participants after the project suggested that they felt that the slide show was an important part of the performance and one stated, 'some people have never seen the Congolese map, so for them to see it's big and to learn about the resources the country has and stuff, it was good, it would have been different without it'.

If this intervention had not taken place the play would have maintained its triangular melodramatic structure, the vertices of which Schinina calls the Villain (perpetrator), the Good Guy (victim) and the Saviour (Schinina, 2002: 102). Schinina discusses this triad in relation to his theatre work in Kosovo where he showed how much the complexities of that war undermined the triangular relationship of bad guy, victim and saviour that the outside agencies kept trying to impose. He sees his theatre work as a way to challenge these oversimplistic conceptualisations, a way 'to break the triangle and to build the circle' (Schinina, 2002: 105). The slide show in *A Letter from Home* had the effect of breaking the triangle, making the roles of all the parties involved much more complex, especially those of the state players involved. Western economies clearly stand to gain from the mineral wealth of places like Congo but are they the villains if they pay fairly for those resources? African governments should be rich given the mineral wealth of that continent but are they the villains for not passing that wealth on to their people or the victims of Western bullying and exploitation, unable to get beyond their histories of colonialism? The 'victims' seemed to be standing on stage in front of us and yet the danced courtroom challenge momentarily elevated the Wana from her victim status.

These metatheatrical strategies where the relationship between actor and character slips in and out of focus, as it did when we watched the young woman dance, create a sense of uncertainty. Are we in the audience watching Wana at that moment, or a vulnerable refugee, or a young African woman with an incredible talent for dance? Similarly, when we are taken by surprise and pulled away from the comfort not only of our theatre seats but of our assumption of the benign intents of our institutions, we might begin to see our role in a different light. And it is impossible to pass all responsibility on to our institutions because we enjoy the benefits which have emerged from the industry that was built on the back of African colonialism. We become implicated, no longer able to assume a position of objective superiority and the villain, victim, hero triad is undermined. Self-reflexivity is especially important in creating work with refugee groups and comes about when practitioners acknowledge the extent to which they are embedded in what Hall calls, 'dirty truth – truth implicated in the hard game of power' (Hall, 1996:314). This knowledge undermines any attempt to create a simple 'heroic' role in relation to the asylum seeker's supposed victimhood, potentially destabilising or, at least partially, levelling the ground on which participants and facilitators meet.

As long as people are subjects, says McLane (1996: 107) 'we will say our lives in order to have or live our lives'. This chapter shows how many refugee and non-refugee artists have tried and continue to try to create an environment where refugees themselves can 'say their lives'. Nervousness about the negative stereotyping of refugees and the need to create a positive image sometimes leads to an overprotective approach perhaps based on a fear that audiences will not like what they hear unless the message is adequately managed. This can happen at large-scale events like festivals where the performative aspect of the event speaks on a civic or even national level and organisers feel the need to mediate or curate refugee stories and performances in order to maximise the impact of these potentially very valuable opportunities.

Individual refugee performers who are responsible only for themselves can take more risks in the public arena when they expose themselves *as* refugees and as people who have suffered or been tortured. Using their training and experience as artists they are in a position to create potentially powerful pieces of performance that have the added impact of allowing audiences to meet the authentic subject of the drama and, in some cases, enter into discussion with them.

The smaller more intimate studio performances, exemplified by *A Letter from Home* and *Nyubani Wapi?Where is Home?*, lie somewhere between these two bodies of work. The participatory practices involved in these pieces aim to give space and time to refugees to articulate their own sense of themselves and their experiences. An element of 'protection' is necessary for participants but not on the same scale as those performing at the more open public festivals. These projects can also discuss much more complex material where the apparently easy 'togetherness' of 'us' and 'them' alluded to in the opening quotation can be critiqued and problematised to show how 'we' can only exist in the conditions of possibility provided by 'them'. 'They' are created by the needs of the West and in order to protect 'our' standards of life, a challenging global image. The final chapter examines the deixis of 'us' and 'them' in order to suggest a possible way forward, not in the realm of geopolitics, but in the small scale, the local and the hospitable.

Conclusion: Face to Face or Shoulder to Shoulder?

> You surprise me by coming to me. Even if I invented you,
> your coming disturbs my world. Indeed, your entering into
> my dwelling place interrupts the coherence of my economy;
> you disarrange my order in which all things familiar to me
> have their proper place, function and time. Your emergence
> makes holes in the wall of my house (Peperzak, 1997: 66).

Since the early 1990s governments, and many citizens, have become increasingly alarmed by the number of refugees from the poorer nations of the world and by the changing face of refugees which has challenged the traditional image of 'the refugee' as a European subject who is fleeing religious or political persecution. State suspicions that the right to protection historically afforded to refugees was being abused by economic migrants led many Western governments to exercise hostile and increasingly exclusionary legislation to attempt to maintain their borders and to minimise disruption on political, social and economic levels. This situation has been exacerbated by a geopolitical condition in which concerns about exploitation have become enmeshed with fears of terrorism as part of a complex picture which challenges the integrity of what has been called the 'holy trinity of nation, territory and citizenship' (Stoianova, 2007: 22). None of this has taken place in a calm or measured way and rapid expansion in the scope and severity of government responses to the situation has created a sense of crisis which is in the interests of these governments to instigate and perpetuate, if only because they can then be seen to manage it.

One of the main ways in which Western governments were seen to be 'handling the refugee crisis' was to distinguish between 'real refugees', those who fitted the historical and political picture set out in international law of the 1951 Refugee Convention, from those who were thought to be abusing the system. In most Western states migrants who claim to be refugees are classed as 'asylum seekers' until such time as they can prove their legitimate right to the title of 'refugee' which is achieved through the credible performance of a story of individual persecution sufficient to convince various legal actors in the country of refuge.

The politics of asylum in this unique historic moment have combined with a newly vigorous political theatre to create a strand of work that questions and expands both the boundaries of theatrical form and the ways in which theatre seeks to influence political and social debate. There have been many experiments with verbatim theatre, for example, pushing that form in new directions which sometimes interact with documentary theatre in the staging of different kinds of documents, and with filmed and other actuality, as well as with speech. These experiments can be seen in the work of Sidetrack Performance Group's *Citizen X* with its staging of extracts from letters sent by refugees in Australia's detention centres spoken as the actors perform quotidian tasks from everyday domestic life. It can also be seen with Banner Theatre's *They get free mobiles...don't they?* when refugees and activists were filmed about their experiences and extracts inserted into a cabaret-style agit prop format. In *CMI (A Certain Maritime Incident)* by version 1.0 the emphasis placed on the words of politicians from extracts of parliamentary speech showed how questions of ethics and responsibility can be obscured by military and political language and rhetoric.

In these examples verbatim extracts are presented with little attempt to disguise them but at other times they are subsumed into a dramatic narrative as in *Le Dernier Caravansérail* by Théâtre du Soleil and *Crocodile Seeking Refuge* by Sonja Linden, for example. However, it is not enough to talk simply of formal developments in theatrical and other art forms, although these are considerable. Innovation and experimentation in refugee theatre has been introduced in the main to expedite and enhance the engagement of this theatre with its audience. The need for strong and immediate impact coupled with the perceived necessity to educate and inform, as well as to entertain, means that questions of audience are uppermost in the minds of theatre makers who create work concerning refugees: who is the audience thought to be, what kind of information people might need or be prepared to accept, what kind of theatre will have the greatest impact?

Although some of the refugee theatre practices discussed have been dealt with separately in other places I have been particularly interested to gather these together to investigate the ways in which they 'speak' to each other. I have been concerned to examine theatrical performances by refugees themselves and what happens when they are drawn explicitly into dialogue with other theatre forms that concern refugees. Those who might be classed as 'refugee artists' (despite the complexities that such terminology raises) can be seen as somewhere between these two worlds. Professional performers and directors in their previous lives, they are often forced to re-negotiate their artistic location in their new home through the channels of social and community theatre. Artists and performers like Silva, Shafaei, Al Qady and Seremba have used their training and experience to create work in their new homes that directly references their experience as refugees. Others, like Blanchard, have used occasions like Refugee Week and programmes like Exodus to maintain existing skills and to showcase their talents, partly in an effort to gain better understanding for refugees and asylum seekers, and partly to seek their own professional development. Most refugees are not artists but many have nevertheless responded to calls to share their stories and experiences in participatory drama workshops and to create performances based on discussions and creative discoveries made together in the rehearsal room. Projects like *A Letter from Home* and *Nyubani Wapi?Where is Home?* are two named examples but there are many other small- scale grass roots projects initiated in places to which refugee have fled.

All of these works, as well as the many others previously discussed, provoke questions about theatrical representation and the most effective and responsible way to present refugees and stories of suffering. The process of performing biographical narratives, specifically in the case of refugees, is full of creative and ethical challenges. The difficult nature of many of these stories has often led practitioners to reflect on how to avoid what Salverson calls 'an aesthetics of injury' (Salverson, 1999: 37) which emphasises the victimhood of the refugee subject by maintaining the dramatic logic of the tripartite structure of good guy (victim), villain and hero, also identified in work with refugees by Schinina (2002) and Edmondson (2005). The effect of bureaucratic performance on these biographical stories also has an impact not only on how stories are being shown but on the ways in which theatre makers become responsible for decisions about which narratives to stage and which to reject. The implicit need for narratives of trauma means that theatre makers may feel that other more complex narratives must be rejected because they do not fulfil the needs of bureaucratic performance.

Similarly, strong ethical challenges are presented when theatre makers attempt to portray violence on stage. Some performers have chosen the chill of the literal, albeit obscured, representation of violence in the depiction of lip sewing for example. In *There is Nothing Here* (2002) by Afshin Nikouseresht and Dave Kelman the actor sits in a cell with his back to the audience lit in silhouette and is seen to be pulling thread through his lips (Gilbert and Lo, 2007: 200). Others have chosen a more metaphorical approach seen, for example, when a character in *The Waiting Room* sews the lips of a teddy bear (Gilbert and Lo, 2007: 200). As one of the makers of *I've got something to show you* (2005) we were faced with the question of how best to represent the suffering of asylum seeker Esrafil Shiri (mentioned in Chapter 3) who set fire to himself in 2003 when he learned that his claim for asylum was likely to fail and who died of his burns three days later. Indeed, the question of how best to represent Esrafil himself as the absent subject of the play presented an ethical and creative challenge which was eventually overcome by deciding not to show him in any literal physical sense. He was represented by an empty chair on which was placed a rucksack evoking his action of carrying a bottle of petrol to the place where he decided to set fire to himself, the offices of a refugee charity in Manchester. His violent act was symbolically re-enacted by the performers who turned his gesture of dousing himself in petrol into the evocation of a ritual cleansing with water at the end of the piece (Jeffers, 2009).

Many theatre makers have experimented with immersive forms of theatre which aim to give audiences a more physically demanding experience than usual in a bid to create empathy. This also exempts them from having to enter into the difficult ethical questions discussed above as they eschew the need to represent refugees by asking their audiences instead to 'become' the refugee subjects of their pieces. Taking the journey of a refugee, stepping into the refugee's shoes, seeing the world through the eyes of a refugee are all strategies that have yielded rich and interesting results. In *The Container* by Clare Bayley the audience sat in such close proximity to the actors that they emerged apparently feeling as though they too had undertaken a journey in the cramped conditions of a shipping container. The story of *Pericles* was staged in such a way that the audience followed the action through a series of experiences and encounters which referenced some of the locations that refugees may find themselves in on their journeys.

Rejecting this strategy entirely Shafaei chose to place himself as a refugee subject at the centre of *Refugitive* in his after show discussions showing how engagement outside the dramatic frame is an effective way to reach and challenge audiences. The opportunity of a face to face encounter with a 'real' refugee created a strong dramatic move in a system where refugees are routinely incarcerated and where official strategies deliberately obscure the humanity of refugees. Sellars also attempted to engage audiences by reviving the democratic possibilities exemplified in ancient Greek theatre and putting *The Children of Herakles* into a programme of debate, education and awareness-raising.

Maintaining a broad definition of the theatrical allows us to understand how activists have made use of the dramaturgy of theatrical structures and gestures to create performances of activism around refugees and asylum seekers. Citizen activists are concerned to draw attention to inequalities, injustices and even the cruelty of national legislations in their approach to asylum seekers. Some of these actions have been highly imaginative and provocative, like the projection onto that most iconic Australian structure the Sydney Opera House that reminds Australian citizens that they are 'all boat people'. This, as well as pieces like *Tampa* by Mireille Astore (Astore, 2005), reminds Australians that contemporary 'boat people' are dying just off the beaches on which they sunbathe and play. Astore's voluntary caging also references the incarceration of so many asylum seekers and imprisoned activists who have maimed their own bodies in an attempt to send their voices outside the walls of their prisons so they will not be forgotten. This seems to be the impulse behind Mike Parr's work also when he disfigures his own body in the gallery space with direct reference to the damaged bodies of asylum seekers in remote prisons well beyond Australia's cosmopolitan centres.

I have suggested that the act of bureaucratic performance has inflected and infected all performances made by and about refugees and asylum seekers in a complex range of ways. As a condition of bureaucratic performance all asylum seekers are compelled to perform stories that conform to expectations that emerge from the necessity to demonstrate persecution both in the past and in the future (should they return to their country of origin). Furthermore, they are compelled to re-tell and perform those stories not only in the moment of claiming asylum but also beyond that in the public arena where certain narratives are both explicitly and implicitly required. The requisite narratives need to be based on persecution as that is the ground on which 'genuine' asylum seekers distinguish themselves from economic migrants. Persecution narratives require their tellers to be frightened, traumatised and vulnerable because to be otherwise raises suspicions that the speaker does not need asylum and is simply spinning an asylum-seeking yarn to encourage residence in more economically developed countries rather than being returned whence they came.

Shame, hospitality and risk

Theatre makers in these states have generated a body of work that often positions their responses to the situation in terms of shame, especially when the theatre makers and audiences are not themselves refugees. Shame is induced when audiences see theatre that reminds them of asylum seekers' suffering under what those citizens feel to be unfair and cruel legislation being carried out by their governments in their name. Williams, the director of *CMI (A Certain Maritime Incident)*, describes the importance of this emotion in seeking to 'undo these performances of refugee policy, not with reasoned argument, but with unspeakable shame' (Williams, 2008: 203). In a similar vein Gilbert and Lo (2007: 204) suggest that Australian audiences go to see plays about refugees less to hear refugees' stories than to 'publically enact their shame'. In another example a critic of *The Bogus Woman*, a play about an African asylum seeker by Kay Adshead, claims 'You can't possibly come away from it without feeling a deepening sense of shame about Britain's treatment of asylum seekers' (Aston, 2003: 12). Perhaps something of this concern motivated Sellars, discussed in Chapter 2, who took the opposite approach with *The Children of Herakles* refusing the possibility of shame but this seems to be the exception.

There is a problem with an over-emphasis on the shameful outcome of refugee theatre. If I go to see refugee theatre simply in order to re-enact my shame I could be forgiven for thinking that refugee theatre is ineffective because it is speaking to audiences who already understand the issues, in common parlance 'preaching to the converted'. Converted audiences know what to expect and going to the theatre to look only for the familiar, my feelings of shame, feels uncomfortably ritualistic. If shame is the *sole* outcome of seeing plays about the injustices meted out to asylum seekers there is a danger that the effect will be enervating, sapping energy and leading only to despair and lack of action. Shame, disgrace or dishonour may be a *necessary* effect of refugee theatre but they should not be the *only* effect because, if shame is all that is produced, the result will be stasis.

Rather than being purely a location for expressions of shame about the behaviour of our governments, or indeed only a site for 'ideological persuasion', it is important to point out that outrage and knowledge need to act *with* shame to create what Gilbert and Lo call 'a prelude to ethical community' (Gilbert and Lo, 2007: 203). Williams describes how version 1.0 intended to 'stage an ethical problem that persists no matter how "converted" to the cause any spectator might be' (Williams, 2008: 203). Bearing the persistence of the ethical problems of hospitality, responsibility and risk in mind I will conclude by considering questions of ethics in relation to theatre and performance that positions refugees and asylum seekers as subjects at their centre but I am also concerned to go beyond this. In placing theatre *about* refugees in relation to theatre and performance that refugees and asylum seekers make *themselves* I will show how the ethics of hospitality can be deepened and extended.

In order to make this point it is necessary to return to ideas about hospitality, responsibility and risk which have underpinned a great deal of the discussion. I will use the ideas of Levinas because this takes my argument to a notion of ethics where the responsibility to act is challenged by the responsibility to Otherness 'which presupposes both an engagement with the other and a more inclusive self/other encounter' (Puggioni, 2006: par. 1). Levinas is concerned with creating a system of ethics that is not totalising, in which the Other is always unknowable. The demands made by the Other on the self are infinite, manifested in the moment when I pass the Other on the street and wish they were absent, wincing at my own indifference

(Critchley, 2008: 56). Levinas' notions of ethical encounters with the Other are very demanding, stressing the obligation to give without asking for, or even expecting, reciprocity. Derrida has called *Totality and Infinity* by Levinas 'an immense treatise on hospitality' (Derrida, 1999: 21) and in Levinas' view home is the place where the self is able to re-collect, re-group, plan and seek material and physic sustenance necessary to leave the home and move into the world. Paradoxically, however, the home achieves its full dignity only when the Other is welcomed into it (Gauthier, 2007: 160).

> To dwell is not the simple fact of the anonymous reality of being cast into existence, as a stone one casts behind oneself; it is a recollection, a coming to oneself, a retreat home with oneself as in a land of refuge, which answers to a hospitality, an expectancy, a human welcome (Levinas, 1969: 156).

Just as the Levinasian face to face encounter gives meaning to freedom, because without the Other I would not know the meaning of freedom (Davis, 1996), the unconditional welcoming of the stranger into one's house generates the movement from egotism to altruism and awakens in the self the possibility of ethical responsibility. Home and nation are conflated by Levinas who says

> To shelter the other in one's own land or home, to tolerate the presence of the landless and the homeless on the "ancestral soil" so jealously, so meanly loved – is that the criterion of humanness? Unquestionably so' (Levinas, 2007: 86).

The moment of welcome generates the knowledge of the host's 'own exilic status' (Gauthier, 2007: 164) whereby the home takes on the characteristics of something closer to the inn, placing it beyond the domain of exclusive ownership and dominion. There is no option but to open up one's home in this way because our status as moral actors, even as human subjects, 'stands or falls with our treatment of the strangers who present themselves on our doorstep' (Gauthier, 2007: 165).

However, state actors have proved reluctant to offer hospitality to the refugee Other, bound up as they are in protecting borders and economic systems. This means that '[r]esponsibility lies unclaimed in the "lost property" room' (Miller, 2004: par.41) and, when it is noticed, it is more often 'claimed' by individual citizens and by authorities on a local level who undertake small-scale, ethical actions: for example, the Italian mayor of Badolato in Italy who accommodated 20 Kurdish refugee families in abandoned houses in his municipality (Puggioni, 2006); French musician Manu Chao and the band Têtes Raides who write and perform songs about *metissage* or pluralism and raise funds for *sans-papiers* (Lebrun, 2006); dawn vigils by Scottish citizens in Glasgow to stop immigration snatch squads from taking asylum seeking families into detention (Qureshi, 2007); French citizens who take in the children of asylum seekers to avoid them being detained with their parents (Bell, 2006; Burke, 2006); the growing number of people in Britain who give spare rooms in their houses to destitute asylum seekers who have been refused asylum but who cannot return to their country of origin (Saner, 2010). These 'small scale' contingent actions are, paradoxically, huge for those concerned, both for the individual asylum seekers who gain valuable support or shelter and for the citizens who open up their homes to strangers, sometimes even breaking the law to do so in the case of the French citizens who shelter children. They all show how these small moments of hospitality can 'still do at least a partial justice to the infinite and unconditional hospitality of the ethical moment' (Miller, 2004: par.47). The people who undertake these actions show how it is possible to stage even an incomplete and compromised hospitality by responding to the face of the refugee and answering the call to ethical responsibility for the Other.

The work of theatre makers who concern themselves with refugees and asylum seekers can be seen as the theatrical equivalent of the small-scale, radical actions of the citizens described above. This is demonstrated on a practical level when actors in companies like Actors for Refugees in Britain and Australia freely donate their time to giving performances of refugees' dialogue at meetings and other events. In these theatre events artists hope that, by representing refugees and their stories to an audience, they will evoke responsibility for the Other on the part of that audience. The call to attention and to responsibility in the theatre sets up the conditions where communication is possible (Erickson, 1999) and which for Levinas was at the root of any possible ethical action. But I am running ahead of myself and want to pause for a moment to consider briefly the general ethical possibilities for theatre before considering refugee theatre specifically.

Ethical encounters

The postmodern urge to *not know* emerging from Levinas' (and Lyotard's) mistrust of knowledge in a post-Holocaust world suggests possible ways in which the uncertain and ephemeral nature of theatre may prove useful in an economy of representation in which uncertainty is valued. Paradoxically it is theatre's lack, lack of action, lack of authority or certainty that invests it with a peculiar power. Theatre produces a 'doubtful performative [which] does not even produce an object, is deceptive as an action, and deceives even when the illusion is openly disturbed or destroyed' (Lehmann, 2006: 179). Playwright David Mamet claims that theatre changes nothing (Mamet, 1994: 386) so maybe my case is that theatre simply fails better. Theatre is permitted to, may even be compelled to, profess ignorance by remaining open to doubt. Thus when the performer represents the body of the refugee as a paradigmatic Other it is not to 'teach' the audience a lesson 'but to expose her own limits, to lay bare her own face before others and before herself' (Erickson, 1999: 11). In an ethical moment of performance the performer's responsibility is to not know and to lead the audience into a similar space of not knowing. Theatre also exists, as is so often pointed out, in a troubled relationship to time and perhaps the Levinasian encounter 'can only occur fleetingly, in powerfully altering moments' (Burvill, 2008: 241). This means that the temporary, doubtful and transient nature of theatre perhaps makes it more appropriate to look for moments of change and to see hopeful positions in the fleeting and the uncertain just as we might read hope into the small scale and local acts discussed above.

Creating theatre about refugees and asylum seekers constitutes an ethical engagement where Levinas' notion of the Saying 'strives to keep open the space of indeterminacy in order to stand against the closed "Said" of the government's language' (Burvill, 2008: 241). The Said is seen in the illocutionary speech act of the government where saying occurs in the same moment as achieving that which was stated: 'the Secretary of State is not satisfied that you qualify for asylum' effectively condemning the asylum seeker to 'failure' from that moment. The Saying of the asylum seeking subject creates only the wishful performative of the perlocutionary speech act, *I claim asylum* which has little power in the face of the Said and the certainties of the bureaucratic machine that is the asylum system. As a result of this political impotence many people seeking asylum turn to modes of expression that are totally unfamiliar and alien to them. Depending on their situation they may feel they have no alternative other than to use their bodies to 'speak' to the inhumanity of the Said of bureaucratic performance and turn in on themselves, to depression and even self-harm. Many theatrical encounters concerning refugees explore this space between statements of fact, the Said of the government's language in the form of bureaucratic performance, and the Saying in the voice of asylum seekers which shows other conditions of possibility. In theatrical performance the variety of approaches and techniques that can be pressed into service to tell refugee stories make this a much more flexible and productive form. It also allows the refugee subjects concerned or involved a much greater degree of agency than the irrevocable acts of self-harm into which some refugees are forced.

If we accept that the face to face encounter is the basis of reason, society and ethics (Davis, 1996: 49) it is possible to read potency in the theatrical moment when we are compelled to respond to the face of the refugee in performance. Theatrical re-tellings of refugee stories in this way of thinking create the possibility of a face to face encounter which has the potential to set up dialogue and understanding. In encountering the refugee Other face to face we are also compelled to speak because, as Levinas reminds us, 'it is difficult to be silent in someone's presence' (Burvill, 2008: 241) but in speaking I am already answering for the Other. However, in a theatrical context as an audience member I have a right, even a responsibility, to be silent and to listen so my speaking is delayed and the Other maintains the freedom to speak uninterrupted. Theatre shows the possibilities inherent in staging the Saying by providing an 'ethical encounter with alterity' (Ibid.: 236). The speaking face of the refugee Other in the face of the silent audience shows how theatre can operate to keep open the space of indeterminacy against the Said. Hervé seemed to know this when he strode on stage proclaiming 'I am Hervé. I am not a refugee'. This deliberately provocative challenge to the audience seemed to demand a response but in the moment of theatre sitting with my fellow audience members I am compelled to remain silent and reflect on what Hervé and his colleagues might mean.

This seems a hopeful position in the face of the enforced silence and invisibility said to characterise refugeeness. It also helps to suggest how I might respond to the mutilated face of the refugee Other who has deliberately prevented himself from speaking and who shows me a face which has been unbearably marked and de-faced. Whatever my feelings I am placed in a position of having to speak *for* him, of voicing his anguish to an uncomprehending audience. The self-mutilation of refugee subjects has been represented on stage but 'theatre stops short of turning it into an absolute' and '[w]hile actors want to realize unique moments, they also want to *repeat* them' (Lehmann, 2006: 137 emphasis in original). This is what makes the performances of the pain of the solo performers and their engagement with their audiences so potent. Being in a position of being able to act and re-enact their pain gives them agency and, in using their training as performers and artists, they can place refugee stories in front of audiences who might not be in a position to hear them otherwise.

Face to face

Explicitly addressing the face to face encounter within a dramaturgical frame suggests that the vast majority of performance styles across cultures and time have been dominated by a 'presentational attitude' (Erickson, 1999: 12) whereby the performer faces the audience members who look back. Erickson suggests that one of the most important lessons for theatre that emerges from Levinas' ideas of face to face contact lies in the non-reciprocity of the relationship between performer and audience. Whether performers and audience are there for each other or not their relationship is not reciprocal, moment for moment, because of my inability speak up as an audience member in the moment of performance. This leads me to suggest that the Levinasian dramaturgy implied in the face to face meeting of actor and audience might be better configured as being with or alongside the Other but the challenge lies in how to ethically engage with the Other in a theatrical context and 'how to address otherness without resorting to moral maxims or notions of community' (Wade, 2009: 16) or togetherness.

If the separation between self and Other is essential for maintaining an ethical relationship, the collapsing of those boundaries,

perhaps in discourses of togetherness at refugee festivals, is not helpful in understanding how I can exist in an ethical relationship to the
refugee Other. Seeking to gain a deeper understanding I move to theatrical representations of refugeeness where stories of refugees and
asylum seekers might extend my knowledge and understanding of
their position. In refugee theatre I am apparently confronted by the
face of the refugee Other, but whose face am I looking at when I
encounter that face in theatrical performance?

I will move to completion by comparing two moments of face to
face encounters with refugee subjects in performance. The first is the
moment at the end of *Refugitive* when Shafaei delivers an eight stanza
poem which, as the light fades, he holds his hands out and recites
directly to the audience (Burvill, 2008: 237). The poem is Auden's
Refugee Blues with some slight alterations, most notably the replace-
ment of 'German Jews' with 'refugees' in one stanza. The second
moment occurs when the actor Noma Dumezweni 'held the gaze of
individual spectators for *real*' in *The Bogus Woman* (Aston, 2003: 12,
emphasis in original). On both occasions individual audience members were compelled to make eye contact with representatives of refugee Others on stage. The audience is faced with a moment in which
the autonomy of the subject 'is called into question by the fact of the
Other's demand by the appeal that comes from their face' (Critchley,
2008: 56). But whose face was the audience looking at 'for real'?

The face of the refugee on stage is often a representation in the
shape of an actor embodying a refugee subject, but this is not always
the case. The audience knows that Dumezweni is an actor but *not* the
refugee subject of the play whereas Shafaei is both the actor of the
play *and* its refugee subject. This is not to diminish the potential
impact of theatre created by non-refugee actors to create something
that is both powerful and immediate. I have no desire to set up any
kind of hierarchy of efficacy. Neither is it remotely suggesting that it
is in some way unethical for actors to represent refugees on stage. It
is, nevertheless, really important to draw attention to the possibilities inherent in seeing the face of a refugee in performance which is
also a face that I can encounter *as a refugee* beyond the moment of
performance. The gaps and spaces implicit in looking and seeing can
open up productive visual communication in which the process of
seeing 'becomes a circulation of energy between and among rather
than an artificial and inadequate bridge between a subject and an

alien world' (Oliver, 2001: 221). An actor who embodies a refugee in a powerful piece of theatre therefore can still act as a witness to refugee stories in such a way as to engage and guide an audience. However, the 'circulation of energy' between and among subjects both *in and beyond* the theatrical moment is perhaps more potent than the 'inadequate bridge' of the face to face encounter between self and Other purely within the theatrical moment. Dumezweni is a powerful actor whose performance might move audiences and, in doing so, inspire them to emotions which may act as an incentive to action. However, audiences also know that, no matter how affective the piece, the bridge created by their face to face encounter in performance cannot be transformed into anything other than that. The relationship between audience member and refugee Other stops at the moment when the play ends.

Shoulder to shoulder

In Australia the Men's Shed movement[1] shows how communal activity and work generates a sense of community and shared understanding among vulnerable people where the *face to face* interaction of a talking therapy is often rejected. In the Men's Sheds men have found community and a sense of purpose through working shoulder to shoulder, alongside each other, with many even claiming that these activities have prevented suicide among this vulnerable group of older white and indigenous men. This leads me to suggest that shoulder to shoulder is a more hopeful proxemic position that emerges when we consider the face to face encounter between audiences and performers in refugee theatre. Audiences sit or stand shoulder to shoulder in the face to face theatrical encounter. Thinking about the ways in which I sit shoulder to shoulder with my fellow audience members suggests Levinas' third party, the body which brings my face to face encounter with the refugee performer into the social and political arena. When the 'thou is posited in front of a we' (Levinas, 1969: 213) I discover the Other and a host of potential Others is revealed to me (Davis, 1996: 52). In watching theatre about refugees I make that journey of discovery shoulder to shoulder with fellow audience members because the 'host of potential Others' is made up of fellow citizens. In gaining a better understanding of the ways in which refugees are treated in the name of protecting state borders, in the name of protecting us as citizens, we gain some understanding of our role in this and ways in which we can choose to be complicit or not.

In the participatory model of theatrical production the 'host of others' is as likely to be made up of refugees and asylum seekers as it is of fellow citizens. In offering a stage on which refugees can re-enact the stories that matter to them we enter into a set of relationships which have been called 'a complicated ballet of proposals, expectations, careful interpretations of seemingly infinite offers' (Rosello, 2001: 127). As a theatre maker I cannot escape the fact that it is in my 'gift' to be able to offer theatre as a space for reflection and expression. In offering the means to place the stories that emerge before an audience, I am also offering an implicit guarantee of an audience that will be sympathetic to them.

At the same time, the offer of a 'hospitable stage' on which refugee stories can be re-enacted is just that, a stage, not substantial, not 'real'. Refugees who accept the offer understand that speaking their story in front of an audience will probably not materially affect their political standing in this place of refuge but standing shoulder to shoulder with those refugees and asylum seekers brave enough to accept the invitation reminds us that there can be no hospitality without risk. That risk is taken on both sides because, in the truly hospitable encounter, both host and guest must be prepared to be changed. Standing shoulder to shoulder with refugees in theatre, and in activism, shows how refugees also constitute 'the third party': we with them and them with us. Our very presence in the act of listening to refugee stories constitutes a form of commitment through an act of trust and generosity on our part as listeners. An even greater level of trust and generosity is needed on the part of those refugee speakers brave enough to share their thoughts, opinions and experiences with an audience. In truth, we can offer very little but to listen and to amplify these stories by giving them a voice through theatre. We can only ever offer to stand together on the threshold, on the stage, in the place for exchanging stories and, like Janus, look both forwards and back at the same time.

Notes

Preface

1. Indices of Multiple Deprivation 2010, Manchester Chief Executive's Department, April, 2011.
2. Readers should assume that the names of all refugees and asylum seekers have been changed throughout this book with the exception of those refugee artists whose names are already in the public domain.
3. Authorities struggle to 'manage' asylum seekers while their claims for asylum are being examined and legislations deal with this in a variety of ways. Australia, for example, introduced the controversial policy of mandatory detention of asylum seekers in 1992. In the UK asylum seekers have been involuntarily dispersed to urban centres outside London and the south east.
4. I have attempted throughout this book to use terminology that emphasises the humanity of those refugees and asylum seekers under discussion rather than dwelling on the terms that describe their legal status.
5. See Thompson, Hughes and Balfour (2009) and Jeffers (2010) for more information.
6. The asylum seeker's name was Esrafil Shiri and interested readers can find out more about this project in *Get Real. Documentary Theatre Past and Present* which is edited by Alison Forsythe and Chris Megson (2009).
7. It has been suggested that Greater Manchester hosts more asylum seekers than any other conurbation outside London. In 2007 more than 5700 asylum seekers were being supported by the authorities in Greater Manchester according to Exodus in their report 'Developing and celebrating refugee arts across Greater Manchester'. November 2004–October 2007 (unpub. report).

Introduction: Stories, Words and Points of View

1. The terms refugee and asylum seeker are legal terms. A refugee is someone who has been recognised as needing the protection of the state to which they have fled, having faced persecution in their country of origin. An asylum seeker is someone in the process of proving their refugee status and who has not yet been officially recognised as a refugee. I will use the term 'refugee' as a generic marker but will differentiate refugees from asylum seekers when it is necessary to do so.
2. See http://www.rsc.ox.ac.uk for further information.

3. Practitioners and artists in community and participatory arts have been influential to this study. They include Janine Waters (Waters Edge Arts); Magdalen Bartlett, Cilla Baynes, Kooj Chuhan, Erin McNeeney, Ian Marsh, Katherine Rogers and Yasmin Yaqub (Community Arts North West); film maker Alan Amin and musicians Jean Azip and Pat Mackela among many others.

4. Mobiles is the common British abbreviation for mobile phones and concerns one of the most persistent asylum myths in the UK that the government give free mobile phones to asylum seekers.

1   Refugees, Crisis and Bureaucratic Performance

1. Using terminology in which an abbreviated title stands for a group of people is distasteful to many and no less offensive than calling asylum seekers 'illegals' as so often happens at border controls but these terms are somewhat foisted on any writer who is exploring this area.

2. 'Guiding Principles on Internal Displacement' United Nations Office for the coordination of Humanitarian Affairs http://www.reliefweb.int/ocha_ol/pub/idp_gp/idp.html (accessed 19 July 2010).

3. Keynote address at Refugee Studies Centre's 25th Anniversary Conference, University of Oxford, 7 December, 2007.

4. http://www.unhcr.org.protect/PROTECTION/3b66c39e1 (accessed 12 January 2007).

5. Cartagena Declaration on Refugees http://www.unhcr.org/refworld/docid/3ae6b36ec.html (accessed 19 July 2010).

6. See http://www.unhchr.ch/html/menu3/b/o_c_ref.htm for a full list of signatories.

7. http://www.unhcr.org/statistics/STATISTICS/48f742792.pdf (accessed 12 January 2009).

8. http://www.refugeecouncil.org.au/arp/stats-02.html (accessed 13 January 2009).

9. The fact that many refugees do not manage to jump this first hurdle at the border perhaps gives the figure of asylum seekers less potency in the United States than in Europe, Australia and the UK (Salter, 2006: 171).

10. It is impossible within the scope of this study to adequately represent the volume of information available. Interested readers should visit www.icar.co.uk.

11. http://www.icar.org.uk/?lid=5026 (accessed 9 January 2009).

12. http://www.news.ulster.ac.uk/releases/2003/790.html (accessed 9 January 2009).

13. http://www.ipsos-mori.com/content/polls-02/attitudes-towards-asylwn-seekers-for-refugee-week-ashx (accessed 13 January 2009).

14. http://english.aljazeera.net/news/asia-pacific/2008/11/200811442221296425.html (accessed 12 January, 2009).

15. http://news.bbc.co.uk/1/hi/world/europe/3600421.stm (accessed 25 March 2009).

16. Citing the 'golden door' from the poem by Emma Lazarus inscribed at the foot of the Statue of Liberty, Senator Edward Kennedy insisted that '[t]he "golden door" must stay open' (Staeger, 2004: 7).
17. Conversation with author (15 December 2005). In this and all subsequent spoken quotations by refugees I have chosen not to indicate where they are using non-standard English.
18. Reasons for Refusal letter of 5 October 2001 (documents in possession of the author).
19. Conversation with author (15 December 2005).
20. 'Asylum toddlers get fingerprinted', http://newsvote.bbc.co.uk/mpapps/ pagetools/print/news.bbc.co.uk/l/hi/ uk_politics/47 (accessed 6 June 2006).
21. 'Exclusive: We will tag new asylum seekers', http://www.mirror.co.uk/ printable_version..cfm?objectid=16752417&siteid=94762 (accessed 19 May 2006).
22. 'Voice ID device to track failed asylum seekers', http://politics.guardian. co.uk/print/0,,329431136–110247,00.html (accessed 6 June 2006).
23. Conversation with author (10 December 2005).
24. Reasons for Refusal letter of 5 October 2001 (documents in possession of the author).

2 Hosts and Guests: National Performance and the Ethics of Hospitality

1. Readers are directed to Gilbert and Lo's chapter on 'Performance and Asylum' in *Performance and Cosmopolitics*, 2007 and to the special edition 'Performance and Asylum' in *Research in Drama Education*, Volume 13, June 2008.
2. This was seen when Joy who was doing the course in refugee radio discussed in the Preface was furiously lobbying the British Home Office for her right to remain when it was, in fact, the Home Office that was funding the radio project on which she was enrolled.
3. In October 2001 353 asylum seekers drowned trying to get to Australia. SIEV stands for Suspected Illegal Entry Vessel and the X means unknown. See www.sievx.com for further details.
4. For a further critique of humanitarian schemes in relation to refugees see Rajaram (2003) 'Humanitarianism and Representations of the Refugee', *Journal of Refugee Studies*, 15: 3.
5. http://www.independent.co.uk/news/uk/politics/asylum-the-facts-539414.html (accessed 2 December 2009).
6. Benefits is a shorthand term used in the UK to describe any public money distributed by the government. Single asylum seekers get £5 per day in the UK which is just over half what the government estimates people need in order to survive (Alan Travis, *The Guardian*, London, 9 October 2010).
7. Conversation with the author (10 December 2005).
8. http://www.bannertheatre.co.uk (accessed 27 February 2007).
9. Interview with Dave Rogers, Director of Banner (18 July 2006).

10. Press release from Banner Theatre 24 May 2007.
11. Programme note. *They get free mobiles...don't they?* Wythenshawe Forum, Manchester 14 June 2007.
12. Interview with Dave Rogers, Director of Banner (18 July, 2006).
13. Some plays have taken a humorous or satirical approach to questions of asylum. Six of One in London produced *Skinless* in 2005, an experiment in the use of burlesque theatre to re-present refugee stories. Tim Lafferty's play *I'm an asylum seeker get me into here*, performed at The Olive Branch Theatre in London in 2005, experimented with form, as four asylum seekers in a reality TV house compete for the ultimate prize of the right to stay in Britain, as determined by the vote of the theatre audience. These kinds of plays are, however, in the minority.
14. Scouse is the name popularly given to the dialect of Liverpool.
15. An abbreviation of Received Pronunciation sometimes referred to as BBC English.
16. http://www.iceandfire.co.uk (accessed 27 February 2007).
17. Jackson, International Practitioners Seminar, In Place of War, University of Manchester, April, 2005.
18. Interview with Claudia Chidiac, Director of *Asylum*, Sydney. (16 September 2006).
19. McEvoy (2006) offers a visual reproduction of parts of the programme.
20. http://www.americanrepertorytheater.org/inside/articles/articles-vol-1-i2-balm-ancient-words (accessed 30 April 2010).
21. Ibid.
22. http://www.hotreview.org/articles/real-children.htm (accessed 30 April 2010).
23. http://www.whatsonstage.com/news/theatre/london/E8821057831292/RSC&%2365533;s+Cardboard+Pericles+Takes+Refuge+at+Elephant.html (accessed 7 May 2010).
24. Sangatte was a refugee centre in Calais, northern France from which a number of refugees made the perilous journey through the Channel Tunnel to England. It also formed the background for one of the scenes of *Le Dernier Caravansérail*.

3   Taking up Space and Making a Noise: Minority Performances of Activism

1. http://www.antimedia.net/nooneisillegal/sea%20of%20chairs.htm (accessed 19 March 2010).
2. http://www.boat-people.org/1_about.htm (accessed 19 March 2010).
3. http://www.boat-people.org/1_about.htm (accessed 16 July 2010).
4. http://www.ncadc.org.uk/campaigns/winning.htm (accessed 19 August 2007).
5. Conversation with author, 31 March, 2005.
6. 'Zaidah and Sharif Must Stay' campaign leaflet.
7. Many torture survivors at the Medical Foundation for the care of Victims of Torture are prepared to go as far as to compare the psychological 'tor-

ture' of their life in the UK as an asylum seeker with physical torture in their country of origin.

8. http://www.noborders.org.uk and http://www.noii.org.uk. These policies and ideas also gain support with some scholars in refugee studies (Cohen, 2003; Schuster, 2003; Marfleet, 2006;).

9. http://www.revolutionarycommunist.org (accessed 23 March 2010).

10. NADC report on the event (unpub.doc).

11. Conversation with author, 31 March, 2005.

12. Speech by Fazil Kawani, Refugee Council at vigil for Bereket Johannes, rejected asylum seeker who killed himself in detention: http://www.refugeecouncil.org.uk (accessed 29 February 2006).

13. '120 Immigration Detainees on Hunger Strike at Campsfield IRC' http://www.indymedia.org.uk/en/2006/06/342930.html (accessed 23 June 2006).

14. 'Immigration Detainees at Risk of Self Harm Doubles' http://www.communitycare.co.uk (accessed 6 June 2006).

15. 'In memory of Bereket Johannes' http://www.ncadc.org.uk/newszine66/bereket.html (accessed 27 January 2006).

16. 'Asylum seekers kills himself so child can stay in Britain' http://www.praxis.org.uk/readnews.aspx?1d=61 (accessed 5 December 2005).

17. 'Gay plea to halt deporting of Iranian' http://guardian.co.uk (accessed 29 February 2006) This formed the basis for the play *I've got something to show you* which was staged in June 2005 as part of *In Place of War*.

18. 'Asylum seeker "set himself alight"' http://newsvote.bbc.co.uk (accessed 8 February 2006).

19. 'Lip sewing chicken dinner advertisement' http://www.abc.net.au/stories/s635561.htm (accessed 12 August 2006).

20. http://www.socialistworker.co.uk (accessed 18 August 2007).

21. http://www.demotix.cam.news/546906/afghan-refugees-hunger-strike-sewn-lips-Athens (accessed 24 January 2010).

22. 'Iranian asylum seekers in Greece sew up lips in protest' http:www.haartz.com/news/international/Iranian-asylum-seekers-in-greece-sew-up-lips-in-protest-1.310854 (accessed 24 January 2010).

23. The White Australia Policy is so called because it restricted non-white immigration to Australia from 1901 to 1975 when it was formally revoked.

24. Mike Parr at Midnight. A Performance Protocol http//.members.iinet.net.au/~postpub/8ball/isshe%2028/Parr=_Malevich_A_Political_Arm_.html (accessed 7 April 2010).

4 'We with Them and Them with Us': Diverse Cultural Performances

1. http://www.refugeeweek.org.uk/Aboutus/background.htm (accessed 2 July 2007).

2. The aims of Exodus Festival are: To challenge negative representations of refugees and asylum seekers in Greater Manchester through arts and culture; to develop and support the sustainable arts and culture of refugees

and asylum seekers in exile; to create excellent quality sustainable events in Greater Manchester, showcasing refugee arts and culture that targets a wide new audience; to support community cohesion among Manchester's diverse communities through cultural exchange; to link refugees and asylum seekers into Manchester's cultural calendar, both mainstream and alternative; to raise the profile of Manchester as a vibrant international city; to create a voice for refugees and asylum seekers in Greater Manchester.

All other information about the Exodus Festival is taken from http://www.can.uk.com/exodus/exodus_main.htm unless otherwise stated.

3. Interview with Cilla Baynes by Jenny Hughes, *In Place of War*, September 2004.
4. Lisa Lowe discusses the competing narratives of a multicultural festival in Los Angeles in her book *Immigrant Acts*, 1996.
5. See, for example www.oldham.gov.uk/es/about_community_cohesion.pdf
6. *Nyubani Wapi?* is the Swahili translation of the play's English title.
7. Interview with two security guards, Exodus Festival, Manchester, 2006.
8. Interview with audience member, Exodus Festival, Manchester, 2006.
9. Interviews with performers at Exodus Festival, Manchester, 2006.
10. Interviews with performers at Exodus Festival, Manchester, 2006.
11. These and all subsequent quotations from Blanchard were recorded by the author at the Exodus Festival in 2007.
12. Interview with Redley Silva http://www.inplaceofwar.net
13. *The Drama Review: TDR* devoted a special edition to the growing form in 1979 although the term has not subsequently enjoyed widespread use.
14. Conversation with author (10 December 2005).
15. Interview with Redley Silva by Jenny Hughes, July 2006.
16. Shahin Shafaei in talk given to Symposium 'Performance of Asylum', University of Sydney, 10 September 2006.
17. Ibid.
18. Part of the publicity for Actors for Refugees in Australia.
19. Shahin Shafaei in talk given to Symposium 'Performance of Asylum', University of Sydney, 10 September 2006.
20. Creative Exchange is a charity which is concerned to create networks and support projects in which arts and culture can influence social policy and practice http://www.creativexchange.org/about (accessed 4 January 2008).

Conclusion: Face to Face or Shoulder to Shoulder?

1. http://www.mensheds.com.au/ (accessed 23 April, 2010).

References

Adshead, K. (2001) *The Bogus Woman*, London, Oberon.

Afrocats (2005) *Nyubani Wapi?Where is Home?* (unpub.ms.)

Agamben, G. (1998) *Homo Sacer. Sovereign Power and the Bare Life*, Stanford, Stanford University Press.

Ahmed, S. (2000) *Strange Encounters. Embodied Others in Post-Coloniality*, London and New York, Routledge.

Ahmed, S. (2004) *The Cultural Politics of Emotion*, Edinburgh, Edinburgh University Press.

Ahmed, S. & Stacey, J. (Eds.) (2001) *Thinking Through the Skin*, London and New York, Routledge.

Al Qady, T. (2006) *Nothing but Nothing: One Refugee's Story* (unpub.ms.).

Alibhai-Brown, Y. (2002) *Celebrating Sanctuary*. London, London Arts.

Anderson, P. & Menon, J. (Eds.) (2009) *Violence Performed. Local Roots and Global Routes of Conflict*, Basingstoke, Palgrave Macmillan.

Ankori, G. (2003) Dis-orientalisms: displaced bodies/embodied displacements in contemporary Palestinian art In Ahmed, S., Castaneda, C., Fortier, A.-M. & Sheller, M. (Eds.) *Uprootings/Regroundings. Questions of Home and Migration*, Oxford, Berg.

Anzaldua, G. (Ed.) (1990) *Making Face, Making Soul. Creative and Critical Perspectives by Women of Color*, San Francisco, Aunt Lute Books.

Arbabzadh, N. (Ed.) (2007) *From Outside In. Refugees and British Society*, London, Arcadia Books.

Arendt, H. (1986 [1951]) *The Origins of Totalitarianism*, London, Andre Deutsch.

Aston, E. (2003) Feminism and Asylum Theatre. *Modern Drama*, 46: 1, 5–21.

Astore, M. (2005) Tampa: when gazes collide. In Coulter-Smith, G. & Owen, M. (Eds.) *Art in the Age of Terrorism*. London, Paul Holberton Publishing.

Athwal, H. (2006) *Driven to Desperate Measures*. London, Institute of Race Relations.

Austin, J. L. (1976 [1962]) *How to Do Things with Words*, Oxford, Oxford University Press.

Austin, S. (2005) 'Mike Parr and the disruptive rupture: the condemned and punished body as a political strategy in Close the Concentration Camps' *Double Dialogues, Anatomy and Politics*, Issue 6, Winter 2005. Available at http:www.doubledialogues.com/archive/issue_six/austin.html (accessed 21 January, 2010).

Bacon, C. (2005) *The Evolution of Immigration Detention in the UK: The Involvement of Private Prison Companies*. Oxford, Refugee Studies Centre.

Baily, J. (1999) Music and refugee lives: Afghans in Eastern Iraq and California. *Forced Migration Review 6*. Oxford, RSC.

Balint, R. (2005) Front Door, Back Door: seascapes and the Australian psyche, Available at http://www.histroy.ac.uk/ihr/Focus/Sea?articles/balint.html (accessed 3 November, 2009).

Barnes, S. (Ed.) (2009) *Participatory Arts with Young Refugees,* London, Arts in Education.

Bassett, K. (2003) Pericles, The Warehouse, *The Independent,* London. (3 August 2003)

Bayley, C. (2007) *The Container,* London, Nick Hern Books.

Belfiore, E. (2002) Art as a means of alleviating social exclusion. Does it really work? A critique of instrumental cultural policies and social impact studies in the UK. *International Journal of Cultural Policy,* 8: 1, 91–106.

Bell, S. (2006) Underground network hides children facing deportation, *The Scotsman,* Edinburgh. (24 January 2006)

Bhabha, H. K. (1994) *The Location of Culture,* London and New York, Routledge.

Billig, M. (1995) *Banal Nationalism,* London, Thousand Oaks and New Delhi, Sage.

Billington, M. (2001) Theatre Review: Credible Witness, *The Guardian,* London. (15th February, 2001)

Blaker, C. (2003) *Senses of the City. London's support for refugees 1999–2002.* London, London Arts.

Blommaert, J. (2001) Investigating Narrative Inequality: African asylum seekers' stories in Belgium. *Discourse and Society,* 12, 413–449.

Bogad, L. M. (2006) Activism. Tactical carnival: social movements, demonstrations and dialogical performance. In Cohen-Cruz, J. & Schutzman, M. (Eds.) *A Boal Companion. Dialogues on Theatre and Cultural Politics.* London and New York, Routledge.

Bonney, J. (Ed.) (2000) *Extreme Exposure,* New York, Theatre Communications Group.

Boyd, A. (2002) Irony, meme warfare, and the extreme costume ball. In Shepard, B. & Hayduk, R. (Eds.) *From ACT UP to the WTO. Urban Protest and Community Building in the Era of Globalization,* London and New York, Verso.

Bracken, P. J. (2001) Post-modernity and Post-traumatic Stress Disorder. *Social Science and Medicine,* 53, 733–743.

Bracken, P. J., Giller, J. E. & Summerfield, D, (1997) Rethinking Mental Health Work with Survivors of Wartime Violence and Refugees. *Journal of Refugee Studies,* 10, 431–442.

Brah, A. (1996) *Cartographies of Diaspora. Contesting identities,* London and New York, Routledge.

Bramwell, A. C. (Ed.) (1988) *Refugees in an Age of Total War,* London, Unwin Hyman.

Branigan, T. (2003) Refugee Vows to Continue Hunger Strike, *The Guardian,* London (30 May 2003).

Brisbane, K. (2005) Political Fictions. *Two Brothers.* Sydney, Currency Press.

Broun, A. (2003) Refugitive at The Cellar this week, Sydney, 23 August 2003. Available at http://www.mailarchive.com/leftlink@vitnet.com.au (accessed 25 July, 2005).

Burke, J. (2006) French defy state childsnatchers, *Observer,* London. (4 June 2006).

Burnside, J. (Ed.) (2003) *From Nothing to Zero. Letters from Refugees in Australia's Detention Centres,* Melbourne, Lonely Planet Publications.

Burvill, T. (2008) 'Politics begins as ethics': Levinasian ethics and Australian performance. *Research in Drama Education,* 13: 2, 233–244.

Butler, J. (1993) *Bodies That Matter,* London and New York, Routledge.

Butler, J. (1995) Burning Acts. In Parker, A. & Kosovsky-Sedgwick, E. (Eds.) *Performativity and Performance.* London and New York, Routledge.

Butler, J. (1997) *Excitable Speech. A Politics of the Performative,* London and New York, Routledge.

Butler, J. (1999) *Gender Trouble,* London and New York, Routledge.

Campbell, E. & Clark, C. (1997) Gypsy Invasion: a critical analysis of newspaper reaction in Czech and Slovak Romani asylum seekers in Britain in 1997. *Romani Studies 5,* 10.

Carlson, M. (1996) Brook and Mnouchkine. Passages to India? In Pavis, P. (Ed.) *The Intercultural Performance Reader.* London and New York, Routledge.

Carlson, M. (1996) *Performance. A Critical Introduction,* London and New York, Routledge.

Caster, P. (2004) Staging Prisons. Performance, activism and social bodies. *The Drama Review,* 48: 3, 107–116.

Charteris-Black, J. (2006) Britain as a container: immigration metaphors in the 2005 election campaign. *Discourse and Society,* 17, 563–581.

Choate, E. T. (2006) Performance Review. Le Dernier Caravansérail, Théâtre du Soleil, Lincoln Center Festival. *Theatre Journal,* 58: 1, 95–99.

Cohen, S. (2002) *Folk Devils and Moral Panics,* London and New York, Routledge.

Cohen, S. (2003) *No One is Illegal. Asylum and Immigration Control Past and Present,* London, Trentham Books Ltd.

Cohen-Cruz, J. (2002) At cross purposes: the Church Ladies for Choice. In Shepard, B. & Hayduk, R. (Eds.) *From ACT UP to the WTO. Urban Protest and Community Building in the Era of Globalization.* London and New York, Verso.

Cohen-Cruz, J. & Schutzman, M. (2006) *A Boal Companion. Dialogues on Theatre and Cultural Politics,* London and New York, Routledge.

Conquergood, D. (1985) Performing as a Moral Act: Ethical Dimensions of the Ethnography of Performance. *Literature in Performance,* 5, 1–13.

Conquergood, D. (1992) Performance Theory, Hmong Shamans and Cultural Theory. In Reinelt, J. G. & Roach, J. R. (Eds.) *Critical Theory and Performance.* Ann Arbor, MI, The University of Michigan.

Conquergood, D. (2002) Performance Studies Interventions and Radical Research. *The Drama Review,* 46: 2, 145–156.

Cox, J. W. & Minahan, S. (2004) Unravelling Woomera: lip sewing, Morphology and dystopia. *Journal of Organisational Change and Management,* 17: 3, 292–310.

Crawley, H. (2009) *Understanding and Changing Public Attitudes.* Swansea, Centre for Migration Policy Research.

Cresswell, T. (2004) *Place. A Short Introduction,* Oxford, Blackwell.

Critchley, S. (2008) *Infinitely Demanding. Ethics of Commitment, Politics of Resistance,* London and New York, Verso.

Daly, M. (1986) *Beyond God the Father: Toward a Philosophy of Women's Liberation,* London, The Women's Press.

Daniel, E. V. & Knusden, J. C. (Eds.) (1995) *Mistrusting Refugees,* Berkley, CA, University of California Press.

Das, V., A. Kleinman, M. Lock, M. Ramphele and P. Reynolds (Eds.) *Remaking a World. Violence, Social Suffering and Recovery,* Berkley, CA, University of California Press.

Davis, C. (1996) *Levinas. An Introduction,* Cambridge, Polity Press.

De Certeau, M. (1984) *The Practice of Everyday Life,* Berkeley and Los Angeles, CA, University of California Press.

Deleuze, G. & Guattari, F. (1987) *A Thousand Plateaus,* London, Continuum.

Derrida, J. (1992) *Acts of Literature,* London and New York, Routledge.

Derrida, J. (1999) *Adieu to Emmanuel Levinas,* Stanford, CA, Stanford University Press.

Derrida/Dufourmantelle (2000) *Of Hospitality,* Stanford, CA, Stanford University Press.

Derrida, J. (2000a) Hostipitality. *Angelaki. Journal of the Theoretical Humanities,* 5, 3–18.

Dolan, J. (1993) Geographies of Learning: theatre studies, performance and the 'performative'. *Theatre Journal,* 45: 4, 417–425.

Dolan, J. (2006) *Utopia in Performance,* Theatre Research International, Cambridge University Press.

Dona, G. & Berry, J. W. (1999) Refugee Acculturation and Re-acculturation. In Ager, A. E. (Ed.) *Refugees: Perspectives on the Experience of Forced Migration.* London and New York, Continuum.

D'Onofrio, L. & Munk, K. (2004) *Understanding the Stranger.* London, ICAR.

Dummett, M. (2001) *On Immigration and Refugees,* London and New York, Routledge.

Dunn, K., M, Klocker, N. & Salabay, T. (2007) Contemporary Racism and Islamaphobia in Australia. *Ethnicities,* 7: 4, 564–589.

Edmondson, L. (2005) Marketing Trauma and the Theatre of War in Northern Uganda. *Theatre Journal,* 57: 3, 451–474.

Edmondson, L. (2009) The Politics of Displacement and the Politics of Genocide, In Anderson, P. and Menon, J. (Eds.) *Violence Performed: Local Roots and Global Routes,* Basingstoke, Palgrave Macmillan.

Eggers, D. (2006) *What is the What?: The Autobiography of Valentino Achak Deng,* New York, McSweeney's.

Erickson, J. (1999) The Face and the possibility of an Ethics of Performance. *Journal of Dramatic Theory and Criticism,* 13: 2.

Faulkner, S. (2003) Asylum seekers, imagined geography and visual culture. *Visual Culture in Britain,* 4: 1, 93–144.

Fekete, L. (2001) The emergence of xeno-racism. *irr news,* Available at http://www.irr.org.uk/2001/september/ak000001.html (accessed 19 July 2010).

Feldman, A. (1994) On Cultural Anesthesia: from Desert Storm to Rodney King. *American Ethnologist,* 12: 2, 404–418.

Filewood, A. (2007) Theatrical Migrations and Digital Bodies: the Migrant Voices project. *Conference on Performance and Asylum.* Royal Holloway University of London.

Filewood, A. & Watt, D. (2001) *Workers' Playtime. Theatre and the Labour Movement since 1970,* Sydney: Currency Press.

Finney, N. (2005) *Public Attitudes to Asylum.* London, ICAR.

Fisek, E. (2008) Le Dernier Cartoucherie: refuge and the performance of care. *Research in Drama Education,* 13: 2, 205–210.

Foucault, M. and J. Miskowiec (1986) Of Other Spaces, *Diacritics,* 16: 1 (22–27).

Forced Migration Review (FMR) (1999) *Culture in Exile.* Oxford, Refugee Studies Centre, December, 1999.

Forsythe, A. and Chris Megson (Eds.) (2009) *Get Real. Documentary Theatre Past and Present,* Basingstoke: Palgrave Macmillan.

Gauthier, D., J. (2007) Levinas and the Politics of Hospitality. *History of Political Thought,* 28: 1.

Gener, R. (2002) Who will speak for the children? Peter Sellars Children of Herakles gives theatrical shelter to refugee kids lost in the system. American Theatre. Available at http:www.highbeam.com/doc/1G1-95261528.html (accessed 7 September 2005).

Gibney, M. J. (2002) Security and the ethics of asylum after 11 September. *Forced Migration Review,* 13, 40–42.

Gibney, M. J. (2006) 'A Thousand Little Guantanamos' Western states and measures to prevent the arrival of refugees. In Tunstall, K. E. (Ed.) *Displacement, Asylum, Migration.* Oxford, Oxford University Press.

Gibson, S. (2003) Accommodating Strangers: British hospitality and the asylum hotel debate. *Journal for Cultural Research,* 7: 4, 367–386.

Gilbert, H. & Lo, J. (2007) *Performance and Cosmopolitics. Cross-Cultural Transactions in Australasia,* Basingstoke, Palgrave Macmillan.

Gilbert, H. & Tompkins, J. (1996) *Post-Colonial Drama. Theory, Practice, Politics,* London and New York, Routledge.

Goffman, E. (1990 [1963]) *Stigma. Notes on the Management of Spoiled Identity,* London, Penguin.

Goldsmith, B. (2002) Asylum Seekers Sew Lips Together, *The Guardian,* London (19 January, 2002).

Gould, H. (2005) *A Sense of Belonging. Arts, Culture and the Integration of Refugees and Asylum Seekers.* London, Creative Exchange Network.

Green, T. (2004) *The Kindness of Strangers,* London, Oberon Books.

Greenslade, R. (2005) *Seeking Scapegoats. The Coverage of Asylum in the UK Press.* London, IPPR.

Guss, M. (2000) *The Festive State: Race, Ethnicity and Nationalism as Cultural Performance,* Berkley and Los Angeles, University of California Press.

Haedicke, S. C. (2002) Un Voyage pas comme les Autres sur les Chemin d'Exil. *Theatre Topics,* 12: 2, 99–118.

Hall, S. (1996) Ethnicity: identity and difference. In Eley, G. & Suny, R. G. (Eds.) *Becoming National*. Oxford, Oxford University Press.

Hall, S. (2000) Conclusion: the multicultural question. In Hesse, B. (Ed.) *Un/stettled Multiculturalisms. Diasporas, Entanglements, Transruptions*. London, Zed Books.

Harrell-Bond, B. & Voutira, E. (2007) In Search of 'Invisible' Actors: barriers to access in refugee research. *Journal of Refugee Studies*, 20: 2, 281–298.

Harrow, M. & Field, Y. (2001) *Routes across Diversity. Developing the Arts of London's Refugee Communities*. London, London Arts.

Harte, L. (2006) Migrancy, Performativity and Autobiographical Identity. *Irish Studies Review*, 14: 2, 225–238.

Hazou, R. (2008) *Refugitive* and the theatre of dys-appearance. *Research in Drama Education*, 13: 2, 181–186.

Heddon, D. (2008) *Autobiography and Performance*, Basingstoke, Palgrave.

Ho, A. (2003) *Stranger in a Strange Land: Refugitive at Barr Arbour*, ABC New England North West. Available at http:www.abc.net.au (accessed 19 September 2005).

Hoad, T. F. (Ed.) (1996) *Concise Dictionary of English Etymology*, Oxford, Oxford University Press.

Honig, B. (2001) *Democracy and the Foreigner*, Princeton and Oxford, Princeton University Press.

Howett, C. J. (1996) Written on the Body? Representation and resistance in British Suffragettes accounts of forcible feeding. In Foster, T., Siegal, C. & Berry, E. E. (Eds.) *Bodies of Writing, Bodies in Performance*, New York, New York University Press.

Hudson, C. (2010) 'Immigration minister Chris Brown condemns "distressing" act and braces for more protests' *Herald Sun*, 19th November 2010. Available at http://www.heraldsun.com.au/news/national (accessed 12 January 2011).

Hughes, H. & Roman, D. (Eds.) (1998) *O Solo Homo!*, New York, Grove Press.

Human Rights Watch (2001) *No Safe Refuge: The Impact of September 11 Attacks on Refugees and Asylum Seekers in the Afghan Region and Worldwide*. London, Human Rights Watch.

Hume, L. & Mulcock, J. (Eds.) (2004) *Anthropologists in the Field. Cases in Participant Observation*, New York, Columbia University Press.

Hutton, C. & Lukes, S. (2004) *Fugitive Arts. Arts and refugees in the South East of England*. Brighton, Arts Council England.

ICAR (2004) *Media Image Community Impact. Assessing the Impact of Media and Political Images of Refugees and Asylum Seekers on Community Relations in London*. London, ICAR.

ICAR (2006) *Reflecting Asylum in London's Communities: Monitoring London's Press Coverage of Refugees and Asylum Seekers*. London, ICAR.

Jackson, M. (2006) *The Politics of Storytelling. Violence, Transgression and Intersubjectivity*, Copenhagen, Museum Tusculanium Press.

Jeffers, A. (2008) Dirty Truth; personal narrative, victimhood and participatory theatre work with people seeking asylum. *Research in Drama Education*, 13: 2, 217–223.

Jeffers, A. (2009) Looking for Esrafil: witnessing 'refugitive' bodies in *I've got something to show you*. In Forsythe, A. & Megson, C. (Eds.) *Get Real. Documentary Theatre Past and Present*. Basingstoke, Palgrave Macmillan.

Jeffers, A. (2010) Performance in Place of War. In Skartveit, H.-L. & Goodnow, K. (Eds.) *Museums New Media and Refugees. Forms and issues of participation*. Oxford, Berghahan Books.

Jermyn, H. (2004) *The Arts of Inclusion*. London, Arts Council England.

Kafka, F. (2005) *The Complete Short Stories*, London, Vintage.

Kaldor, M. (2001) *New and Old Wars. Organized Violence in a Global Era*, Cambridge, Polity Press.

Kalra, V., S., Kaur, R. & Hutnyk, J. (2005) *Diaspora and Hybridity*, London, Sage Publishers.

Kearney, R. (2002) *On Stories*, London and New York, Routledge.

Kenney, D. N. & Schrag, P. G. (2008) *Asylum Denied. A Refugee's Struggle for Safety in America*, Berkley, CA, University of California Press.

Kern, M. (2004) What Remains? Visual arts and refugees. *Refugee Week*. Available at http://www.refugeeweek.org.uk/Events/Examples+of+Refugee+Week+events/Refugee+Week+Blog/Margareta+Kern (accessed 19 July 2006).

Kibreab, G. (1999) Revisiting the debate on place, identity and displacement. *Journal of Refugee Studies*, 12: 4, 384–410.

Kidd, B., Zahir, S. & Khan, S. (2008) Arts and Refugees: history, impact and future. London, Arts Council England, The Baring Foundation, The Paul Hamlyn Foundation.

Kilby, J. (2001) Carved in Skin. Bearing witness to self-harm. In Ahmed, S. & Stacey, J. (Eds.) *Thinking Through the Skin*. London and New York, Routledge.

Kirshenblatt-Gimblett, B. (1998) *Destination Culture: Tourism, Museums and Heritage*, Berkley, University of California Press.

Kristeva, J. (1982) *The Powers of Horror. An Essay on Abjection*, New York, Columbia University Press.

Kundnani, A. (2001) In a Foreign Land: the new popular racism. *Race and Class*, 43: 2, 41–60.

Kurashi, Y. (2004) Theatre as Healing Space. Ping Chong's Children of War. *Studies in Theatre and Performance*, 24: 1, 23–36.

Kushner, T. & Knox, K. (1999) *Refugees in an Age of Genocide. Global, National and Local Perspectives during the Twentieth Century*, London, Frank Cass.

Kustow, M. (2003) Wondrous Strangers. *The Guardian*. London, 18 June, 2003.

Kwon, M. (2004) *One Place After Another. Site-specific art and locational identity*, Cambridge, MA, Massachusetts Institute of Technology.

Kyambi, S. (2005) *Asylum in the UK*, ippr, London. Available at http://www.ippr.org.uk/comm/files/asylum-factfile-feb05.pdf (accessed 19 July 2010).

Lebrun, B. (2006) Banging on the Wall of Fortress Europe. Music for Sans-papiers in the Republic. *Third Text*, 20: 2, 711–721.

Lehmann, H.-T. (2006) *Postdramatic Theatre*, London and New York, Routledge.

Levinas, E. (1969) *Totality and Infinity*, Pittsburgh, PA, Duquesne University Press.

Levinas, E. (2007) *In the Time of the Nations*, London and New York, Continuum Press.

Lewis, M. (2005) Asylum. Understanding Public Attitudes. London, ippr.

Lewis, P. & Taylor, M. (2006) What really happened at Harmondsworth? *The Guardian*, London, 13 December 2006.

Liddell, C. & Manchester, H. (2005) Radio for Refugees. A Model for Community Development. Manchester, Home Office/Radio Regen/Allfm. (unpub.ms)

Linden, S. (2003) *I have Before Me a Remarkable Document Given to Me by a Young Lady from Rwanda*, London, Ice and Fire.

Linden, S. (2005) *Crocodile Seeking Refuge*, London, Aurora Metro Publications.

Loshitzky, Y. (2006) Journeys of Hope to Fortress Europe. *Third Text*, 20: 6, 745–754.

Lowe, L. (2006 [1996]) *Immigrant Acts. On Asian American Culture Politics*, Durham and London, Duke University Press.

MacAloon, J. J. (1984) *Rite, Drama, Festival, Spectacle. Rehearsal toward a Theory of Cultural Performance*, Philadelphia, PA, Institute for the Study of Human Issues.

MacCallum, M. (2002) *Girt by Sea. Australia, Refugees and the Politics of Fear*, Melbourne, Black Inc.

Malkki, L. (1995) *Purity and Exile. Violence, memory and national cosmology among Hutu refugees in Tanzania*, Chicago, Chicago University Press.

Malkki, L. (1995a) Refugees and Exile: from "Refugee Studies" to the national order of things. *Annual Review of Anthropology*, 24, 495–523.

Malkki, L. (1996) National Geographic: The rooting of peoples and the territorialization of national identity among scholars and refugees. In Eley, G. & Suny, R. G. (Eds.) *Becoming National. A Reader.* Oxford, Oxford University Press.

Malkki, L. (1996a) Speechless Emissaries: refugees, humanitarianism and dehistoricisation. *Cultural Anthropology*, 11: 3, 377–404.

Mamet, D. (1994) *A Whore's Profession. Notes and essays*, London, faber and faber

Manne, R. (2004) *Sending Them Home. Refugees and the Politics of Indifference*, Melbourne, Black Inc.

Marfleet, P. (2006) *Refugees in a Global Era*, London, Palgrave Macmillan.

Maric, V. (2009) *Bluebird. A Memoir*, London, Granta.

MARIM (2007) *Good Practice in Integration.* Manchester, Manchester City Council. (unpub.ms.)

Marranca, B. (2005) Performance and Ethics. Questions for the 21st century. *Performing Arts Journal*, 79, 36–54.

Marrus, R. M. (1985) *The Unwanted. European Refugees from the First War through the Cold War*, Oxford, Oxford University Press.

Massey, D. (1994) *Space, Place and Gender*, Cambridge, Polity Press.

McAfee, B. (1998) Instead of Medicine. Report of the Bosnian Mental Health Pilot Project. London, Refugee Action.

McEvoy, W. (2006) Finding the Balance: writing and performing ethics in Theatre du Soleil's Le Dernier Caravanserail. *New Theatre Quarterly,* 22: 3, 211–226.

McGray, D. (2003) Out of the Mouths of Babes, *Washington Post Magazine,* Washington DC, 2nd February, 2003.

McKenzie, J. (2001) *Perform or Else. From Discipline to Performance,* London and New York, Routledge.

McLane, J. (1996) The Voice on the Skin: self-mutilation and Merleau-Ponty's theory of language. *Hypatia,* 11: 4, 107–119.

McMaster, D. (2001) *Asylum Seekers,* Melbourne, Melbourne University Press.

Meikle, G. (2003) We are all Boat People: a case study in internet activism. *Media International Australia,* 107, 9–18.

Merheb, N. (Ed.) (2006) *The State of the World's Refugees. Human Displacement in the New Millennium,* Oxford, Oxford University Press.

Miller, J. G. (2006) New Forms for New Conflicts. Thinking about Tony Kushner's Homebody/Kabul and Théâtre du Soleil's Le Dernier Caravansérail. *Contemporary Theatre Review,* 16: 2, 212–219.

Miller, J. G. (2007) *Ariane Mnouchkine,* London and New York, Routledge.

Miller, P. (2004) Truth Overboard: what does it mean for politicians and statesmen to assume responsibility for their words of mass destruction? *borderlands,* 3: 1.

Mistiaen, V. (1999) Be Humiliated, Abused, Bullied...for just £4 a go, *The Guardian,* London, 24th March 1999.

Moorehead, C. (2005) *Human Cargo. A Journey among Refugees,* London, Chatto and Windus.

Nicholson, H. (2005) *Applied Drama. The Gift of Theatre,* London, Palgrave Macmillan.

Nield, S. (2006) On the Border as Theatrical Space. Appearance, dis-location and the production of the refugee. In Kelleher, J. & Rideout, N. (Eds.) *Contemporary Theatres in Europe. A Critical Companion.* London and New York, Routledge.

Nield, S. (2008) The Proteus Cabinet or We are Here but not Here. *Research in Drama Education,* 13: 2, 137–145.

Nobili, S. & Reynolds, G. (2005) *Evaluation of Escape to Safety.* Lancaster, Global Link Development Education Centre.

Nordstrom, C. (1997) *A Different Kind of War Story,* Philadelphia, PA, University of Pennsylvania Press.

Nyers, P. (2003) Abject Cosmopolitanism; the politics of border protection in the anti-deportation movement. *Third World Quarterly,* 24: 6, 1069–1093.

Nyers, P. (2006) *Rethinking Refugees. Beyond States of Emergency,* New York and London, Routledge.

O'Kelly, D. (1996) Asylum! Asylum! In Fitz-Simon, C. & Sternlicht, S. (Eds.) *New Plays from the Abbey Theatre 1993–1995.* New York, Syracuse University Press.

Oliver, K. (2001) *Witnessing. Beyond recognition,* Minneapolis, MN, University of Minnesota Press.

Oliver, M. (2003) Second refugee protests by stitching up eyes, *The Guardian,* London. 8th July, 2003.

Orenstein, C. (2002) "A Taste of Tibet" The nuns of Khachoe Ghakyil Nunnery and Theatre du Soleil. *Asian Theatre Journal,* 19: 1, 212–230.

O'Riordan, B. (2005) Revenge attacks bring second night of race violence to Sydney, *The Guardian,* London, 13 December 2005.

O'Riordan, B. (2005) When the sand ran red, *The Observer,* London, 18 December 2005.

Parker, A. & Kosovsky-Sedgwick, E. (1995) *Performativity and Performance,* London and New York, Routledge.

Parkin, D., Caplan, L. & Fisher, H. (Eds.) (1996) *The Politics of Cultural Performance,* Providence, Berghahn Books.

Patraka, V. M. (1999) *Spectacular Suffering. Theatre, Fascism and the Holocaust,* Bloomington, IN, Indiana University Press.

Peck, J. M. (1995) Refugees as foreigners: The problem of becoming German and finding home. In Valentine, E. D. & Knusden, J. C. (Eds.) *Mistrusting Refugees.* Berkley, CA, University of California.

Pedersen, A., Watt, S. & Hansen, S. (2006) The role of false beliefs in the community's and the federal government's attitudes toward Australian asylum seekers. *Australian Journal of Social Issues,* 41: 1, 105–124.

Peperzak, A. T. (1997) *Beyond. The Philosophy of Emmanuel Levinas,* Evanston, IL, Northwestern University Press.

Pirouet, L. (2001) *Whatever Happened to Asylum in Britain? A Tale of Two Walls,* New York and Oxford, Berghahn Books.

Prosser, J. (2001) Skin Memories. In Ahmed, S. & Stacey, J. (Eds.) *Thinking Through the Skin.* London and New York, Routledge.

Puggioni, R. (2006) Refugees reception and the construction of identities: encountering Kurdish refugees in Italy. *borderlands,* 5: 2.

Pugliese, J. (2002) Penal System: refugees, ethics and hospitality. *borderlands,* 1: 1.

Pupavac, V. (2008) Refugee Advocacy, Traumatic Representations and Political Disenchantment. *Government and Opposition,* 43: 2.

Qureshi, R. (2007) Something Remarkable, *The Guardian,* London, 13 April 2007.

Rajaram, P. K (2003) Humanitarianism and Representations of the Refugee. *Journal of Refugee Studies,* 15: 3.

Rancière, J. (2010) *Dissensus: On Politics and Aesthetics,* London and New York: Continuum

Ranger, T. (2005) The Narratives and Counter-narratives of Zimbabwean Asylum: female voices. *Third World Quarterly,* 26: 3, 405–421.

Rayson, H. (2005) *Two Brothers,* Sydney, Currency Press.

Refugee Action (2007) *Directory for Arts and Refugees.* South East England.

Reinelt, J. G. & Roach, J. R. (Eds.) (1992) *Critical Theory in Performance,* Ann Arbour, MI, University of Michigan Press.

Richards, M. (2005) Sewing and Sealing: speaking silence. In Coulter-Smith, G. & Owen, M. (Eds.) *Art in the Age of Terrorism.* Southampton, Southampton Solent University.

Rieff, D. (2002) *A Bed for the Night. Humanitarianism in Crisis,* London, Vintage.

Rogers, D. (2002) *Migrant Voices* Banner Theatre, (unpub.ms).

Rosello, M. (2001) *Postcolonial Hospitality. The Immigrant as Guest,* Stanford, Stanford University Press.

Rosen, H. (1998) *Speaking from Memory. The Study of Autobiographical Discourse,* London, Trentham Books.

Rotas, A. (2004) Is Refugee Art Possible? *Third Text,* 18: 1, 51–60.

Salter, M.B. (2006) The Global Visa Regime and the Political Technologies of the International Self: Borders, Bodies, Biopolitics, *Alternatives: Global, Local, Political,* 31: 2, 167–180.

Salverson, J. (1996) Performing Emergency: Witnessing, Popular Theatre and the Lie of the Literal. *Theatre Topics,* 6: 2, 181–191.

Salverson, J. (1999) Transgressive Storytelling or an Aesthetics of Injury: Performance, Pedagogy and Ethics. *Theatre Research in Canada,* 20: 1.

Salverson, J. (2006) Witnessing Subjects: a fool's help. In Cohen-Cruz, J. & Schutzman, M. (Eds.) *A Boal Companion.* London and New York, Routledge.

Saner, E. (2010) Our guest the asylum seeker, *The Guardian,* London, 25 June, 2010.

Scarry, E. (1987) *The Body in Pain. The Making and Unmaking of the World,* Oxford, Oxford University Press.

Schechner, R. (2002) *Performance Studies. An Introduction,* London and New York, Routledge.

Schechner, R. (2002a) Theatre in Times/Places of Crisis: a Theoretical Perspective In Bernardi, C., Dragone, M. and Schinina, G. (Eds.) (2002) *War Theatres and Actions for Peace. Community-Based Dramaturgy and the Conflict Scene,* EuresisEdizioni, Milan

Scheer, E. (2008) Australia's Post-Olympic Apocalypse? *PAJ Performing Arts Journal,* 30: 1, 42–56.

Schinina, G. (2002) Cursed Communities, Rituals of Separation and Communication as Vengeance In Bernardi, C., Dragone, M. and Schinina, G. (Eds) (2002) *War Theatres and Actions for Peace. Community-Based Dramaturgy and the Conflict Scene,* EuresisEdizioni, Milan

Schinina, G. (2004) Here we are. Social theatre and some open questions about its development. *The Drama Review,* 48: 3, 17–31.

Schmid, E., Harris, R. & Sexton, S. (2003) *Listen to the Refugee's Story. How UK Foreign Investment Creates Refugees and Asylum Seekers.* Peace in Kurdistan, 2003.

Schrag, P. G. (2000) *A Well-Founded Fear. The Congressional Battle to save Political Asylum in America,* London and New York, Routledge.

Schuster, L. (2003) *The Use and Abuse of Political Asylum in Britain and Germany,* London, Frank Cass.

Scott-Flynn, N. (2007) The Evaluation of Refugee Week 2007. London, Refugee Week.

Sellers, S. (1994) *The Hélène Cixous Reader,* Routledge: London and New York.

Seremba, G. (2000) Come Good Rain In *Along Human Lines. Dramas From Refugee Lives.* Winnipeg, Blizzard Publishing.

Shacknove, A. E. (1985) Who is a Refugee? *Ethics,* 95, 274–284.

Shafaei, S. (2003) Refugitive (unpub.ms.).

Shepard, B. & Hayduk, R. (2002) *From ACT UP to the WTO. Urban Protest and Community Building in the Era of Globalization,* London and New York, Verso.

Shevstova, M. (1999) Ariane Mnouchkine in Tibet, *PAJ: A Journal of Performance Art,* 21: 3, 72–78.

Shimakawa, K. (2002) *National Abjection. The Asian American body on Stage,* Durham and London, Duke University Press.

Shuman, A. & Bohmer, C. (2004) Representing Trauma: political asylum narrative. *Journal of American Folklore,* 117: 466, 394–414.

Silva, R. (2003) *Twisted Things* (unpub.ms.). http://www.lines-magazine.org/Art_Aug03/Ridley_Play.htm (accessed 8 June 2007).

Smith, S. & Watson, J. (2001) *Reading Autobiography,* Minneapolis, MN, University of Minnesota Press.

Soto-Morettini, D. (2005) Trouble in the House: David Hare's Stuff Happens. *Contemporary Theatre Review,* 15: 3, 309–319.

Staeger, R. (2004) *Asylees,* Philadelphia, PA, Mason Crest Publishers.

Stern, C. S. & Henderson, B. (1993) *Performance Texts and Contexts,* London, Longman.

Stoianova, M.B. (2007) *Writing the Subject of International Relations: Why the Poem?* (unpub.ms)

Summerfield, D. (1999) Sociocultural Dimensions of War, Conflict and Displacement. In Ager, A. E. (Ed.) *Refugees: Perspectives on the Experience of Forced Migration.* London and New York, Continuum.

Summerfield, D. (2002) Effects of war: moral knowledge, revenge, reconciliation and medicalised concepts of 'recovery'. *BMJ,* 325: 1105. Available at http://www.bmj.com/content/325/7372/1105.full

Taylor, D. (1997) *Disappearing Acts. Spectacles of Gender and Nationalism in Argentina's "Dirty War",* Durham and London, Duke University Press.

Taylor, D. (2003) Bush's Happy Performative. *The Drama Review,* 47: 3.

Teichmann, I. (2002) *Credit to the Nation. Refugee contributions to the UK.* London, The Refugee Council.

Thompson, J. (2005) *Digging Up Stories,* Manchester, Manchester University Press.

Thompson, J., Hughes, J. & Balfour, M. (2009) *Performance in Place of War,* London, New York, Calcutta, Seagull Books.

Tompkins, J. (2006) *Unsettling Space. Contestations in contemporary Australian Theatre,* Basingstoke, Palgrave Macmillan.

Turner, V. (1988) *The Anthropology of Performance,* New York, PAJ Publishers.

Turton, D. (2003) Conceptualising Forced Migration. *Refugee Study Centre Working Paper,* 12.

Tyler, I. (2006) Welcome to Britain: the cultural politics of asylum. *European Journal of Cultural Studies,* 9, 185–202.

Verstraete, V. and Cresswell, T. (2002) *Mobilizing Place, Placing Mobility: The Politics of Representation in a Globalized World.* Rodopi: Amsterdam. p. 18.

Wade, L. A. (2009) Sublime Trauma: the violence of the ethical encounter. In Anderson, P. & Menon, J. (Eds.) *Violence Performed. Local Roots and Global Routes Performed.* Basingstoke, Palgrave Macmillan.

Wehle, P. (2004) Children of the world. Ping Chong's travels. *Performing Arts Journal, 76*, 22–32.

Wehle, P. (2005) Théâtre du Soleil. Dramatic Response to the global refugee crisis. *Performing Arts Journal, 80*, 80–86.

Wertenbaker, T. (2002) Credible Witness. *Timberlake Wertenbaker: Plays 2.* London, faber and faber.

Whittaker, D. J. (2006) *Asylum Seekers and Refugees in the Contemporary World,* London and New York, Routledge.

Williams, D. (1999) *Collaborative Theatre. The Théâtre du Soleil Sourcebook,* London and New York, Routledge.

Williams, D. (2008) Performing Refugee Policy in Politics and Theatre. *Research in Drama Education, 13*: 2, 199–204.

Wills, S. (2002) Un-stitching the Lips of a Migrant Nation. *Australian Historical Studies, 118*, 71–89.

Winder, R. (2004) *Bloody Foreigners. The Story of Immigration to Britain,* London, Little Brown Books.

Younge, G. (2006) *Stranger in a Strange Land. Encounters in the Disunited States,* London, The Guardian.

Zard, M. (2002) Exclusion, terrorism and the Refugee Convention. *Forced Migration Review, 13*, 32–34.

Zetter, R. (1999) International Perspectives on Refugee Assistance. In Ager, A. E. (Ed.) *Refugees. Perspectives on the Experience of Forced Migration.* London, Continuum.

Zolberg, A. (2002) Foreword. In Marrus, R. M. (Ed.) *The Unwanted. European Refugees from the First World War through the Cold War (Politics, History and Social Change).* Philadelphia, PA, Temple University Press.

Zolberg, A. R., Suhrke, A. & Aguayo, S. (1989) *Escape from Violence. Conflict and the Refugee Crisis in the Developing World,* New York and Oxford, Oxford University Press.

Index

Titles of contemporary plays are presented in the language in which they were originally written. Where plays are published the date refers to the date of publication.